Economic theory of the industry

Economic theory of
the industry

MICHAEL WATERSON

University of Newcastle upon Tyne

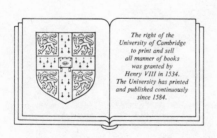

The right of the
University of Cambridge
to print and sell
all manner of books
was granted by
Henry VIII in 1534.
The University has printed
and published continuously
since 1584.

CAMBRIDGE UNIVERSITY PRESS

Cambridge
London   New York   New Rochelle
Melbourne   Sydney

Published by the Press Syndicate of the University of Cambridge
The Pitt Building, Trumpington Street, Cambridge CB2 1RP
32 East 57th Street, New York, NY 10022, USA
296 Beaconsfield Parade, Middle Park, Melbourne 3206, Australia

First published 1984

Printed in Great Britain at the
University Press, Cambridge

Library of Congress catalogue card number: 83-20916

British Library Cataloguing in Publication Data

Waterson, Michael
Economic theory of the industry.
1. Industrial organization (Economic theory)
I. Title
338   HD2326
ISBN 0 521 24438 2 hard covers
ISBN 0 521 28686 7 paperback

AN

Contents

Contents

Preface

In recent years, industrial economics (or industrial organisation) has undergone substantial changes. Probably one of the most fundamental is the way in which economic theorists have moved into the area. As a consequence, the range of models used in positive analysis has been extended and normative analysis has become markedly more explicit. A body of theory has achieved sufficient common currency as not to warrant referencing, yet this theory is beyond most intermediate microeconomics texts. (One of the clearest examples is mention of 'Cournot–Nash' equilibrium.) Essentially, the intention of this book is to make the link between intermediate microeconomics and current journal debates in the area.

The intended readership will consist mainly of final year undergraduates and first year graduates studying industrial economics. They will not, however, find all they may wish to know about on the subject herein, in two main senses. First, there are theoretical areas not covered, because they are outside the core area of the theory of the industry, as usually understood. Thus, the theory of the firm is largely neglected and the whole area of regulation is eschewed. Price discriminatory practices probably receive insufficient attention, as does the impact of uncertainty. Second, empirical work, and particularly anecdotal evidence, is suppressed, though some empirics emerge in Chapter 10. There are positive benefits in this. Most importantly, the reader should be able to glean theoretical insights much more readily than in the more usual type of industrial economics text which adopts the approach of broad overall coverage.

Prerequisites

As I have already implied, the reader of this book is assumed to have the economic background of (at most) an intermediate microeconomics course. Some early topics may well have been encountered already, though probably not in the way treated here. Concerning mathematics, the analysis is largely informal, emphasising intuition. It is no more difficult than that in most other industrial economics texts and anyone who has attended a course in quantitative methods for economists should have little difficulty. Nevertheless, the student who has no knowledge of partial differentiation will find some parts of the book difficult to follow, and functional notation is quite extensively used. Integration, however, is only occasionally employed, and discussion of dynamics is kept at a heuristic level. Little is assumed in the way of statistical technique apart from the ability (for chapter 10) to read a regression equation, but an appreciation of elementary statistical notions such as mean, variance and probability distribution is assumed.

Acknowledgements

I have built up substantial (intellectual) debts in the course of writing this book. In particular, I would like to thank Ingo Böbel, Steve Davies, Kevin Keasey and Norman Strong, each of whom gave very generously of their time in reading and commenting upon the manuscript. In their very different ways, each helped to improve the content of the book; Steve Davies also had a hand in its structure. Other colleagues who read smaller portions of the book but whose comments, nevertheless, were very valuable, include Paul Geroski, Bruce Lyons, Graham Loomes and George Yarrow. Useful comments were also obtained from two of my students, Bong-Ho Shin and Paul Simpson, both of whom read through much of the text.

I would also like to acknowledge a debt to the teachers who first interested me in the subject, namely Keith Cowling and Basil Yamey. Additionally, Sally Waterson helped with the bibliography and Lynda Morgan typed the manuscript.

I absolve all these people from any errors.

1

Introduction: the analytical framework

This book does not tell you how to run a business. It does try to explain how economists, as outsiders, have thought about the motivations and constraints facing the firm as a result of it being in an industry. Thus to a large extent, we view the firm as maximising profits subject to constraints imposed from without – actions of other firms which affect its marginal revenue or (to a lesser extent) its marginal cost and thus influence its profit-maximising calculus.

Of course this book, like any other, is predicated on certain beliefs. We consciously push the firm's motivational mechanisms and internal structures into the background in order to focus on external structure. We also assume that such a study is worthwhile in the sense that the polar analyses of competition and monopoly are not the whole story. More positively, we believe a body of theory regarding the industry has been built up which is not covered in most microeconomics texts, yet is referred to and recognised by practitioners in the field of Industrial Economics/Industrial Organisation. One manifestation of this is that the days are largely gone when the explanation of an empirical specification in the area could be prefaced by the words: 'elementary economic theory suggests that . . . '

There are four other matters we should discuss by way of introduction. The first is the concept of the industry, with which is associated a discussion of the practical difficulties of industrial classification. Secondly we have a methodological section on the predominant method in this field, namely the Structure–Conduct–Performance approach. This leads in section 3 to a discussion of the welfare framework commonly adopted in industrial economics. The last main topic is a very brief discussion of alternative methodologies and their impact both on the positive and the normative analysis. The chapter closes with a few notes on reading material relevant to the chapter and some comments to guide the reader through the book.

1. The concept of the industry

If life were simple, firms would each produce only one product and there would be no subtleties such as product differentiation. The world would consist of groups of firms producing easily identifiable things such as cement, pure sulphur, chocolate, copper pipe and motor oil. There would then be little difficulty about the concept of the industry.

However, firms do make things which differ, to a greater or lesser extent, from other firms' products, and they do produce a range of products. A question then arises as to how the industry is to be defined. Possibly, particular characteristics are specific to certain goods.[1] Or, if a group of products can be identified between which cross-elasticities of demand are high, yet the cross-elasticity of demand between any one of them and an outsider is low, then that group can be considered as an industry from the consumer's point of view. From the producer's point of view, cross-elasticities of supply are also important. Usually though, no specific break in the chain of elasticities can be identified, and in any case the concept lacks rigour because of the vague nature of 'low' and 'high'. Nevertheless, we can all think of numerous examples of well-defined industries (e.g. cigarettes and shoes) so that, though the economy cannot necessarily be parcelled up into disjoint sets of firms satisfying various consumer demands, we can conceive of a large range of cases where a group of firms interact with each other while having qualitatively different relationships with outsiders. That indicates the concept has wide applicability.[2]

Practical problems with industry classification schemes

Although classifications differ between industrialised countries, the basic principles behind them are rather similar. They allocate a certain range of numbers to a particular broad category of industry (e.g. clothing) and successively subdivide this to produce finer detail (e.g. men's outerwear; trousers). In the U.S., the system involves a series of digits rather like the Dewey system for library classification except that there is no decimal point, so that people talk of the 'three digit' level etc. Two digit descriptions identify broad areas of manufacturing while 7 digit categories are usually specific products. In the U.K. a similar method is used except that there is a dual classification scheme: the 'SIC order' (roman numbers) and the MLH (minimum list heading – a three digit number), which is the main level of disaggregation. Below this is the 'product level' of classification. The international scheme is conceptually similar to the American.

All classification schemes of this type run into problems which make difficulties for empirical workers wishing to use them in cross-sectional studies of theoretical industries. It may be useful to mention some of these problems at this stage, though in general they only become relevant in understanding corrections employed by empirical workers.

Because the data are collected from firms, it is natural for substitution in supply to be emphasised at the expense of substitution in demand. This occasionally leads to absurdities such as cane and beet sugar being in separate 4 digit categories in the U.S. But more generally, things which may be closely substitutable in the eyes of consumers but involve different materials (e.g.

aluminium foil and waxed paper dishes for use in home freezing) are unlikely to be classified together. Relatively modern goods, for example things made of plastic, also can be haphazardly classified, both on the demand and even the supply side.

Unfortunately also (from the statistician's point of view), many firms do not fit into neat categories. Some may have only a small portion of their activity in manufacturing industry. Others are predominantly manufacturers but produce an extraordinarily wide range of products: an example is Unilever. Now, a firm will probably be classified according to the largest segment of its activity. This can create a divergence between classification using the firm as a statistical unit and classification using the plant as a basis (in the U.K., the 'enterprise' and 'establishment' methods of classification). It also means there will be a difference between classification of an industry in terms of the firms who mainly produce for it, and classification on the basis of the product. These differences can be measured (and so extensive divergences guarded against) by means of 'specialisation' and 'exclusiveness' ratios, the former being the proportion of sales of an industry which consist of its principal products, while the latter is the extent to which establishments in an industry are responsible for the total output of the appropriate industry.

Another problem arising in open economies is the fact that details are only collected from domestic firms. The state of competition can be drastically affected by imports (consider, for example, the motor industry in most Western countries). In addition, if domestic firms are substantial exporters they may face rather different conditions in their export markets.

Lastly, even in the best-designed classification schemes, there are always product areas which defy convenient classification or are so multifarious as not to warrant it – an example in the U.K. is the category 'miscellaneous metal manufactures'. In both the U.K. and the U.S., category numbers ending in 9's tend to be remainder categories.

2. The structure–conduct–performance paradigm

In most areas of economic analysis there are predominant methodologies or ways of looking at things. In the case of Industrial Economics, the structure–conduct–performance paradigm (or framework) fills this role.

The basic idea can best be explained by means of an example. We take the case of a monopolist maximising profits. He thus equates marginal cost with marginal revenue, which is related to price and the elasticity of demand via the well-known condition:

$$MC = MR = p(1 - 1/\eta) \tag{1.1}$$

where η is the own-price elasticity of demand (written as a positive number). Rearranging:

$$\frac{p - MC}{p} = \frac{1}{\eta} \tag{1.2}$$

Thus the *price–cost margin* is equal to the inverse of the elasticity of demand. Moreover, if marginal cost equalled average variable cost, we could multiply numerator and denominator by output to show that the ratio of profit (plus fixed costs) to sales revenue was also equal to the reciprocal of demand elasticity (see chapter 2).

Now (1.2) is, strictly speaking, an equilibrium relationship and so carries no implication about causality. Yet it is natural to see causation flowing from the right-hand side – the demand elasticity – to the left-hand side – the price–cost margin or profit–revenue ratio – thus from basic conditions, via structure (monopoly) to performance. Conduct was embodied in the assumption that the monopolist was able to choose output to maximise profits.

The paradigm becomes more exceptionable when extended beyond this simple idea. Structural variables such as concentration (a measure of relative firm sizes), barriers to entry, extent of vertical integration and so on, are identified. Conduct is widened to include advertising and research and development expenditures as well as pricing. Performance can take on a normative as well as a positive dimension (as we see in the next section).

Now this framework would be of little use if conducts were free to vary, since it is easier to observe structural and performance variables (like concentration and profitability) than to divine conducts like collusion. The strongest position to take is therefore that conducts are themselves determined by structure[3] so that prediction runs directly from structure to performance.

However, this one-way causation scheme strictly implies that structure is immutable, or at least subject only to exogenous shocks. Fairly basic concepts like the one we started with – demand conditions – can probably bear such an interpretation reasonably well. However, the extent to which an industry is concentrated in the hands of a few firms or is vertically integrated can and does change. To some extent, such changes may reflect the influence of basic factors such as cyclical fluctuations, cost structures and so on, and to that extent the paradigm may be upheld. But, in addition, performance and conduct variables can influence structure, as when high profitability induces entry. More generally, factors like advertising and product differentiation, which we have identified as conduct variables, do not fit easily into the scheme.

An alternative methodology to use while still retaining an essentially neoclassical framework would be the comparative-static approach based upon reduced-form reactions to truly exogenous influences. It may be that this comes increasingly into favour in this area. On the other hand, given that certain structural features change relatively slowly, such a methodology might involve intensive effort to little effect.

Perhaps then, we can retain a modified structure–conduct–performance approach which takes into account the possibility of reverse linkages. Indeed, this is the approach essentially adopted in this book. One theme running through it is that we start with topics (such as oligopoly) incorporating a strong structure–conduct–performance emphasis, graduate to those (such as advertising) where the linkage is weaker, and close with theoretical discussion on the topic of reverse causations and basic influences on structure.

3. The welfare basis in industrial economics

This book does not purport to be a treatise on general equilibrium and welfare economics. Rather, we assume the reader has at least some knowledge of the elegant analytics involving the *Pareto principle*: That all 'reasonable men' would agree a change in the direction of improving one group's welfare involving no reduction in others' welfare is unambiguously welcomed. To run through this very quickly indeed, application of the Pareto principle in production and exchange leads to the utility-possibility frontier locus of efficient outcomes amongst which one may be chosen by means of some apparatus such as a social welfare function. Further, we remind the reader that atomistic profit-maximising firms trading with utility-maximising consumers in a decentralised world will lead automatically to a *Pareto-optimal* outcome — one on the utility-possibility or welfare frontier (though not necessarily the one the social welfare function would lead us to).

The foregoing assumes the absence of externalities and increasing returns, among other things, but if we can make these heroic simplifications, the basic point is that Perfect Competition has some justifiable claim as a method of economic organisation ensuring economic efficiency. However, we should also point out that the 'General Theory of the Second Best' implies it may not be worthwhile striving for a position nearer to satisfying certain of the optimality conditions if they cannot be satisfied elsewhere. Nevertheless, under specific assumptions (i.e. given enough separability in the model) such an attempt is worthwhile. It really is on this last position that the welfare basis in Industrial Economics lies, for the standard approach is normally rather partial in nature.[4] Like the analysis briefly outlined, it is also essentially static.

Since industrial economics is really concerned with analysing cases where markets are to some extent imperfect, the focus is usually on situations where price does not accord with marginal cost. For convenience let us analyse the case of a representative individual facing a price rise. Then, assuming the price of a given good is increased, and nothing else changes, the individual would become worse off. It might well be relevant to enquire how much she would need to receive as compensation for the change. Alternatively, we might ask how much she would be willing to pay to avert the change. These two concepts are known as the compensating and equivalent variations respectively. Unfortunately in general they do not coincide, nor are they easily measurable. However, if the benefits obtained from consuming the good are a relatively small part of the consumer's budget, and if the income elasticity is not too large, then it can be shown (Willig, 1976) that both measures may be quite well approximated by a more rudimentary concept – *consumer surplus*, the area under the consumer's demand curve above price.

Any change in the price facing the consumer is likely also to lead to a change in the welfare of the producer(s) of the good, in supernormal profits and/or in rents accruing to scarce resources. In assessing any price change, we would want to take account of this. However there is the question of the appropriate weighting to be attached to gains/losses in producer surplus as against consumer surplus. It is the usual practice in industrial economics to weight these equally (without any particular justification).

The common criterion for assessing whether a particular move is worthwhile therefore becomes whether the change in welfare measured as the sum of producer and consumer surplus without regard to distribution is positive, i.e. whether,

$$\Delta W \equiv \Delta \text{ Producer surplus} + \Delta CS > 0$$

(where CS is consumer surplus). This is sometimes known as the Kaldor–Hicks criterion: after such a change the gainers could compensate the losers, though they need not do so. If, as in most cases, all the producer surplus may be picked up as supernormal profit (Π), then a move is worthwhile when:

$$\Delta W = \Delta \Pi + \Delta CS > 0 \tag{1.3}$$

The case against monopoly

Suppose an industry which is perfectly competitive becomes monopolised. Assume that it is subject to constant costs, so the supply curve for the competitive industry is horizontal and is at the same level as marginal cost for the monopolist, so $S = MC_1$ in figure 1.1. Then with a competitive equilibrium at $D = S$, price under competition is at that level also ($= p_c$) and output is Q_c. Consumer surplus is the whole of the area above the supply curve under the demand curve. When the industry is monopolised and marginal revenue is set equal to marginal cost, then output is at the level Q_{m1} and price, read off the demand curve, is at p_{m1}. Some people might argue that the higher price is in itself a 'bad thing'. Others might point out that output has fallen and, with it, quite possibly, also has employment. (These resources have been released for potential use elsewhere though, so monopolisation does not cause unemployment in a general equilibrium sense.) However economists' condemnation of monopoly is on neither of these grounds but rather on the criterion established above in (1.3).

What has happened is that consumer surplus has decreased to become the area above p_{m1} under the demand curve. Producer surplus (supernormal profit) has increased from zero to become the rectangle between p_{m1}, p_c; 0 and Q_{m1} marked Π_1. The net change is the loss of the shaded area, called a *deadweight welfare loss*, because it is (a partial equilibrium approximation to) the loss to society as a whole. It arises from people who previously

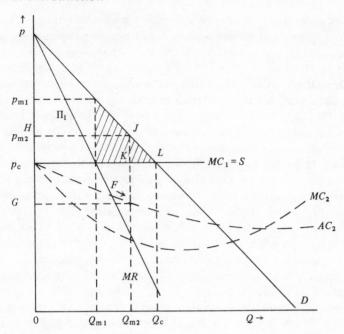

Figure 1.1

bought the product at p_c but valued it at between p_c and p_{m1}. They gained consumer surplus from their purchase but are now unable to.[5]

Under some simplifying assumptions, it is possible to measure this area of loss. To take the simplest case, assume a straight line demand law so that the shaded portion is a triangle. As is well known, its area is half the base multiplied by the height. But with a straight line demand curve, marginal revenue has the same origin on the price axis but is twice as steeply sloping,[6] so it will cut the length of the supply curve to Q_c in half and the monopolist's output is half that under competition (so $0Q_{m1} = Q_{m1}Q_c$). Thus the base and the height of the triangle are equal to the base and the height of the rectangular profit area. Consequently the deadweight welfare loss triangle may be operationally measured as half the area of profit Π_1. This is the basis of most partial equilibrium calculations of monopoly welfare loss. One twist which has been introduced is that, if monopoly rents are available, there will be wasteful competition for them. Thus, some people have argued that some part or all of the area of profit earned represents another loss to society, (see e.g. Posner, 1975).

Notice, incidentally, that if the monopolist is able to discriminate perfectly between consumers, assessing their willingness to pay exactly, then the demand curve becomes the effective marginal revenue curve and everyone who is willing to pay above marginal cost is served. The monopolist captures all the former consumer surplus and there is no deadweight loss. Therefore a perfectly discriminating monopolist should receive no condemnation from the economist as economist. Yet in the legal frameworks of many countries, price discrimination is frowned upon equally as much as monopolistic pricing practices, if not more so. A partial economic justification is that imperfect price discrimination can on occasion produce a greater welfare loss (Yamey, 1974) than monopoly pricing (though it often leads to less loss). In addition, it could plausibly be argued that, since the monopoly profits are greater here than in the normal case, the consequent wasteful competition to capture them will be greater. In general though, the reason for the legal condemnation of price discrimination is more likely to be equity than efficiency.

Returning to the case of the monopolist selling at a single price, we should remove one *ceteris paribus* assumption which may often be untrue. The justification for a more monopolistic structure may be to achieve scale economies. In that case, the supply curve under competition need not coincide with the monopolist's marginal cost schedule. For example, suppose that each firm under perfect competition is unable to obtain any scale economies because of its small size, so supply is again along S in figure 1.1. However, if the industry was monopolised, the monopolist's plant would, by assumption, be large enough to allow substantial scale economies, so that AC_2 and MC_2 would be his average and marginal costs respectively. Choosing the output at which marginal cost equals marginal revenue, that is Q_{m2}, leads to a price p_{m2} and profits equal to the area of the rectangle *FGHJ*.

If the scale economies were very extensive, then a price below p_c and output above Q_c could result. Clearly then, monopoly would be preferable to competition. Even in the case depicted, it looks as though monopoly would be preferable on the basis of a criterion like (1.3), since the increase in profit *FGHJ* is much larger than the fall in consumer surplus *JKL*. In general, in looking at a situation where an industry becomes more monopolised but as a result increased scale economies can be achieved, society faces a trade-off between increased producer surplus and reduced consumer surplus. This is known as the *Williamson trade-off* after the author (1968) who first set it out in detail.[7] He found analytically that the reduction in costs required to offset monopolisation of an industry rarely seemed large; using various sensible-sounding parameter values, it was of the order of 5%.

We should note that if, on Williamson trade-off calculations, the monopoly (or, a more monopolistic structure) turns out better, this does not mean it is optimal. Within the partial framework we are employing here, it would be better still if price were to be set equal to marginal cost; output would be expanded enormously in the case depicted in figure 1.1 and price would be extremely low. The difficulty is how to capture these benefits because, unfortunately, this scheme would involve the producer in losses unless he were able efficiently to discriminate between customers. Hence we have the economist's justification for nationalising areas subject to very extensive scale economies, if necessary funding them partly out of general taxation. Legitimate[8] European examples might include certain aspects of rail transport, telecommunications and postal services, electricity distribution and so on. A compromise solution adopted in the U.S. is to regulate the industry in an attempt to keep prices relatively low, yet not bear the burden of losses. There are problems as well as benefits in both these forms of organisation, but since they are essentially associated with the incentive structure of the firm they are not our concern in this book.

Although the analysis in the subsequent chapters is largely positive, many of the topics covered bring fresh ramifications to the basic ideas laid out above and thus many chapters include a section on the implications for welfare measured in the way outlined.

Biases against products

As well as the problem of prices not being in line with marginal costs, market operation can also lead to biases against particular types of products. The basic point is that a seller cannot capture all the surplus arising from production on the basis of charging the same price to all. Thus, the introduction of a product will increase social welfare (CS + Π) by more than the increase in producer surplus (Π). The distinct possibility arises that there will be some cases where consumer and producer surplus together amount to more than the cost of introducing the product, so production is socially worthwhile, yet the firm cannot capture enough surplus to make it worthwhile to her. But products are not subjected equally to this constraint, since the proportion of total surplus capturable by the firm varies with certain characteristics of the product. Prime among these is the elasticity of demand.

To see this, notice that the *gross* surplus accruing from the introduction of the product may be thought of as the area (shaded in figure 1.2) under the demand curve up to profit maximising output Q_m, formally as:

$$GS = \int_0^{Q_m} D(Q) \cdot dQ \tag{1.4}$$

(of course, variable and fixed costs must be subtracted from this to get net surplus). Total revenue accruing to the firm may, by definition, be written as the integral of the area under the marginal revenue curve up to Q_m:

$$TR = \int_0^{Q_m} MR(Q) \cdot dQ \tag{1.5}$$

But marginal revenue and price, $D(Q)$, are related as in (1.1). Thus if, to take the simplest case, demand elasticity is constant, we may write (1.5) using (1.4) as:

$$TR = (1 - 1/\eta) \int_0^{Q_m} D(Q) \cdot dQ = (1 - 1/\eta) \cdot GS \tag{1.6}$$

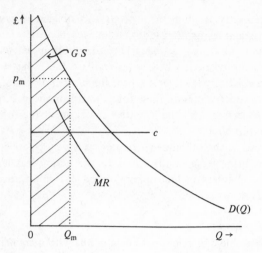

Figure 1.2

Therefore, the more elastic is demand, the larger the fraction of gross surplus which may be captured by the firm. Consequently, if two products have equal fixed and variable costs and the same accrual of gross surplus, the one with the larger elasticity is likely to be more profitable, a bias against products with inelastic demands. One product might be produced and not another, despite their equal contributions of gross surplus, and product i might be produced rather than j when j would have contributed the greater amount of total surplus. It is also fairly apparent that a high fixed cost is likely to militate against a product's introduction.

Actually, we have somewhat simplified the analysis (which is based on papers by Spence, 1976b, and Dixit and Stiglitz, 1977) in neglecting the effect of cross-elasticities of demand. However it is reasonably clear, even in our simplified model, that the number and type of products actually succeeding in the market can vary widely from what would be socially desirable. This can be an important source of social welfare loss, though one which is very difficult to measure. Some illustrative calculations by Spence (1976a) indicate that it can rival, or even much exceed, the size of the normal welfare loss due to pricing above marginal costs on existing products which normally receives much more attention. The point recurs in chapter 6.

4. Alternative schools of thought

We have neither the space nor the patience to provide an overview of historical developments in the field of industrial economics. Nevertheless, although neoclassical methods of analysis are largely used in industrial economics, and the content of this book reflects that bias, other schools of thought have contributions to make, and we ought at least to acknowledge this, at the risk of merely providing caricatures of the alternative views.

To start with a caricature of the *neoclassical view* of the industrial scene, it is a picture of a relatively static and certain world in which information is generally cheap and agents are rational, though not necessarily all-seeing. It focuses on equilibrium, on market failures and upon profit as an *ex post* indicator of such failures. The pinnacles of its analytics are probably in its predictions regarding industrial performance and in the calculation of welfare trade-offs connected with these.

The Austrian school

The contrast with the Austrian viewpoint could hardly be more marked. Though there are differences of detail within the Austrian school, the essential message is that the world is in a constant state of flux. The idea of competition is broadened to what neoclassicists more commonly call rivalry or non-price competition, that is to competition in product specifications, advertising and so on. Competition is viewed as a process rather than a state. Thus, profits are not signs of market failure but a necessary part of the market at work. It is implicit in the Austrian scheme that there is a perfectly elastic supply of entrepreneurs and the entrepreneur has a key role as arbitrageur — a person who takes advantage of differences in prices and gaps in product specifications.

The major consequence of all this is that there is no specific optimal position against which an economy can be compared. As a result, Austrians would view the calculation of deadweight loss triangles as an extremely limited exercise. They would emphasise rather more the welfare gains, in terms of producer and consumer surplus, as new markets are opened up, albeit by monopolists. This point becomes important in chapter 8 on technical change.

Their other main area of influence is in regard to barriers to entry. Their views on these will receive attention in chapter 4 but, to preview very briefly, they have adopted the Chicagoan view of consumers as extremely footloose individuals. As a consequence they see the main barriers to entry into industries not in terms of things created by established firms but rather in legal impediments imposed by government fiat.

In general, the Austrians have tremendous faith in market processes, but much less faith in the efficiency of public bodies. The consequence is that one can gain an impression from some of their writings of everything which unfettered operation of the market mechanism brings about being naturally optimal. This neglect of legitimate problems in welfare economics relating to externalities, increasing returns, public goods and so on is unfortunate, but they do provide a provocative challenge to static theory.

The Marxian viewpoint

In contrast to the Austrian view, the positive aspects of Marxian analysis in industrial economics are largely in accord with neoclassical ones. We may notice, for example, that the neoclassical concept of the firm's price-cost margin provides a rough equivalent to the Marxian ratio of surplus value to total product of the firm.

However, Marxists do not adhere at all to the strict version of the structure conduct performance approach in which structure is relatively slowly changing. Instead they stress the drive to increase the surplus by actively seeking to gain monopoly power – to monopolise markets, to gain the advantages of size, to differentiate their product from those of others, to cut out competition from small firms. Nevertheless, they believe tacit collusion amongst big and powerful firms is relatively easy to achieve. Thus the standard paradigm undergoes changes in emphasis, while still retaining the basic concepts we shall examine in later chapters – oligopoly, barriers to entry, concentration and so on.

Also, the Marxist view of the internal workings of the firm is more developed than the standard neoclassical view. Some aspects of this analysis have common strands with Williamson's hierarchical picture of the firm which we have shortly to consider, but there is more emphasis on internal conflicts, particularly over how much of the firm's surplus should be distributed to the operatives as against the managerial and capitalist classes. In their model there is no identity of interest regarding basic objectives.

Lastly, a major difference, which has something in common with the views of Galbraith (*New Industrial State*, 1969) is that the modern, large, maybe multinational corporation cannot be analysed in isolation from its political and social background – it impinges far too deeply onto everyday life for that. Thus they (if maybe not he) would see the calculation of the deadweight loss triangle as a rather limited exercise from two standpoints. First, it ignores questions of distribution between the monopoly capitalist and consumer and employees. Second, it only captures in a rather partial and puny way the (arguably) vast political and social influence large firms have upon our life. The focus both in Baran and Sweezy's *Monopoly Capital* (1968), and in Galbraith's *New Industrial State*, is not on the position of the firm within the industry, but on the large size of the largest corporations *per se*, vying in economic size (and, by analogy, power) with governments of medium size countries.

Behavioural theories

Finally, we come to a rather heterogeneous group of beliefs related to the view that optimising behaviour cannot be taken for granted[9] in a world of uncertainty and large limited-liability companies. We refer to these, roughly, as behavioural theories, though that term is often reserved for one among the group.

Most closely related to theories of optimising behaviour is Williamson's (1975) discussion of hierarchies within the firm. In theory the 'peak co-ordinator' (the equivalent of an entrepreneur within a large joint-stock company) wishes to control the firm in such a way as to maximise profits, assuming his personal remuneration depends upon this. However he encounters the basic problem of 'bounded rationality': he faces physical limits on his powers of dealing with information flows and limits on his ability to communicate precisely with subordinates. There is then the possibility of 'opportunistic behaviour', where subordinates misrepresent their positions to put themselves in a better light. Williamson's analysis enquires closely into the manifestations and effects of such behaviour, also into how the internal structure of the firm can be more optimally ordered to surmount some of the problems of controlling a large complex organisation. The rich detail this produces means that market influences on the firm tend not to be emphasised. Nevertheless, we will encounter his ideas on hierarchies again in this book, most particularly in discussing vertical integration, where the firm supplants the market, an area where they have been quite extensively developed.

In a rather similar manner to Williamson, the 'X theory' specifies that there is something, called 'X-inefficiency', which prevents firms from operating on their theoretical cost functions. In looking at the mechanisms which give rise to this though, the emphasis is shifted slightly. Rather than stressing co-ordination difficulties, it focuses on individuals seeking to minimise their own effort subject to constraints. The constraints are more explicitly not only internal but also external. Thus, lack of product market competition can make X-inefficiency larger than it would otherwise be. The main consequence is that an additional factor comes into the 'Williamson trade-off' of the previous section.[10] If an industry becomes more monopolised, although costs may be reduced because more advantage can be taken of scale economies, at the same time they may be increased because of lessening product market pressure.[11] The difficult question is the extent to which this will occur; only rough estimates have been produced.

Finally, there are some theories which suggest no real attempt is made to maximise profits. Instead, firms 'satisfice', or set targets below what could be achieved. Again, there could be considered to be only a qualitative difference between this and Williamson's view expressed earlier: If a peak co-ordinator seeks to maximise profits but is constrained in doing so by pressures inside the firm, the outcome may well be similar to that if she had instead been content to achieve a 'satisfactory' level of profits. In other words, the 'satisfactory' profit might be defined as that level achieved by some optimal (long-run sustainable?) amount of struggle against hierarchical inefficiencies. Nevertheless, the concept of satisficing behaviour has led to a particular behavioural model, developed by Cyert and March (1963). In this view, uncertainties are manifold, so the firm works mainly within the short-term, reconciling production, sales and profit plans, producing targets and re-examining the plans if the targets cannot be met. One of the important uncertainties concerns the reaction of rivals and thus the industrial environment a firm faces. However, by the very nature of the theory, it cannot provide explanations for and predictions about particular actions of the firm.

One group of theories of the behavioural type which do give rise to a prediction about a particular target a firm sets are the various 'cost plus' or 'average cost' pricing models. The basic idea is that price is equal to average cost plus some fixed, or at least stable, 'reasonable' percentage markup.[12] Thus a satisfactory, or target, price is set.

There are several variants, with the variation arising mainly through differing bases for calculating average cost. For example, there is 'full average cost' (including fixed costs) and 'normal cost'. Some logical difficulties are caused with the former, since in order to know average fixed costs, an estimate of sales volume will have to be made, yet this should itself depend on price. Thus it is probably more sensible to say that some idea of 'normal', or at least planned, range of output is envisaged in such theories. One quite careful specification is developed by Godley and Nordhaus (1972).

Another group of views goes under the title of the 'administered pricing hypothesis': that those firms in industries where market power is concentrated in a few hands have some latitude in pricing behaviour which allows them to set prices administratively. Exactly how this power is exercised is not entirely clear, since the same term has meant slightly different things at different times and the original hypothesis (see Means, 1962) was essentially non-testable. However, the main suspicions are of prices not fully moving in accord with pressures of demand (high or low) and of a willingness to pass on wage increases.

Actually, if average variable cost is roughly constant (and so equal to marginal cost) and if the elasticity of demand remains fairly constant, then the prediction for a monopolist under a cost plus theory or even perhaps under the administered pricing hypothesis would accord well with the prediction coming from equation (1.1) which assumes profit maximisation. Thus the finding that price is apparently set by such an alternative method is not necessarily inconsistent with profit maximisation. To distinguish between the alternatives, one could look to see whether as an industry structure changes over time the markup also changes or whether across a group of industries the markup varies with industry structure. Cost-plus theories[13] therefore provide a null hypothesis in tests along these lines inspired by neoclassical analysis, which are discussed in chapter 10.

Notes on the literature

In the case of some of the topics covered here, the most accessible literature is the introductory chapters of other texts. To avoid excessive advertising of rivals, they will not be listed here. Having said that, the most extensive discussion of the structure–conduct–performance paradigm is probably Scherer (1980, ch. 1).

The standard framework of General Equilibrium Theory and welfare economics is covered in intermediate microeconomics textbooks. In addition a popular diagrammatic exposition is Bator (1957). Rowley (1973, Chs 1–5) sets out the particular frame of reference used in industrial economics, developed, as we have said, from Williamson (1968). Schmalensee (1981*b*) provides a fairly general analysis of the welfare economics of third degree price discrimination, which we merely mentioned above.

Some of the theories of the firm which were *not* discussed here are those of Baumol (1959), Marris (1964), Williamson (1964) and Yarrow (1976). A useful analysis is provided by J. Williamson (1966). A few microeconomics texts (e.g. Koutsoyiannis, 1979) also discuss them. Spence (1975) gives a useful brief survey of the internal organisation literature.

As far as the alternative schools of thought are concerned, a textbook which takes the Austrian viewpoint is Reekie (1979). A Marxian view is provided in Cowling (1982). The hierarchical analysis of the firm is expounded in Williamson (1975) while *X*-inefficiency was first introduced by Leibenstein (1966).

Guides to the book

We have already discussed at length one unifying theme in industrial economics, namely the structure–conduct–performance approach, and the plan of the book is heavily influenced by that paradigm. The early chapters, numbers 2 to 4, are the ones most strongly embedded in the structural view of industry, structure being represented by firm numbers, barriers to entry and so on, and chapter 5 largely takes this approach. Chapters 6 to 8 emphasise conducts other than price, such as advertising behaviour, and take interrelationships between structure and conduct more seriously, while chapter 9 considers determinants of structure. Thus, we initially follow the paradigm, but increasingly draw away from it.

Another general theme running through the book is that a limited number of specific models of oligopoly behaviour provide the building blocks upon which much of industrial economics has been constructed, because they capture the basic concept of interdependence. It is therefore logical to start by developing the theory of oligopoly. As a consequence though, the areas which have been developed furthest theoretically are presented quite early in the text. Readers need not anticipate that, if they find the first few chapters rather rigorous, things are going to get worse. They are more likely to get better, as later analyses, as well as drawing on the early theory, also draw increasingly on the empirical tradition.

Chapters 2 and 3 consider classical and game-theoretic analyses of oligopoly respectively, focusing mainly on homogeneous product industries. There, entry to the industry is either considered blockaded or free. In chapter 4 this dichotomy is bridged when the analytics of entry barriers are considered. Chapter 5 extends the field of the foregoing analyses into the area of vertical pricing relationships. The three subsequent chapters provide extensions into other planes of rivalrous behaviour. Chapter 6 considers analyses of product differentiation whilst chapter 7 covers the closely related topic of advertising behaviour. Chapter 8 extends rivalry into the sphere of dynamic competition in discussing R and D activity. In chapter 9 we discuss theories of the determinants of the structural elements which we essentially took as given in chapter 2. The book closes with a chapter briefly surveying cross-sectional empirical work in the fields covered theoretically.

2

Classical theories of oligopoly

It is quite common in Industrial Economics texts to start the first substantive chapter with descriptions of some aspects of industrial structure. By contrast, we shall start in this chapter with theoretical models of industry which are fairly abstract, in that they make rather naive assumptions about entry into the industry and, initially, they assume all the forms are identical, making a homogeneous product. No one would pretend this closely mirrors reality. However, it is important to consider such models at this early stage for two main reasons. First, they capture a key feature of modern industrial society, the interdependence amongst particular groups of firms, and second, they provide the structure upon which more complex models can be constructed.

The quintessential feature of an oligopoly is interdependence: the actions of all the individual firms in an industry are affected by the actions of the other firms. It is this interdependence which gives rise to many of the theoretical problems in modelling oligopoly behaviour. Hence, although the cases of perfect competition and pure monopoly have been solved to the satisfaction of the vast majority, oligopoly has features making simple solutions unlikely.

In this chapter we consider the classical theories of oligopoly using calculus methods and then go on in chapter 3 to enquire into the contribution of game theory. Product differentiation enters at this stage only in a rather superficial way but receives further consideration in chapter 6. Even if we can specify the exact number and size of firms producing an undifferentiated product though, we have to consider the possibility that entry may be feasible at certain prices. Moreover, the mere potential of entry may be enough to alter established firms' behaviour. We take entry here either to be impossible or to be completely free, but the topic is covered in detail in chapter 4. Again, behaviour may be affected by the presence of powerful buyers from, or powerful sellers to, this industry. Such factors are left until chapter 5. At present we only intend to discuss the theory of oligopoly in pure form.

Our method of exposition is to discuss the interdependence assumptions in a model with homogeneous products in section 1 before turning to differentiated product cases in section 2. There is some discussion of stability of solutions in section 3 and of the normative aspects of oligopoly theory in

17

section 4. The chapter closes, as do all subsequent ones, with some notes on the literature.

1. Classical theories with undifferentiated products

To put the problem of interdependence of producers in oligopoly into sharpest relief, let us consider a simple model where there are N sellers of a standardised product with a single selling price in a market with no possibility of entry, inputs being purchased at given prices and outputs sold to price-takers. Industry inverse demand is therefore a function of total output which is simply the sum of individual outputs, say $p = f(Q)$; $Q = \Sigma_i \, q_i$. Thus, each firm will have a profit function:

$$\Pi_i = p(Q) \cdot q_i - C_i(q_i) \qquad i = 1, 2, \ldots, n \qquad (2.1)$$

where each firm has a (possibly different) cost function $C_i(q_i)$. For maximum profits we will require:

$$\frac{d\Pi_i}{dq_i} = p + q_i \frac{dp}{dQ} \cdot \frac{dQ}{dq_i} - C_i' = 0 \qquad (2.2)$$

and

$$\frac{d^2\Pi_i}{dq_i^2} < 0, \qquad \text{for all } i.$$

The first-order condition will receive greater attention in a moment; for the while simply note that it is a version of the familiar marginal revenue equals marginal cost condition. Thus the second-order condition, which we have refrained from writing in full, states that the slope of the marginal revenue function must be less than the slope of the marginal cost function. This will be true if the marginal revenue curve is negatively sloped and the marginal cost curve is positively sloped, horizontal, or less negatively sloped than the marginal revenue function. We assume one of these holds and in general, in fact, we will not be unduly concerned to enquire into second order conditions in this book.

Returning to the first-order condition (2.2) then, there is an immediate question about the term dQ/dq_i. In words, it is the effect the ith firm's output will have on the other firms' outputs. In order to solve its own maximisation problem the ith firm has to make some assessment of this term. Recalling the definition of Q, it may be expanded to read:

$$\frac{dQ}{dq_i} = \frac{dq_i}{dq_i} + \frac{dQ_i}{dq_i} \equiv 1 + \lambda_i$$

where Q_i is the output of the other firms. Thus each firm has to make some guess or conjecture about how the others will react to its output changes, i.e. the size of dQ_i/dq_i, or λ_i, as we have written it for brevity. It is called the *conjectural variation* term. We can easily see that the firm's conjecture about interdependence is of crucial importance in evaluating (2.2) and is at the heart of the oligopoly problem. Different oligopoly theories, in fact, can be viewed as assuming different conjectures about λ_i, as we see in a minute.

First though, we enquire into what we can say in general. To take the simplest case, assume all the firms have the same cost function (or, differ only in the level of their fixed costs, which will not enter into (2.2)) and, in addition, assume they all make the same conjectural variation assumption. In that case the firms will be identical in size at equilibrium for the simple reason that there is no difference between the equations (2.2) for each of them. Rearranging slightly, we have:

$$\frac{p - C'}{p} = -\frac{q_i}{Q} \cdot \frac{Q}{p} \cdot \frac{\mathrm{d}p}{\mathrm{d}Q} \cdot (1 + \lambda)$$

$$= \frac{s_i(1 + \lambda)}{\eta}. \tag{2.3}$$

where η is the modulus of industry price elasticity of demand and s_i the share of the ith firm in industry output. But since all firms are the same size, $s_i = 1/N$, so we have that the firm's and the industry's *price-cost margin* may be written:

$$\frac{p - C'}{p} = \frac{(1 + \lambda)}{N\eta}. \tag{2.4}$$

By analogy with the case of monopoly, it is natural to think of the industry's structure (firm numbers and demand conditions) determining its performance (the price-cost margin) through firm-determined conduct (profit maximisation and the belief about λ). The price-cost margin is often called the *Lerner index* of monopoly power.

The more general version of (2.3) where we allow marginal costs to vary between firms and allow them to entertain different conjectures about their rivals is easily seen by the same manipulation to yield:

$$\frac{p - C_i'}{p} = \frac{s_i(1 + \lambda_i)}{\eta}. \tag{2.5}$$

Here there is no reason for all firms to be the same size even if the λ_i are equal. Also the price-cost margin will differ between firms in general.

If we can observe industry but not firm magnitudes, it is natural to think of aggregating (2.5) across firms in a relevant manner. Now if marginal cost is equal to average variable cost,[1] the difference between revenue and marginal cost times output is profit plus fixed cost. In symbols, rewriting (2.1) to separate out fixed costs (F_i):

$$\Pi_i = p(Q) \cdot q_i - C_i'(q_i) \cdot q_i - F_i$$

so that:

$$\Pi_i + F_i = p(Q) \cdot q_i - q_i \cdot C_i'(q_i)$$

and therefore, summing across all firms in the industry, we note that:

$$\Pi + F \equiv \Sigma_i(\Pi_i + F_i) = \Sigma p(Q) \cdot q_i - \Sigma q_i C_i'(q_i)$$

Thus, rearranging (2.5) by multiplying through by q_i and summing:

$$\frac{\Sigma pq_i - \Sigma C_i' \cdot q_i}{p} = \frac{\Sigma s_i(1 + \lambda_i)q_i}{\eta}$$

then dividing by Q, and rearranging the right hand slightly:

$$\frac{\Sigma pq_i - \Sigma C_i' \cdot q_i}{pQ} = \frac{\Sigma s_i^2(1 + \lambda_i)}{\eta}$$

we can express the industry (gross) *profit to revenue ratio* as:

$$\frac{\Pi + F}{R} = \frac{\Sigma s_i^2(1 + \lambda_i)}{\eta} = \frac{H}{\eta}(1 + \mu) \tag{2.6}$$

where μ is defined as $\Sigma s_i^2 \lambda_i / \Sigma s_i^2$, a weighted sum of conjectural variation terms and $H = \Sigma s_i^2$. In fact H is known as the *Herfindahl index of concentration*. If, because all C_i' and all λ_i are the same, all s_i are the same, then $H = 1/N$ and (2.6) degenerates to the simpler case of (2.4). In general though, all firms will differ in size. The Herfindahl index is a particular way of aggregating firms' shares to obtain a representation of how concentrated an industry is into the hands of a few firms when, because their sizes differ, the number of firms in an industry becomes an ambiguous measure of competition. We discuss concentration indices in much more detail in chapter 9; at the moment we think of *concentration*, as measured for example by the Herfindahl, as simply a structural feature being a representation of *the extent to which market power is vested in a few firms*. Again then, in (2.6) structure (H and η) determines performance (the profit–revenue ratio) via conduct (μ) according to the straightforward paradigm, and different oligopoly theories involve different conducts. Later, in chapter 9, we shall have cause to modify this viewpoint on concentration.

When the number of firms tends towards infinity, their perceived interdependence is presumably negligible (and also their own effect on industry output is negligible). The values of λ and μ tend towards zero, and H tends towards zero. Thus from (2.4) and (2.6) price becomes equal to marginal cost and the profit–revenue[2] ratio tends to zero, so we reach a result equivalent to the perfectly competitive one. Similarly in the case of a monopoly there are no direct rivals so $\lambda_i = 0$, N is unity and so is H. The price–cost margin and profit–revenue ratio equal the reciprocal of industry demand elasticity. These are polar cases; we are interested in the intermediate oligopoly situations as illustrated by (2.4) and (2.6).

Cournot's theory

Cournot's (1927) theory of oligopoly assumes each firm considers that the other firms' output will not change as a result of the firm in question changing his output (though that his own output will influence the industry output level). This means that $\lambda_i = 0$ for all i, so $\mu = 0$; the conjectural variations term is zero. From (2.5) we have:

$$(p - C_i')/p = s_i/\eta \tag{2.7}$$

for each firm, implying that the larger is C_i', the smaller is s_i. With equal marginal costs, each firm's price cost margin would equal $1/N\eta$. Equation (2.6) simplifies to:

$$(\Pi + F)/R = H/\eta \tag{2.7a}$$

It is thus a particularly straightforward solution.

The set of equations represented by (2.7) each relate functionally a particular firm's output q_i and others' output Q_i. Thus they indicate how a firm would choose his output level for any given output by the other firms and so define a set of *reaction functions*. They should all intersect at positive outputs to give the equilibrium solution. A duopoly example drawn assuming linear demand and total cost functions (for simplicity) is shown in Fig. 2.1. These reaction functions might be considered heuristically as defining a path to equilibrium. Thus if we were to start (conceptually) with firm 1 producing

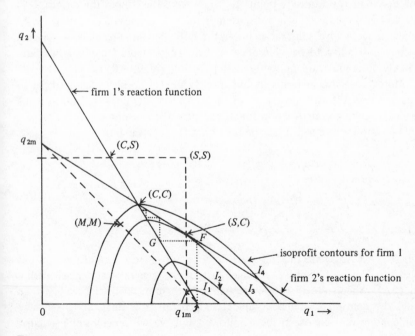

Figure 2.1

the monopoly output q_{1m} and firm 2 producing nothing, then firm 2 would choose a point F on his reaction function as preferable, whereupon 1 would choose point G, and so on until the Cournot point (C, C) is reached. More generally, this point would be achieved starting from anywhere on either reaction function (but see also section 3). Critics have pointed out the naivety of this sequential process in which each firm's underlying assumptions are continually falsified. More recently though, attention has focused on the equilibrium independent of the path.

We may also superimpose on figure 2.1 sets of curves each describing combinations of the two firms' output yielding a given level of profit to one of the firms. These are called *isoprofit contours*.[3] Thus they originate from the monopoly position and represent lower levels of profit as they move further into the diagram. The maximum level of q_2 reached on each of firm 1's contours is on firm 1's reaction function. This is because the reaction function plots the optimal output for firm 1 given a level for firm 2's output.

Stackleberg's Theory

The reaction functions are utilised by the leader in Stackleberg's (1952) theory of oligopoly. The aim of the Stackleberg leader is to choose that point on the other's reaction function offering maximum profits. Such a point is shown at (S, C) for firm 1 in the figure, and involves more profits for her than the Cournot point. If firm 2 were the leader, the point (C, S) would be chosen, while if both attempt to lead, the result is a point (S, S) which may involve substantial losses for both parties. Stackleberg believed such a possibility to be widespread and thus considered 'economic warfare' a likely outcome of oligopoly (see Fellner, 1949, pp. 99–101).

More generally, in terms of our model, let us consider a case where all but one firm act as 'followers'. For them, we have $dQ/dq_i = 1$. However, the leader, knowing their reaction functions, uses them to obtain a more favourable position for herself. If she be the mth firm, then she has:

$$\frac{dQ}{dq_m} = \frac{d}{dq_m}(q_m + Q_m)$$

$$= 1 + \frac{\sum\limits_{j \neq m} d\, \psi_j(q_m)}{dq_m},$$

where the $\psi_j(q_m)$ are the followers' 'reduced form' reactions[4] to m's output changes. This is obviously a special case of the general result given earlier in (2.5), where not all the λ_i are equal. With more potential leaders than one, the analysis becomes complex. In general, it is difficult to see why someone would choose to be a follower, but we will encounter particular instances.

Collusion

Another special case which can be developed from the general model is the limiting case of collusion, which receives more detailed attention in chapter 3. Here each firm knows that, if he raises or lowers output, the others will do likewise. Thus if the firm in question has a particular share of the market s_i, he expects the others to react to any expansion or contraction according to the ratio of their shares of the market compared to his, i.e. $\lambda_i = (1 - s_i)/s_i$. Consequently from (2.5) we have:

$$\frac{p - C_i'}{p} = \frac{1}{\eta} \tag{2.8}$$

and from (2.6):

$$\frac{\Pi + F}{R} = \frac{1}{\eta}. \tag{2.8a}$$

In other words, the result for both the firm and the industry is equivalent to the result for a monopolist, which would seem preferable to, say, the Cournot outcome from the firm's point of view.

Note that (2.8) implies all firms have the same marginal cost of producing their particular output level in equilibrium, as with the individual plants of a multiplant monopolist. However, if the firms have very different cost functions, their shares of the market will also be very different: more inefficient (higher cost) firms will tend to have smaller shares (as in the Cournot model). It may even not be possible to equate all firms' marginal costs at any output levels at all (for example if one has a constant higher marginal cost than another). This means the high cost firm should stop producing in order for profits to be maximised. Such problems can lead to difficulties within the collusive group, as we see in the next chapter. There may be external difficulties as well.

A suggestive reformulation

Under certain circumstances (see e.g. Clarke and Davies, 1982), it is possible to array industry behaviour on a spectrum between Cournot and collusive behaviour. If we suppose all firms have the same belief about the *proportionate* effect of their output changes on other firms' outputs, α, then:

$$\alpha \equiv \frac{dQ_i}{dq_i} \cdot \frac{q_i}{Q_i} = \frac{\lambda_i q_i}{Q_i}.$$

Hence,

$$\lambda_i = \alpha \left(\frac{Q - q_i}{q_i} \right) = \alpha \left(\frac{1}{s_i} - 1 \right)$$

Substituting this into (2.6), recalling that $\Sigma s_i \equiv 1$, and rearranging, yields:

$$\frac{\Pi + F}{R} = \frac{\alpha}{\eta} + (1 - \alpha)\frac{H}{\eta}. \tag{2.9}$$

In this equation when $\alpha = 1$, we have (2.8a) implying collusion, while when $\alpha = 0$ we have (2.7a) implying Cournot behaviour. Thus α might be thought of as a degree of *apparent collusion* in the industry. A similar concept is used in classifying outcome in heterogeneous product cases in the next section. (See also Cyert and de Groot (1973) for an alternative parameterisation.)

The dominant firm or price leadership model

In this model a group of firms (or a single firm) choose industry price to suit their own joint ends, as with the case of collusion, but they are constrained in doing so by the presence of a fringe of firms who treat price as parametric, (which is not, it should be noted, what Stackleberg followers do).

Since the fringe act like competitive firms would, they can be considered to act according to a supply function relating their sales (Q_s) to industry price:

$$Q_s = Q_s(p).$$

Thus, the demand facing the collusive group is:

$$Q_G(p) = Q(p) - Q_s(p). \tag{2.10}$$

This group will maximise joint profits with respect to price by setting the relationship between price and marginal cost that a monopolist would, i.e.:

$$(p - MC_G)/p = 1/\eta_G$$

where η_G is the elasticity of demand they jointly face. To determine that elasticity, let us differentiate (2.10) then multiply by $(-p/Q_G)$ to yield:

$$\eta_G \equiv -\frac{p}{Q_G}\frac{\mathrm{d}Q_G}{\mathrm{d}p} = -\frac{p}{Q_G}\cdot\frac{\mathrm{d}Q}{\mathrm{d}p} + \frac{p}{Q_G}\frac{\mathrm{d}Q_s}{\mathrm{d}p}.$$

If we define C_G as the share of the collusive group in industry sales (Q_G/Q) so that $(1 - C_G)$ is the share of the fringe, we have:

$$\eta_G = \frac{\eta_I}{C_G} + \left(\frac{1 - C_G}{C_G}\right)\eta_s$$

where η_s is the elasticity of supply of the fringe firms and η_I is the industry elasticity of demand. Finally then, the price–cost margin for the dominant group is:

$$\frac{p - MC_G}{p} = C_G/[\eta_I + (1 - C_G)\eta_s].$$

The index C_G is otherwise known as the G-firm (e.g. CR_4 is the four-firm) concentration ratio. This index will be discussed in chapter 9, along with a related index, the Linda index.

In order for this model to become operational, we have to define how supply of the fringe responds to price. Thus, to take two examples, we might assume (i) a conventional upward-sloping supply curve implying a finite η_s and C_G and so a finite price–cost margin for the industry as a whole (here, assuming the competitive fringe are pricing at marginal cost, the margin for the industry as a whole is that for the dominant group weighted by their share, i.e. $(p - MC)/p = C_G^2 / [\eta_I + (1 - C_G)\eta_s]$), or (ii) that the competitive fringe is a group of importers whose supply is perfectly elastic at the level of marginal cost including tariffs and transport, in which case price settles at that level. One problem with the leadership model is that outcomes vary so much as the assumptions regarding the fringe differ. On this see Ono (1982). Basically, followers benefit from the leader's restriction of output, so leadership has costs as well as benefits.

It is also possible, for example, to incorporate a set of fringe producers into the Cournot model. Again, depending upon what assumption is made, different outcomes will be generated. For example, Lyons (1981) shows that in a model with a fixed share for importers, the profit–revenue ratio for the home producer is:

$$\frac{\Pi + F}{R} = \frac{D}{D + M} \cdot \frac{H_D}{\eta} \tag{2.11}$$

where H_D is the Herfindahl index for home producers and D and M are domestic production and imports, respectively.

The general lesson from this series of models is that within a homogeneous good industry, given that output is the competitive weapon, a determinate solution for the profit–revenue ratio can be obtained and that this in general depends upon the industry elasticity of demand for the good in question and on the established industry structure (firm numbers etc.) but also upon the particular conjectures of the firms concerned[5] (and on the conditions of entry). Varying these will change the outcome in an oligopoly.

Bertrand's model

In contrast to all the above discussion, Bertrand (1883) asserted that even in duopoly, price would fall to the competitive level. The reason is that he assumes each firm chooses a price rather than an output level. Each also, crucially, has enough capacity to fulfil the entire market demand at a price equal to marginal cost (assumed the same for both, for simplicity). Because the products are identical, the firm with the lowest price makes all the sales. Now if firm 1, say, charges a price p_1 greater than marginal cost, firm 2 would undercut him slightly to make all sales. In turn, firm 1 would undercut firm 2 slightly to regain the market. The only equilibrium would be at price equal to marginal cost, where no firm has an incentive either to lower or to raise prices, but where no profits are made. Edgeworth (1925) developed an alternative to this model where the firms faced capacity constraints. In his model, as a consequence, no equilibrium need result.

Consistent conjectures equilibrium

In the Cournot model, each firm believes the others will not react to its output changes (and they do not, at equilibrium), but we know that in fact their reaction functions have a non-zero slope everywhere. In Stackleberg's model, the leader knows the other's reactions, but not vice versa. In Bertrand's model, the reaction is to the other firm's price rather than output. The outcome in each case is very different, but is exogenously given by virtue of the assumptions and never alters in the light of experience. Thus it may be argued that each theory is arbitrary.

Recently, some authors (see Bresnahan, 1981, or Perry, 1982*a*, for example) have suggested that a potentially superior equilibrium concept based upon reaction functions can be generated by requiring that the conjectures involved are consistent. In the Consistent (sometimes called Rational) Conjectures Equilibrium each firm's belief about how the others react, as captured in the conjectural variation, accords with the actual slope of the reaction function in the vicinity of equilibrium. In general the equilibrium is characterised by combined output greater than in the Cournot equilibrium, and sometimes it involves a combined output as great as in Bertrand's model.

The discussion in this section illustrates the wide range of possible solutions to the oligopoly problem. In particular we have seen that, if the firms' products are indeed identical, the choice of competitive weapon (e.g. price, quantity, conjecture) is of great importance in determining the outcome. Nevertheless the differences should not be over-emphasised. The extreme dichotomy between Bertrand and Cournot does not continue when we turn to the more realistic differentiated product cases. Also, as we shall see in our discussion of the Nash noncooperative equilibrium in chapter 3, the concept underlying equilibrium in Cournot, Bertrand and Consistent conjectures is actually very much the same.

2. Heterogeneous products

Several complications arise when we endeavour to extend our model of pricing behaviour to encompass industries producing heterogeneous products; not the least of which is the difficulty of deciding upon the industry boundaries. However, we leave this aside. In addition, firms might not be expected actively to pursue policies, such as advertising, designed to differentiate their product in the consumers' eyes. Under many circumstances though, we can separate pricing and produce location activities logically, and this is the approach adopted here. Product differentiation proper receives attention in chapter 6; our discussion here is only preliminary.

One factor we must consider at this juncture is the possibility that firms are more interested in setting prices than outputs. In contrast to the homogeneous industry situation, more than one price logically may exist in the market at any time. Even in a heterogeneous product industry though, it is not necessarily true that price is the decision variable; as an empirical matter, price, quantity or a mixture of the two may be more important in a given market. Having said this, we ought to view the maximising decision from both standpoints; there can be considerable differences in the outcomes.

At the very least then, we must redefine the ith firm's profit function to read:

$$\Pi_i = p_i q_i - C_i(q_i)$$

where

$$p_i = f_i(q_1, q_2, \ldots, q_n)$$

or, more convenient for price setting:

$$q_i = g_i(p_1, p_2, \ldots, p_n)$$

Notice that it is no longer possible to sum outputs unambiguously to obtain industry output. Thus, if maximisation is by choosing output there is no term equivalent to the dQ/dq_i of the previous section, so industry magnitudes are not easily recovered.

More promising is the approach of maximising with respect to price. Here we shall follow a symmetric oligopoly model developed by Cubbin (1974).[6] From the definition of profit, the first order maximum condition is:

$$\frac{d\Pi_i}{dp_i} = q_i + p_i \frac{dq_i}{dp_i} - \frac{dC_i}{dq_i} \cdot \frac{dq_i}{dp_i} = 0 \tag{2.12}$$

And here:

$$\frac{dq_i}{dp_i} = \frac{\partial q_i}{\partial p_i} + \sum_{j \neq i} \frac{\partial q_i}{\partial p_j} \frac{dp_j}{dp_i} \tag{2.13}$$

In this expression, it is the term dp_j/dp_i (between zero and one) which represents the 'conjectural variation', firm i's belief about the effect of his price change on j's behaviour. We may call it α_{ij}. The weighted average over the industry may then be written:

$$\alpha = \sum_{j \neq i} \alpha_{ij} \cdot \frac{\partial q_i}{\partial p_j} \bigg/ \sum_{j \neq i} \frac{\partial q_i}{\partial p_j}.$$

Substituting this and (2.13) into (2.12) yields:

$$q_i + (p_i - C_i') \cdot \left(\frac{\partial q_i}{\partial p_i} + \alpha \sum_{j \neq i} \frac{\partial q_i}{\partial p_j} \right) = 0 \tag{2.14}$$

Now, just as in the quantity variation model, firm i's *belief* about the relationship between his demand and the industry curve may well be erroneous. In Cournot's homogeneous product case with equal sized firms, the firm's demand curve if the others do not follow suit is (compare (2.7) and (2.8)) simply N times as elastic as his demand curve if they follow. Here, it is more complex. Using the definitional form of (2.13), Cubbin shows that:

$$\eta_I - \eta_{fi} = -\frac{p_i}{q_i} \sum_{j \neq i} \frac{\partial q_i}{\partial p_j} \tag{2.15}$$

where η_I is defined as the industry elasticity of demand, measuring the response of demand when all others change their prices by the same amount (i.e. when $dp_j/dp_i \equiv 1$ in (2.13)), whilst η_{fi} is the firm elasticity, measuring the response facing firm i when all others keep their prices constant.

By rearranging (2.14) to obtain the price–cost margin then substituting (2.15) into the result, we obtain:

$$\frac{p_i - C_i'}{p_i} = \frac{1}{\alpha \eta_I + (1 - \alpha)\eta_{fi}} \tag{2.16}$$

as the general expression for the ith firm's price–cost margin. Again, the actual result depends crucially upon the beliefs of the firms in the industry, and particular beliefs lead to particular models. Most analytical models though, faced with the awesome problems involved in all the products being different, assume some form of symmetry between the firms (e.g. if all set the same price they would all have the same sales).

Before we turn to some particular cases, one important general question we should discuss relates to the role of numbers in the industry, for, in contrast to our general homogeneous product model, as represented by (2.9), neither the number of firms nor a concentration index appears in (2.16). Consider though, using (2.15) to eliminate η_{fi} from (2.16), so obtaining:

$$\frac{p_i - C_i'}{p_i} = \frac{1}{\eta_I + (1 - \alpha)\frac{p_i}{q_i} \cdot \sum_{j \neq i} \frac{\partial q_i}{\partial p_j}} \tag{2.17}$$

Let us assume for simplicity, and ease of interpretation, that $\partial q_i/\partial p_j$ is the same for all j (that is: the particular product i is equally affected by a change in the price of any of its substitutes so they are all equally 'close' to it) and that in equilibrium situations $p_i = p_j$. Then, from (2.17):

$$\frac{p_i - C_i'}{p_i} = \left[\eta_I + (1 - \alpha) \cdot (N - 1)\frac{p_j}{q_i} \frac{\partial q_i}{\partial p_j} \right]^{-1}$$

Now, if the cross-elasticity between products does not fall as their numbers increase (which seems plausible) the second term in the square bracket rises with N, so the margin falls with increasing numbers as long as α is between 0 and 1. In the general case, the suggestion is that numbers do matter.

Chamberlin's small numbers case

This is the case equivalent to full collusion, and so where $\alpha = 1$ in (2.16). However, Chamberlin (1962) points out that there need not be explicit collusion amongst the firms in the industry. It is simply that if the group is small enough (though this is not defined) the firms will not be so naive as to assume that their actions will not have an effect upon their rivals' prices. Therefore, they realise, as with the case of collusion, the full effects of their price changes. Recognition of interdependence will arise again in a game theory context in the next chapter.

Chamberlin's large numbers case

This is the more famous of Chamberlin's theories set out in his book, and is essentially a price-setting equivalent of Cournot, called 'monopolistic competition'. It involves the assumption of symmetry of a very strict kind: uniform demands and costs throughout the whole group. Thus, the concept of the 'representative firm' may be adopted in diagrammatic analysis. He also introduces product differentiation, so that despite potentially large numbers in the industry each firm has a downward sloping demand curve. Both these assumptions have come in for criticism, basically because of the necessarily woolly nature of the concept of the industry. We have mentioned this already in chapter 1 and will not trouble to discuss it again here.

Chamberlin's own analysis is essentially graphical and involves a dd' curve and a DD' schedule as in figure 2.2. The latter is that fractional part of the

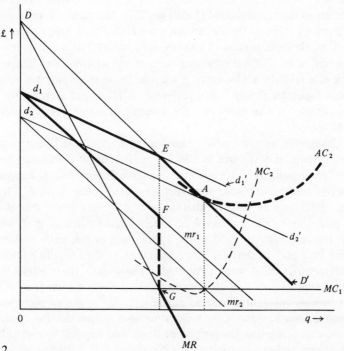

Figure 2.2

market demand curve which accords with the firm's share. It is thus drawn under the assumption that all firms are doing likewise and has an elasticity η_I; it shifts only if numbers of firms in the industry change. The ceteris paribus assumptions underlying dd' are that all other firms' prices are taken as given as well as the number of firms. Its elasticity is therefore η_{fi}. Because there are a large number of firms it is assumed, as in Cournot's theory, that each does not recognise interdependence; i.e. they assume $\alpha = 0$. This means that each firm thinks it is operating on dd' whereas, when they do so, the dd' curve shifts along DD'. Some representative examples are shown in figure 2.2, together with the associated marginal revenue curves. (Ignore for the while the varying thicknesses of line).

In order to explore possibilities more generally, we first examine a standardised version of Chamberlin's model. Here, equilibrium will be reached, as in Cournot's model, when the firm's belief turns out to be realised. For example moving from point E on d_1d_1', each will wish to expand as marginal revenue is substantially above marginal cost. But if they do so, the actual movement will be along DD' and price will be lower than expected. When dd' has shifted as far down as d_2d_2' though, setting $mr_2 = MC_1$ indicates an output at point A which is maintainable since it is on DD'. Thus A is the equilibrium within the present framework.

Instead of working with reaction functions, one can think of very much the same slide of dd' down DD' as happening in Cournot's homogeneous product model, as Archibald (1959) explains. The parallel is not exact though as Webb's addendum (in the reprinted versions of Archibald's paper) shows.

A standardised version of Chamberlin's model thus involves an equivalent assumption to Cournot's by each firm about its rivals and hence a similar type of equilibrium. However Chamberlin chose to employ two assumptions which make his theory rather different: a 'U' shaped average cost function and completely free entry into the industry, resulting jointly in a zero profit equilibrium.

Chamberlin assumes a 'U' shaped average cost curve like AC_2 and so we have a marginal cost curve like MC_2. Thus because of the way we have drawn the figure, point A is the short-run equilibrium here also. It happens that it involves zero profits, since price at A is equal to average cost, so it is the long-run equilibrium as well. If, alternatively, AC_2 were lower than it is drawn, so point A's equilibrium involved supernormal profits, or if it were higher and involved losses, Chamberlin's assumptions of free entry and exit would come into play to shift DD' (and dd') until at the long-run equilibrium the characteristics of A were reasserted, namely each firm selling the profit-maximising level of output given its assumed demand curve ($mr_2 = MC_2$) but not making any profit, because of the tangency of the average cost and the assumed demand curve at the point at which it crosses the true demand curve. Thus, with free entry, the number of firms is determined by cost and demand conditions, and so is endogenous to the model.

One question is whether this tangency equilibrium is inefficient because firms are producing less than an amount representing the lowest point on their average cost curves and so have excess capacity. This is not clear cut, because although costs are incurred as firms introduce more products, at the same time the consumers gain variety and so welfare. The topic is discussed when we consider product differentiation more formally in chapter 6.

The kinked demand curve theory

Using the apparatus developed above, we may also examine the kinked demand curve theory of oligopoly. This is spoken of by some as 'the' theory of oligopoly. However, it is merely a special case of the general conjectural variations model. Essentially the model assumes that the firms each have asymmetric beliefs about others' reactions – that they will follow price cuts but not price rises. Symbolically:

$$\frac{\mathrm{d}p_j}{\mathrm{d}p_i} = \begin{cases} 0 \text{ for } \mathrm{d}p_i > 0 \\ 1 \text{ for } \mathrm{d}p_i < 0 \end{cases}$$

Thus, $\alpha = 0$ for $\mathrm{d}p_i > 0$, $\alpha = 1$ for $\mathrm{d}p_i < 0$. At the going price (say point E in figure 2.2) then, there is a kink in the imagined demand curve. The lower (bold) section of the schedule corresponds to Chamberlin's DD' curve with elasticity η_I, whereas the upper section (also boldly drawn) is the very much more elastic dd' curve (elasticity η_{fi}). This means the marginal revenue curve (bold) is discontinuous over a certain range of prices at the going quantity (between F and G in our figure).

However, the supposed main advantage of the kinked demand curve theory, that is its explanation of infrequent price changes as due to marginal cost changes within the discontinuous range not affecting price, is at the same time its major disadvantage. For the corollary of this is that the theory can attempt little explanation of the extent to which price is above marginal cost. Obviously limits may be prescribed; it is fairly straightforward to deduce that the extent of discontinuity as a proportion of price may be expressed as:

$$\frac{mr_{fi} - MR_i}{p_i} = \frac{1}{\eta_I} - \frac{1}{\eta_{fi}}$$

Within these limits though, the theory is silent. Another questionable point is whether in boom periods firms will still consider that others are reluctant to follow price rises.[7]

In summary, within the sphere of differentiated product models, there are again a wide range of possibilities. However those same factors that proved to be of importance in the homogeneous product cases – industry structure, demand elasticities and conjectures about rivals, are again seen to be important here.

3. Reaction functions and the stability of solutions

In our discussion of various oligopoly models, we have assumed that the firm's second-order conditions for maximisation are satisfied, so the firm has a non-negative optimal output. But this is not sufficient to ensure that the behaviour of the group of firms under consideration (even given that their number is fixed) will have some stability. There are really two questions here. One is whether, in say the price leadership model, the dominant group can maintain its identity. This question of stability of a sub-group is not our concern at the moment, though it will come up in chapter 3. The other question, which we will address now, really relates to the observability of a particular postulated equilibrium for given parameter values. If the equilibrium is (or, all potential equilibria are) unstable then slight shocks will move the firms away from equilibrium and we would not observe it except briefly. Thus it would lose its relevance. In other words, we should enquire how sensible particular models are, not from the standpoint of assumptions about rival behaviour but instead as regards the likelihood of equilibrium.

We saw in figure 2.1 that the Cournot duopoly situation with linear reaction functions had a unique stable equilibrium. A natural problem to be posed is whether in every type of more complex formulation this still holds. Fellner (1949) was somewhat dubious. He noted that in the Cournot model with non-linear demand and cost functions there may be several intersections between demand and cost functions. Under more general conjectural variation assumptions, he observed that 'reaction functions in this extended sense need not intersect for positive outputs, and if they intersect, the point of intersection *need not* be stable' (p. 73).

In analysing such potential difficulties, the main approach has been to inject some dynamics into a simple version of the model under consideration. The problem here is to make the dynamics believable; for example in the Cournot model a stepwise process towards equilibrium involves continuous falsification of the maintained assumption. For this reason many authors suggest only local stability (in the vicinity of equilibrium) is of interest rather than, say, the movement between equilibria involved in figure 2.1.[8]

Much of the work in this area has in fact been done on the Cournot model itself. An early example is Theocharis (1960) who set up a simple sequential model with linear demand curves and constant marginal cost. In it, each firm believes the other firms would maintain their output from the previous period, so that in choosing its own output the firm also determines industry price. He assumed each firm could adjust output completely and instantaneously to the optimal level, the relevant point on the reaction function, i.e. $q_{it} = q_{it}^*$. Thus, as far as the ith firm is concerned, price at time t will be:

$$p_t = f(q_{1,t-1} + q_{2,t-1} + q_{i,t}^* + \ldots + q_{n,t-1})$$

Such a scheme results mathematically in a system of simultaneous difference equations. Without dwelling on the mechanics of this, the general solution for firm i is found to be:

$$q_{it} = A_i(\tfrac{1}{2})^t + B\left(-\frac{n-1}{2}\right)^t + \bar{q}_i \qquad (2.18)$$

Here B and A_i are constant (see e.g. Gehrig, 1981). Thus the first term declines as t increases because the damping effect of increasing powers of $\tfrac{1}{2}$ becomes apparent (e.g. $(\tfrac{1}{2})^6 < (\tfrac{1}{2})^5 < (\tfrac{1}{2})^4$). The second term is much more important. For $n = 2$, the value in brackets is $(-\tfrac{1}{2})$ and so as t increases that term fluctuates between positive and negative values but becomes smaller in absolute value. Hence, as t becomes large, q_{it} approaches $\bar{q}$, just as the path in dotted lines in figure 2.1 does. However, for $n = 4$, for example, the value in the second bracket in (2.18) is $-\tfrac{3}{2}$, so succeeding values of t produce increasing oscillations. Theocharis had discovered the rather surprising result that the model was stable with two firms, gave rise to constant oscillations for 3 and was unstable for any higher number.

Still keeping very much within the Cournot framework other writers (e.g. Fisher (1961), Quandt and McManus (1961) and Hahn (1962)) have concentrated on the adjustment function and the marginal cost specification. Fisher argues that it is consistent with the spirit of the Cournot model for adjustment by the firm in question not to be complete and instantaneous. He posits an adjustment:

$$q_{it} - q_{i,t-1} = K_i(q_{it}^* - q_{i,t-1})$$

Thus the Cournot firm is looking and receiving information while making adjustments as well as afterwards. The character of the information then causes him to change his optimal value before adjustment to the previous value is complete.[9] In addition, Fisher considers the case of non-constant marginal cost using a simple linear function. The conclusions are that increasing marginal costs are a stabilising factor and the slower the speed of reaction the larger the number of firms to cause instability. Intuitively, both increasing marginal cost and a slow reaction speed make the 'rivals output constant' assumption a better approximation, so stability is more likely.

The limiting case of continuous adjustment is the version:

$$\frac{dq_i}{dt} = K_i(q_i^* - q_i)$$

which yields a series of differential rather than difference equations. Here, the firm is continuously reviewing decisions while making adjustments, so adjustment is extremely slow *relative to* the frequency of decision review. It would seem to follow from the existence of such a continuous process that a slow enough adjustment can always be found to produce stability, whatever the number of firms. Interestingly, Hahn shows that whatever the functional form of demand and costs, with a continuous review, stability is automatic as long as the slope of the firm's marginal cost curve is always greater than the slope of the industry demand curve and assuming the marginal revenue of each producer falls if the other producers expand output. Ogukuchi (1964) finds a weaker version of continuous adjustment gives the same results. Seade (1980) points out that Hahn's second condition, though seemingly innocuous, in fact rules out some quite reasonable demand elasticity ranges. However, he is able to widen the range of cases where stability holds somewhat.

The discussion of stability has also gone beyond the basic Cournot model. Seade (1980) finds Hahn's assumptions and model can easily be extended to the case of positive conjectural variations. Hadar (1966) considers a differentiated oligopoly where profits are maximised with respect to output and adjustment is of the Theocharis type. Here increasing marginal cost again has a stabilising effect and the model will be stable as long as the cross-effects of the other firms' products upon the marginal revenue of the firm in question are sufficiently weak. These results hold for a more general variant he develops. Quandt (1967) takes a differentiated oligopoly with price the decision variable and a continuous adjustment. Unlike the quantity model with continuous adjustment, stability does not automatically occur, though it will do so if the effects of others' price changes are relatively small compared to own price changes. Intuitively, if j's price falls below a certain level, there might be quite marked swings away from i's product, which will cause i to react sharply, and so on; but this is less likely the smaller the cross effects.

Obviously, we cannot arrive at any very general conclusions regarding stability. However, for most purposes we will be interested in our models only as descriptions of oligopolistic markets around equilibrium (and indeed it is only then that most of the adjustment mechanisms become believable). In that case continuous review and so calculus methods would seem a reasonable framework to employ and, as we have seen, stability will be a feature of a wide class of models – a comforting conclusion.

4. Some welfare considerations

As we saw in the previous chapter, economists should be concerned about divergences of price from cost from the public policy point of view that they lead to deadweight welfare losses. In implementing an anti-monopoly policy to correct problems arising from the use of excessive market power, the government would presumably consider intervening in ways which influence industry output (e.g. disallowing a merger or splitting up a powerful firm). At the same time, this activity is costly. Thus, the government should intervene to only a limited extent and should attach itself to those projects which show the greatest excess of benefits over costs. Assuming the costs are directly related to the magnitude of the output changes involved, this narrows to the government pursuing changes in which the benefits are most intensive relative to the output change.

Dansby and Willig (1979) have investigated the theory of intervention in the context of oligopolistic behaviour. They find the optimal direction for a welfare-improving policy is directly related to the difference between price and cost in the firm(s) concerned. They then choose a suitable measuring rod[10] to evaluate the relative size of output adjustments and thus find an index ϕ which measures the rate of potential improvements in welfare performance of an industry as outputs q_i^0. This may be written as a simple transformation of the firms' Lerner indexes evaluated at q_i^0:

$$\phi = \left\{ \sum_i \left[\frac{p_i^0 - C_i'(q_i^0)}{p_i^0} \right]^2 \right\}^{1/2}$$

Thus, in a homogeneous product industry with N firms, we may substitute from equation (2.5) to write the *industry performance gradient index* ϕ as:

$$\phi = \frac{1}{\eta} [\Sigma s_i^2 (1 + \lambda_i)^2]^{1/2} \qquad (2.19)$$

They then go on to derive some special cases, for example for a Cournot industry. However the main point, which is evident from (2.19), is that the rate of potential welfare improvement from government intervention depends not only upon market structure (firm sizes and demand elasticity) but also on market conducts (λ_i). Notice in addition that the greatest impact on performance in an industry is likely to be made by affecting those firms with the largest market shares.

We should append a general warning to these points on intervention. Throughout the chapter we have treated costs as exogenously determined. We shall have cause to modify this view somewhat in chapter 9 and consequently shall have more to say on the question of concentration and welfare.

In conclusion, there is no unique model of oligopoly and so no unique welfare implications arising from changing industry structure. In fact, it might seem that a bewildering array of models can be applied to the oligopoly situation. However, though outcomes are manifold, the same features continually crop up: industry demand elasticity, market structure and firms' beliefs about rivals. Hence it is not true that we can say nothing about outcomes in oligopolistic industries; we can make a number of statements of a ceteris paribus kind, for example.

Notes on the literature

There have been several attempts to define that group of firms which constitutes an industry and then to classify industries into various types (e.g.

homogeneous oligopoly). An example is Bishop (1952), which gave rise to an extensive discussion (in *American Economic Review* of 1953 and 1955).

On the exposition of the classical theories of oligopoly, at an intermediate microeconomics level, Henderson and Quandt (1971), Cohen and Cyert (1975) and Koutsoyiannis (1979) are all quite good, though they do not relate the results to the price–cost margin. The basic model used to do this here is set out in Cowling and Waterson (1976), which also derives the relationship involving the Herfindahl index. The dominant firm model is due to Saving (1970). Fellner is also good on Cournot, Stackleberg etc., and in particular has some very useful discussions on reaction functions. The kinked oligopoly demand curve is clearly analysed in Stigler (1968). Many of the topics discussed in the chapter are analysed in Encaoua and Jacquemin (1980), though the reader may find this rather abstract.

Unfortunately, stability in the sense discussed here does not seem to have received a straightforward comparative treatment or survey.

3

Oligopoly: the game theoretic approach

As we saw in chapter 2, there are a large number of potential 'classical' solutions to the oligopoly problem. Given this diversity of outcomes, several approaches to further analysis are possible. One is to use the theory solely in tests where only general results are required, and this is the implicit approach adopted by much of the empirical work covered in chapter 10. An alternative is to try a somewhat different approach, to build a new conceptual framework, in the hope that it will provide new insights or even new solutions. This is what the *theory of games* as applied to oligopoly does. It relates to classical oligopoly theory by providing a different angle on the problem. The focus in game theory is on strategic aspects of behaviour, on the players in the game and the payoffs (profits) they envisage.

Because this approach is relatively novel, we develop the concepts of game theory from basic first principles in the opening section. One of the main conceptual classes of game useful in oligopoly theory, that is non-cooperative games and their equilibria, receives further analysis in section 2. In such cases, the firms cannot make binding agreements amongst themselves. If they are able to do so, we are into the world of cooperative games. These are discussed in section 3, along with other theoretical contributions which, while not always thought as part of the body of game theory, nevertheless use a similar analysis of strategy and of the difficulties of achieving complete cooperative agreement.

A third approach to the oligopoly problem is to attempt to design tests specifically to identify situations in which one or more of the particular theories are most useful. This has been tackled by those developing *experimental oligopoly games*, which are discussed in the final substantive section.

1. Some simple examples

In order to gain some appreciation of the scope and method of the theory of games, without getting too involved with terminology or mathematics, we proceed largely by discussing simple examples and extensions on an intuitive basis. Consider then the simple *payoff matrix* below (table 3.1), where the payments in the table are understood to go to firm A, and the payment to firm B is simply 100 minus the payment to A. This is a *constant sum game*.

Table 3.1. *Payoff to A*

		Strategy for B		Maximise row minima (maximin)
	1	2	3	
Strategy for A 1	45	30	40	30
2	35	10	15	10
3	50	25	20	20
Minimise column Maxima (minimax)	50	30	40	
[Minimum payoffs to B	50	70	60]	

Each firm or *player* in our example has three *strategies* or moves, of which he can make one. Once each player has decided upon his strategy and played it, the game ends and the payoffs are distributed. Thus, having described the 'rules' of the game, we proceed by considering the players' preferences. Let us view the situation first from firm A's point of view, bearing in mind that, by assumption, both firms know everything about the game.

Suppose firm A considers he will have to play first (though in fact plays may well be made simultaneously). In this case firm B has a completely free hand to do as well as she can for herself (and so be as hard as she can on A). What can A do? One very persuasive stratagem would be to consider each of his choices from the point of view of how badly he might do. Thus if he used strategy 1, the least he could obtain would be 30 units, with strategy 2, the lowest is 10 units, and with strategy 3, 20 units. If, as we suggested, he is only interested in comparing worst outcomes, then strategy 1 is best; given that B is assumed to move second, A has ensured himself at least 30 units, he has maximised the row minima, or played his *maximin* strategy.

Alternatively, if B has to move first, and given that the players' interests are completely opposed, she should think in the same way as A. Remember that this time B is interested in the column maxima as these are (to her) minima, when subtracted from 100. The column maxima and consequent minimum payments to B are listed in the table. The obvious choice is strategy 2 which assures A at most 30 units and so B at least 70 units. She in turn has played her *minimax* strategy. And notice that, if both act along these lines, each gets what he expected, the strategy played is the best reply to the opponent (their strategy assumed fixed), and the maximin value is equal to the minimax value. Therefore, this can obviously be considered as an equilibrium solution and moreover, one which game theory has revealed but has not previously been considered by us.

Several questions arise, however. The first and most obvious is as to whether we have cheated by formulating an example in which the maximin payoff is equal to the minimax payoff. The answer is, both yes and no. In a two-person constant (or, conceptually equivalent, zero) sum game with several pure strategies such as: always play strategy number 2, it need not be so. Table 3.1 happened to feature a *saddle point*, that is a position where payoffs in one direction (for example as B's strategy changes) rise as one moves away from it and those in another direction (A's strategy changing, B's fixed) fall as one moves away. This is what gave rise to the equilibrium. If we changed the table by making the payoff to A under his strategy 1, B's strategy 2 to 5 units, there would be no saddle point. However, if the rules of the game allow players not only to choose pure strategies but also *mixed strategies* then, as was first proved by von Neumann (see von Neumann and Morgern-stern, 1953), a saddle point will always exist. Mixed strategies are probabilis-tic combinations where, for example, a player adopts one particular strategy if a fair coin tossed produces heads and another strategy if tails eventuates.

Secondly, there is the question of what happens if there are more than two players. Solutions, it must be admitted, become much more complex. Lastly, and most fundamentally, can an oligopoly game be considered as of the constant sum variety? If we are talking about rivalry over market shares we have a constant sum situation since a gain for one player is a loss for another, but why should there be a fight over market shares regardless of other parameters such as price? Alternatively, we could conceptually add one player who receives the negative of the payoff to the firms, for example, and thereby turn the game into a zero-sum one. This player has no image in the real world though; he cannot be the consumer, because the sum of consumer and producer surplus varies as we move along the industry demand curve. Thus the procedure is of limited use; total profits change with the solution.

Oligopoly, then, is in general an N person, *non-constant sum* and, often, *non-cooperative* game. Non-cooperative means that the players are not able to make binding agreements amongst themselves, and is a sensible rule for most oligopoly situations; it was the usual assumption of chapter 2. Work on models of co-operative or collusive oligopoly, where binding agreements can be made, is reviewed in the third section. The question for the moment is whether there are non-cooperative solutions and, if so, what their properties are. Let us again take a two-firm example with three strategies, where each firm plays only one, and plays are made simultaneously. The firms produce the same product and have identical cost functions so the payoffs will be symmetrical, but we have to write both (with 1's payoff first) in a table since the sum is not constant over cells. Consider then the simple example presented in table 3.2, where payoffs were derived by assuming a demand curve:

$$p = 200 - q_1 - q_2$$

and cost curves given by:

$$c_i = 20q_i, \qquad i = 1, 2.$$

Let us consider the problem in abstract terms first. In this game, the pay-offs are no longer completely opposed, and so the players need not be as

Table 3.2.   *Firm 2's strategies*

		M	C	PMC
Firm 1's	M	(4050, 4050)	(3375, 4500)	(2025, 4050)
strategies	C	(4500, 3375)	(3600, 3600)	(1800, 2700)
	PMC	(4050, 2025)	(2700, 1800)	(0, 0)

actively opposed to one another as in the constant sum game. However, we can easily see that the third strategy, *PMC*, will never logically be employed. For *whatever* strategy 2 plays, firm 1 has a payoff incentive to play either the *C* strategy rather than the *PMC* one (i.e. $4500 > 4050$, $3600 > 2700$, $1800 > 0$), or the *M* strategy rather than *PMC*. The same goes for firm 2. Thus *PMC* is said to be *dominated* by both *M* and *C* whatever transpires and so (by what is known as the 'sure thing' principle), would not logically be chosen by either firm. Hence, we shall continue by restricting choices to strategies *M* and *C*.

Now, let us assume the players are extremely risk averse and again try the strategies equivalent to minimax and maximin. For firm 1, the row minima are 3375 and 3600 respectively. This suggests playing strategy *C* and expecting a payoff of 3600. Since firm 2 is identical, he would make the same decision. Thus, the minimax and maximin point would be (C, C) and the payoff would be that expected. Notice further that if the point (M, M) were envisaged, each player would have an individual interest in playing his *C* strategy if he thought the other would play the *M* strategy. Hence both would, if they believed the other to be a maximin agent, play the *C* strategy. Even if both believed that the other would think like this and so play the *C* strategy, the *best reply* would itself be the *C* strategy, as can be seen in the table. Thus strategy *C* dominates other potentially more favourable ones (here *M*) within the restricted set now being considered. It is only if both are *sure* that the other will play the *M* strategy and they each have an effective way of punishing deviation from this behaviour, that they will play (M, M). But that moves us outside the realm of the rules in the absence of binding agreements.

Such a choice problem (between *M* and *C*) is an example of what is called a *prisoners' dilemma* game. The standard prisoners' dilemma envisaged is that two people are separately interviewed as to a crime they have committed. If one confesses to the implication of both, he gets a low penalty (high relative payoff) in exchange for cooperation, while the other is severely punished. If both confess, however, a high penalty (low relative payoff) will be meted out. Alternatively, if neither confesses, a more minor charge can be success-fully prosecuted and both get a moderate penalty. Assuming there is little honour among thieves, both have a substantial incentive to confess.

Notice that in both stages of describing the game we made use of the dominance concept. However, there is an essential distinction to be made. Both players have an individual as well as a joint interest in playing the *C* (or *M*) rather than the *PMC* strategy. This may be contrasted with the choice between *M* and *C* plays where there is a joint interest in playing (*M, M*) but an individual interest in each playing *C*.

The time has come to reveal that the *M*, *C* and *PMC* strategies are those of setting joint-monopoly, Cournot, and price-equal-to-marginal-cost output levels in our simple duopoly example. Looking at these in a game-theoretic context has revealed the power of the Cournot solution, for if one player utilises his Cournot strategy, the other's best policy is to do likewise. In fact, this is merely a simplified example of what is known as the *Nash non-cooperative equilibrium*, yielding a point such that 'each player's strategy maximises his expected payoff if the strategies of the others are held fixed'[1] (Shubik, 1959, p. 62). What this means in our context is that, even if we were to fill in a plethora of alternative possible strategies between *M* and *C* and between *C* and *PMC* in an *N firm* game, it would still be true that the Cournot equilibrium would be a Nash non-cooperative equilibrium, for Shubik's quotation illustrates just what Cournot firms do. That is, whatever example we wished to pick would illustrate the point that, for all firms, any value in the matrix involving more output for the firm concerned would involve a lower payoff to that firm, which consequently has an individual incentive to move to the Cournot output level. Moreover, outputs smaller than the Cournot level can only be envisaged as leading to higher payoffs if the belief that others will follow the move can be sustained. In sum, no player can gain by *unilateral* departure from the Cournot–Nash point.

But we can be more general even than this. Suppose in a differentiated product industry that price is the decision variable. Then, along the lines of the Chamberlin-type model presented in section 2.2, an equilibrium equivalent to the Cournot equilibrium ($\alpha = 0$) can be determined, where each firm's assumption that the others hold their prices fixed is realised. Since the statement of the Nash non-cooperative equilibrium does not specify a particular decision variable then the equilibrium strategies in this case also give rise to such an equilibrium, often also called Cournot–Nash. In both cases, there is no reason why price and output should fall to the level where price equals marginal cost.[2]

2. Further analysis of non-cooperative equilibria

The realisation that the Cournot point (or its price equivalent) is a non-cooperative equilibrium is a very powerful insight. One obvious extension which we consider is to see whether other non-cooperative equilibria exist apart from the Cournot–Nash point. But moreover it means that any theorem which can be proved for a non-cooperative equilibrium will be valid for a Cournot equilibrium. This provides an alternative approach to proofs of stability and uniqueness for the Cournot model and possibly also for extensions of it involving reaction functions. Let us first turn to work on this question.

Friedman (1977) shows rigorously that a Cournot quantity variation equilibrium *exists* for an N-firm oligopoly under fairly general assumptions regarding demand and cost functions – the most stringent of which is possibly that the industry demand function cuts both price and quantity axes[3] – and assuming that the second-order maximisation condition for the firm holds (see chapter 2). However *uniqueness* of the equilibrium turns out to require rather stronger conditions. These parallel the stability conditions identified by Fisher (1961) (for the case where $k_i = 1$) outlined in section 2.3; that is as the number of firms increases, uniqueness requires more and more sharply increasing marginal cost functions. There is thus a very real possibility that more than one Cournot quantity equilibrium will present itself if the number of firms is large.

Friedman further demonstrates that the Cournot price variation equilibrium similarly exists under fairly general conditions on cost and demand – though the latter have to be expressed in a rather complex form to take account of various boundary possibilities – and assuming the equivalent second-order maximisation condition holds. Uniqueness, in contrast to the quantity model, is far less problematical as it does not depend upon numbers in the industry. The conditions are along the lines of those for stability found by Hadar (1966) (see again section 2.3), and upward sloping marginal cost, plus dominance of the effect of i's price changes on i's marginal revenue over the effect of other firms' price changes on i's marginal revenue, are sufficient.

In the Stackleberg follower–leader model of chapter 2, one firm picks a reaction function, or rule, for choosing a quantity and the other chooses a point on that function. This does not produce a non-cooperative equilibrium though, because at least one firm can do better by playing an alternative strategy[4] (e.g. setting output at the Cournot level rather than picking a reaction function). However the consistent conjectures equilibrium, where each firms picks a quantity and a conjecture, is a Cournot–Nash equilibrium in *conjectures*. There may be other reaction functions which firms want to use, and there is at least a possibility that choosing time-labelled reaction functions (see below) rather than quantities or prices might yield non-cooperative equilibria additional to the Cournot–Nash one, which is the degenerate case in the sense of being the simplest and most obvious strategy. Unfortunately, as Friedman explains, the customary method of proof is of little assistance in indicating such equilibria, for it relies on proving existence without isolating specifically cases other than the degenerate one. Thus this particular approach to dynamic equilibria has not so far proven very tractable within the game theoretic framework. Despite this, substantial insights into many-period models have been gained using an alternative method of attack, to which we now turn.

Within our present set of rules (i.e. in the absence of binding agreements) the Cournot–Nash equilibrium is the only sensible result in a one-period game, for any other play but the Cournot strategy leaves the firm with the strong possibility of a below-Cournot payoff and no possibility of retaliation. But in the 'real world', firms do not normally play a one-period game. Rather they play a series of more or less similar games (and possibly also strategies) year after year. The possibility of some retaliation to unwelcome strategies by other players then arises. Let us investigate these possibilities,[5] starting with a simple example.

Suppose that our players or firms are engaged in (say) three games, like that of table 3.2, all identical. They could choose a strategy for each constituent game at its commencement, but the possibility arises that they choose a strategy to cover all games at the commencement of play. Such a set of similar or identical one-period games might then be considered together as a *supergame*, though some authors reserve this term for an infinite series of games. Because all constituent games are by assumption identical, the supergame is said to be *stationary*. The choice of a strategy to cover all possible plays by opponents at the beginning is called a *supergame strategy*.

One possible supergame strategy would be to decide to play the Cournot quantity move in each period regardless of opponents' 'moves', but interest focuses naturally on alternative plays. In our three-game example though, consider the last period, period three. No retaliation beyond this point can occur, so that for each firm the Cournot move is the best available in this period, and payoffs of 3600 each are received. But then the move in period three has been chosen without reference to payoffs and strategies in previous periods, so that the first and second periods stand alone. Consider now period two. Nothing done here can affect period three, as the best strategy for that period has already been chosen. In that case, the best strategy for period two is that which would hold if period two were the last period, since there is no retaliation available – again the Cournot strategy. Period one then stands alone and the Cournot strategy will be chosen for this also. The argument can easily be extended to a game with any finite number (T) of periods, and is the backward induction argument of Luce and Raiffa (1957).

To get strategies alternative to constant play of the Cournot move we have (at least in theory) to consider an infinite period game. Suppose for simplicity this is again stationary. Here each firm is naturally expected to wish to maximise the expected sum of dismounted future payoffs P_i (which depends on his own and others' strategies S_j) from now till eternity, that is to maximise:

$$\sum_{t=1}^{\infty} \alpha_i^{t-1} P_i(S_{1t}, S_{2t}, \ldots, S_{Nt}), \qquad 1 > \alpha_i > 0$$

The α terms may be considered straightforwardly as discounting parameters in a world of certainty – the higher α_i, the more *highly* firm i values future payoffs, or in terms of an expected payoff in an uncertain world. In the latter case, $1 - \alpha_i$ is the probability (as perceived by i) that the current play is the last. Thus although the game is infinite, the existence of play in any particular period (except the first) is not certain. This interpretation makes the idea of an infinite game more intuitively acceptable. In addition, there would seem no particular reason why α_i could not account for both discounting and probability of continuation.

Again one possible supergame strategy would be to play the Cournot move in every period; this provides a non-cooperative equilibrium. But the alternatives here are many. Because the game is never certain to end, retaliation next period is always possible, so non-Cournot plays can be countenanced. The theorist's skill lies in conjecturing such supergame strategies which will give rise to non-cooperative equilibria. Thus Friedman (1977) considers the case of a player (i) choosing a particular strategy, involving payoffs higher than the Cournot level if all firms follow suit, and maintaining it for as long as others do in fact follow suit. If another player ever chooses not to make that play, however, player i moves to her Cournot strategy for the rest of the game (or until some other play can be agreed upon implicitly). The obvious example, and the case which Telser illustrates for two firms, is for the initial strategy to be the one which jointly maximises profits, all other firms doing likewise. Whilst this is *not* the only possible example, it adds concreteness to our discussion to have this strategy in mind and also provides a link with the next section.

The danger of playing the joint-profit maximising strategy is similar to the classic one of the prisoner's dilemma. Another firm may find he can obtain higher payoffs by playing an alternative strategy, or 'cheating' as Telser (1972) puts it. Cheating can provide a one period higher payoff due to a surprise change of move at the expense of later periods when the Cournot strategy becomes the best play for all. In comparing 'cheating' with joint-profit maximising we can consider that the cheat takes place in the first period; this should be the most profitable time to cheat because successive periods' payoffs are valued less highly.

If there are only two firms, we can illustrate the possibilities involved using the reaction functions of chapter 2, suitably amended (see figure 3.1, drawn for a case like table 3.2). The decision problem is this: if both firms choose the joint-profit maximising strategy and continue to use it, profits for firm 1 are the discounted sum of Π_{12} as a perpetuity, that is: $\Sigma_{t=1}^{\infty} \alpha_i^{t-1} \Pi_{12}$. If firm 2 starts by choosing her joint-profit maximising strategy, but firm 1 cheats, the latter will choose the output associated with the given value $\bar{q}_2$ on her reaction function, yielding profit level Π_{14}. (Note she does *not* choose the Cournot output level as this would yield a slightly lower profit of Π_{13} for the first period). Thereafter, both play the Cournot strategy with associated payoff to firm 1 of Π_{11}. In this case profits for firm 1 are:

$$\Pi_{14} + \sum_{t=2}^{\infty} \alpha_i^{t-1} \Pi_{11}$$

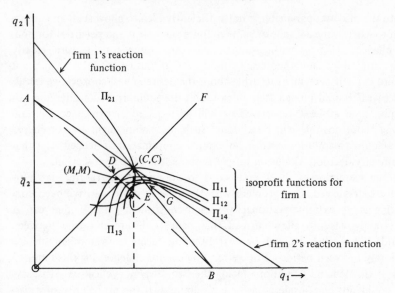

Figure 3.1

The two payoffs to infinity may then be compared. Without doing this explicitly, it is easy to see intuitively that if α is high, the joint-profit maximising case is likely to prevail as it involves more profits at the expense (compared to the alternative) of less in the first period. Thus the joint-profit maximising strategy will provide a non-cooperative equilibrium for suitably high evaluation of future periods (or given a sufficiently high probability of continuing), as assessed by both firms. Hence a particular equilibrium (e.g. the Cournot strategy) may or may not be reached dependent upon the speed of adjustment.

This example may fairly obviously be extended to any number of firms. If even one firm finds it advantageous to play the alternative strategy however, all players move in the next period to the Cournot strategy and continue along that path. Nevertheless it is possible, as Friedman (ch. 8) suggests (but is unable to prove), that a 'balanced temptation equilibrium' exists where all firms have the same discount parameter α and so all have the same temptation to cheat, yet none do so because the one period gain does not outweigh later period losses.

We have been talking in this supergame of 'cheating'. This terminology is not strictly accurate though, for the equilibrium is not cooperative but non-cooperative. That is, for suitably high α values it is in each firm's individual interest in this supergame to play the joint profit maximising strategy on the assumption that others do so. The joint profit maximising equilibrium may thus come about *without* explicit agreement.[6] We could call this collusion by definition if we wished, or we could reserve that term solely for cases where the discount parameter is not sufficiently high to allow such an equilibrium to exist in the absence of some definite agreement and penalties for non-compliance. This semantic point aside, the interesting feature clearly demonstrated by game-theoretic methods, is that mutual self-interest may not require explicit agreement to bring about the desired quasi-cooperative result. One caveat should immediately be noted. If the equilibrium considered is not unique, then at least verbal assent will be required on which equilibrium among those possible will be chosen. Such discussion might be considered tantamount to collusion even if no explicit coordination is needed after that preliminary decision. Collusion proper is discussed in the next section.

Some examples of slight extensions to our supergame results may now briefly be reviewed. One problem with the type of game we have been considering is its extreme stationarity – each constituent game is identical. It is certainly easy to allow instead that payoffs differ arbitrarily between periods. Thus, the demand or cost function facing a firm might change randomly between periods. But we must be careful in delimiting this randomness. If the demand conditions facing the firm display cyclical patterns, say, this could not be considered as true randomness if the probability of a particular game in the next period depended to some extent on the character of the current, and maybe past, constituent games (e.g. if demand is lower in this period than last, it might be likely to be even lower next period). Thus, arbitrary payoffs in constituent games should be distinguished from *stochastic supergames* where past games and/or strategies have some probabilistic influence on the character of the present games. It would not be as easy, and may even not be possible, to show the existence of strategies other than the constant Cournot play for the latter type of game. Another possible model type, which we do not consider, are games which are structurally time dependent, in that payoffs this period are a function of last period's plays as well as those of this period, for example.

One interesting case suggested by Nicholson (1972) is where players have two strategic variables in a supergame of the type we have been considering. His example is pricing and advertising policy. It is possible that retaliation to actions on one of these is slower than for the other, maybe because the relevant information is harder to obtain. Thus it might be that a firm can respond to 'cheating' on price in the next period, but 'cheating' on advertising requires two periods before effective action can be taken. In such a model it is far more likely, for a given discount parameter, that a 'collusive' policy is followed on the quicker reaction strategy variable and a Cournot-type policy on the slower one, since the temporarily higher payments last longer in the latter case. Thus Nicholson suggests that collusion on price is more likely than collusion on advertising policies. Whilst one might argue about the relative lags in these two particular examples, his discussion provides a useful insight into a simple extension of our standard supergame model. Here (and elsewhere), the *state of information* in the market has been shown by game-theoretic methods to be of some importance in gaining insights into oligopolistic behaviour.

So far our discussion of game-theoretic models of oligopoly has been based largely within the classical framework established in the previous chapter. However it is possible to indicate briefly that we may use game theory to move somewhat outside that framework. For example, both Shubik and Telser point out that one tacit assumption of classical oligopoly models, that price discrimination is not practised, should be exposed to some scrutiny. In fact, in many cases price discrimination is unlikely to occur since the opportunity for the oligopolists to segment the market in an appropriate way (by 'labelling' consumers) seldom exists.[7] Nevertheless, Shubik (1959) points out a particular case of a firm setting a price but not being willing fully to satisfy the custom thereby generated. Suppose, for example, this firm's price is lower (for 'equivalent' or identical quality[8]) than his rivals'. If he cannot satisfy the unexpectedly high demand there may be room for the rivals to charge a higher price (for equivalent quality). Other situations can no doubt be envisaged and Telser often reminds us in his work that uniform price should be deduced rather than being assumed.

Shubik's main theoretical contribution in the game theoretic analysis of oligopoly is his work on *games of economic survival*. This is firmly outside the classical framework in that he here relaxes the assumption of perfect capital markets. The firm no longer has unlimited, or even any, powers to borrow money from outside. This means that such factors as the differing kinds of management structure inherent in a capitalist or mixed economy bring about different solutions – the owner of an unlimited liability firm may well be expected to act differently from the owner of a limited liability company, or one which is management controlled. Shubik finds that the 'solution' to such a game is not normally a single determinate point and the asset structure is of great importance in determining the likely payoffs. If the asset structure is 'not too' dissimilar, then it may be neglected, but normally it will matter. Indeed, 'the financial dominance of one firm may be enough to entitle it to the lion's share of a peacefully divided market' (p. 212). From this standpoint he discusses in general terms the Tobacco and Automobile industries. In fact though, the information requirements are tremendous and forbidding for any full empirical study.

3. Cooperative equilibria

When we turn to collusion or cooperative behaviour, it is not necessarily the outcome but rather the rules of the game which are presumed to have altered, to allow open negotiation. The parties concerned (in the non-constant sum game) are now able to make binding agreements between themselves regarding pricing, outputs and so on, that is to form themselves into a *cartel*. However this does not mean there is nothing to be gained from reneging on

the agreements. Thus cartelisation is not without problems. In fact, Osborne (1976) perceived five problems facing a cartel:
 (i) to predict, and discourage, production by non-members;
 (ii) to locate the contract surface, that is the point or set of points providing maximum profits to the group;
 (iii) to choose a point from amongst the set above (that is, how to share);
 (iv) to detect breaches of the cartel agreement;
 (v) to deter breaches which may occur.
We will discuss all of these in turn, concentrating most attention of the final three. However there will be some overlap, since an efficient solution to one of the problems can sometimes help with another.

Production by non-members of a cartel can arise either from firms in the industry which choose not to join the cartel, or as a result of entry into the industry by outsiders attracted by the high profits. As far as non-members within the industry are concerned, one possible assumption is that they constitute a fringe of firms taking price as given, as in the dominant firm model of chapter 2. Alternatively, they may be of some size and importance but may choose, or be forced by insiders, to remain outside the cartel. Both these situations are potentially amenable to analysis as if there were entrants, so we postpone discussion of them until chapter 4, taking the number of firms in the cartel as given.

However it is worth saying that because output of a non-member is not constrained in the way that members' outputs need to be, it will generally prove more profitable to be a non-member than a member, given that there is a cartel. Consequently it is usually in the cartel's interests for non-members either to be absorbed or dissuaded from producing. Nevertheless for certain cost and demand parameters, because of the indivisibilities involved, industry equilibria can exist where it is neither in an individual cartel member's interest to secede nor in an individual fringe member's interests to join, and hence a cartel involving part of the industry is naturally stable.[9]

Theoretically, locating the contract surface is straightforward if (for simplicity) the industry product is homogeneous[10] and if all the firms' cost functions are known. This is the usual assumption in the literature. The problem is then to maximise profits:

$$\Pi = p(Q) \cdot Q - \Sigma_i C_i(q_i); \qquad Q = \Sigma q_i; \qquad i = 1, 2, \ldots, N.$$

with respect to each firm's output, so that:

$$\frac{\partial \Pi}{\partial q_i} = p + Q \cdot \frac{dp}{dQ} - C_i'(q_i) = 0 \qquad \text{for all } i \qquad (3.1)$$

This is the familiar prescription for the multiplant monopolist: set outputs so that the marginal cost of each firm's output is equal to marginal revenue. There may be only one point with this property or there may be many.

Sharing

In the example of table 3.2, since both firms have equal marginal costs of 20 units, equation (3.1) does not give a unique solution for the share of output between the two firms. As a result, the contract surface consists of the whole line AB in figure 3.1 and our earlier selection of point (M, M) as the solution (in both figure and table) might be considered rather arbitrary because there is a problem of how shares will be determined. In general, the situation could be asymmetric and then we must distinguish revenue-pooling or *perfect cartels* from imperfect cartels which can only allocate quotas to members.[11] The former may have equilibria available to them which do not exist for the latter. To take an absurdly simplistic example of an asymmetric situation, let us suppose we were to change the problem of table 3.2 by making B's marginal costs a constant 30 units. The Cournot (non-cooperative) equilibrium would provide profits of (4011, 2844) units respectively. However, a cartel operating according to (3.1) would allocate all production to A's plant, as it is the more efficient at every output level. B would not of course join such a cartel unless it were of the revenue-pooling kind and a *side-payment* of at least 2844 units was paid from A to B out of the total available of 8100.

One solution concept which is useful here is the notion of the *core*. No one could be expected to join a cartel not offering her at least as much as she could obtain without its help given the most pessimistic assumptions about others' (and outsiders') behaviour. This amount is the maximum she would be assured of, supposing she were forced to play a non-cooperative game with all the others acting collusively together. Again, no group of firms S would join a cartel not guaranteeing them at least as much as they were assured of under similar pessimistic assumptions. For any particular game, the *characteristic function* $v(S)$ associates with each possible coalition (including firms acting alone), the set of payoffs it can guarantee itself. The core consists only of those payoffs which cannot be improved upon by any coalition in S. Thus, each individual receives at least as much as he could get by his own actions or by combining in another manner. Payoffs in the core therefore have the formal properties:

$$x_i \geqslant v(i), \qquad \Sigma_S x_i \geqslant v(S), \qquad \Sigma_{I_N} x_i = v(I_N) \qquad (3.2)$$

where x_i is the payoff to individual i and I_N is the set of all players (hence the last equality).

To give some concrete examples, in the duopoly case depicted in figure 3.1, the core is any point on the line AB between D and E. Points between A and D are ruled out, although they maximise joint profit, because firm 1 would do better alone, by setting the Cournot output level. For an analogous reason, the segment BE is not in the core. In the example where 2's marginal cost is 30 units, but firm 1's is only 20 units, the core consists of all those shareouts which promise A at least 4011 units and B (side-payments of) at least 2844 out of the 8100 total. In a triopoly, any two firms would only be willing to join with the third if they can be assured at least of (a) what they could obtain individually and (b) what they could obtain acting together but non-cooperatively against the third. The core, it may be seen, is a potentially powerful tool for use in cooperative games; though it generally will not give a unique answer, it does narrow down the possibilities.

An alternative is the *value approach*. There are various models here, each involving a unique (but possibly different) attainable point on the contract curve, but with different methods for arriving at such a point. The basic consideration is that the share between players should be fair or just. Consequently, though the approach is axiomatic, interfirm comparisons are necessarily made. We discuss the approach in more detail in chapter 5, where it is more appropriate. For the moment we may note that whilst most methods would agree on the half-shares solution in the case of table 3.2's model, they would usually differ in cases like the variant discussed above (with revenue-pooling).

Osborne was concerned only with cartels (like OPEC) which agree on output quotas, rather than perfect cartels. His suggestion for symmetric and asymmetric cases where there is more than one point on the contract curve, was to select that position which minimises the variance of profits when determining shares. Others (e.g. Mills and Elzinga, 1978) have been critical, basically because they do not find the reason for that particular point persuasive.

Detection

The classic paper on detection by colluders is Stigler's (1964) 'Theory of Oligopoly'. He takes the situation (relevant to the U.S. and, to a large extent, the U.K. and other E.E.C. countries) where collusion is illegal so that revenue-pooling is not enforceable. Consequently 'collusion takes the form of joint determination of outputs and prices by ostensibly independent firms . . .' (p. 45) and accurate feedback from co-conspirators would be difficult to enforce. Thus secret price-cutting becomes an attractive temptation and detection of it by others within the collusive group relies largely upon probabilistic evidence about increased sales to a rival. Even in a more openly legal cartel like IATA though, it may be difficult for the participants to allocate exact quotas amongst themselves, so Stigler's analysis is again relevant.

How is a given firm to detect whether someone is price-cutting and, if so, who? Stigler suggests there are three key pieces of information: the behaviour of the firm's own old customers, the behaviour of the old customers of rival firms and the behaviour of new customers. To take the first of these; if there is (as he assumes) a known probability p that a customer will repeat a purchase from the firm which supplied it in the previous period, then the mean (average) number of old customers buying from a given firm in any period is pn_o/n_s, where n_o/n_s is the ratio of old customers to sellers. Around this mean there is a variance.[12] Thus it is possible to assess the likelihood of a given distribution of sales in any period being due to chance, and further to consider whether the distribution is skewed in favour of a particular firm to a suspicious extent. Hence, Stigler derives criteria for accusing erstwhile colleagues of cheating. His other detection methods are similar in concept. Having developed them, Stigler proceeds to relate the probability of detection, and hence potential gains without detection, to the parameters of the model. Thus, the fewer new buyers, the higher the probability of repeat purchase, the smaller the number of sellers, or the larger the number of buyers, the less one firm may gain at the expense of others without detection, so the more likely is adherence to agreed prices. One interesting result thrown up by the theory is that when firms are unequally sized, the Herfindahl index of concentration becomes the relevant measure of inequality 'if we wish concentration to measure likelihood of effective collusion' (p. 55).

Critics of Stigler have attacked the execution of the model rather than the basic idea. McKinnon (1966) points out that an efficient detection mechanism would pool information from the three key areas Stigler suggests in order to evolve more powerful criteria. He also notes that rather than the fixed decision rules Stigler adopts, the approach should consist in balancing the cost of unjustly accusing a rival of price-cutting against the losses from undetected price-cutting. Other people have commented that detection becomes increasingly difficult if more than one firm is cheating, also that the assumptions regarding demand (one purchase per period by old customers regardless, say, of price-cuts) are rather rigid. Cathcart (1979) extends the model to relax this assumption and to allow the seller in question to pool information for a number of periods in order to reduce errors of invalid accusations (but at the expense of increasing the gains from cheating). Nevertheless the basic factors Stigler found relevant retain their importance in all this.

Deterrence

Stigler had little to say on what should be done once cheating has been detected and Orr and MacAvoy (1965) have shown his suggestion was inadequate. Yet detection is not, of course, the same as deterrence. If the cartel is to survive, penalties sufficient to deter others must be imposed on the firm which is found out and the type of penalty which will work in a particular situation depends upon the rules under which the cartel works.

One interesting suggestion for a cartel operating with quota allocations is Osborne's rule: produce

$$q_i = \max \left\{ q_i^o, q_i^o + \frac{s_i}{s_j} \Delta q_j \right\} \tag{3.3}$$

where q_i^0 is the designated quota for i, s_j the designated share of firm j and Δq_j the amount by which j has gained as a result of illicit price-cutting. Equation (3.3) essentially specifies the contract each party to the original agreement signs. Intuitively (and, as Osborne shows, mathematically) the rule has much to recommend it. The idea may be illustrated using figure 3.1 or table 3.2 again. In terms of the figure, as we have seen it might be tempting for, say, firm 1 to increase output from (M, M) so point G is reached. The rule specifies this cannot happen: it confines all output movements to ray OF. Then, if each firm knows all movements will be along OF, the best policy is to remain at (M, M). As Osborne points out, if everyone else obeys the rule, any particular firm will find it best to do so. Consequently amongst that delimited set of strategies represented in (3.3), q_i^0 is the Nash equilibrium.

Unfortunately for the participants,[13] there are various difficulties with Osborne's rule, which may explain why the history of cartel discipline records not quota rules but fines as the popular deterrent. Many of these were in fact anticipated and discussed in Orr and MacAvoy (1965) in the context of a different model. For one thing, Osborne's rule relies upon speedy retaliation along the lines of (3.3). If, as Mills and Elzinga (1978) point out, retaliation may take some time, then we return to the world described in the previous section where it can be profitable to break the binding agreement and move to G even in the knowledge that the agreement will therefore fall through (so that (C, C) is reached). The number of firms party to the agreement has an influence here, as Cathcart shows. Also, Osborne's rule is not valid where because of asymmetric profit contours, sidepayments are required to maintain the cartel point. Holohan (1978) illustrates this with a model where the joint profit maximising point entails less profit to a sub-group of the cartel participants than the Cournot point (in the absence of sidepayments) and the two positions are not on the same ray from the origin. When cheating occurs, one likely eventuality is that (C, C) is reached since it is more profitable than the retaliation point given by the rule on the ray through (M, M). Finally, Rothschild (1981) has pointed out that the intuition developed from geometric treatments may prove misleading in large number situations. He develops an N-firm symmetric model where it may be better not to retaliate at all than to use Osborne's rule. Possibly therefore, a more profitable direction for research is into the area of an optimal fines policy.

4. Experimental gaming in oligopoly

The basic idea behind experimental oligopoly games is that, given the number of forces which affect firms' actions in the real world, and given the plethora of oligopoly theories, to design a test of a *particular* oligopoly theory in the real world verges on the impossible. The experiment thus assists by modelling a simplified version of the real world in a laboratory setting in order that pointers to the factors of relevance to manufacturers in making their decisions can be discovered. We shall briefly discuss some of these experiments in terms of the insight they offer: the work we consider is that by Fouraker and Siegel (1963), Friedman (1963), Hoggatt (1967), Murphy (1966), Dolbear *et al.* (1968), Lowes and Pass (1970), and Friedman and Hoggatt (1980).

There are several factors common to all work of this type: the cost and demand functions take fairly simple algebraic forms (usually, linear), each firm has one decision variable, the number of firms in the market is usually very small, subjects play in 'games' lasting for many bids or 'periods', and no direct communication is allowed between players (see Friedman 1969). Most experimenters allow their subjects a few trial runs before the 'real' situation begins. The participants are often paid a sum proportional to the profit they have made. Among the many factors differing between experiments, we shall focus on three: the number of players, the state of information and the decision variable used. Experimenters generally did most of their work with 2, 3 or 4 person games, though Dolbear *et al.* have an experiment involving 16 players. We should note that in the Dolbear and Friedman experiments the structural effects of changes in the number of players were minimised by making the market size increase as the numbers increase. This has the effect of isolating behavioural characteristics for investigation (see Sherman 1971).

The information given can be characterised either as complete (where payoffs to all parties given the respective decision variable values are specified) or incomplete (where payoffs only to the particular individual concerned are divulged).[14] The decision variable used is either price or quantity; where price is the relevant variable the experimenter has specified differentiated products except in some experiments by Fouraker and Siegel, and Murphy.

Fouraker and Siegel, whose work was very influential, perform two types of oligopoly experiment, using both information states. In their 'quantity adjuster' models, their participants tend to arrive at Cournot contracts when they have incomplete information, although there are outcomes below as well as above this position and, compared with duopoly experiments, there tends to be more dispersion around the Cournot level in their triopoly tests. With complete information the contracts are, rather intriguingly, more diverse than in the incomplete information experiments. Their 'price adjuster' models follow similar patterns, though this time, as the products are undifferentiated the incomplete information contract tends to be at the Bertrand price.

In an interesting re-run of Fouraker and Siegel's price adjustment experiment with incomplete information, Murphy amends and extends the profit tables to allow bids below the Bertrand price level (which involve the players in losses). He finds that 'the change in the profit table only has greatly increased the amount of cooperation at the expense of competitiveness. The new results are more like those from (their) complete information experiment . . .' He also notes that 'as more trials were run, the tendency towards cooperative ruling prices became more pronounced' (both quotes p. 301).

Friedman's work is based on price adjustment with product differentiation, and the aim is to discover how much cooperation takes place in complete information models. In fact, however, he considers that his experiments are unable to yield any real evidence on the matter.[15] He does note though that 'In comparing the *F-S* complete information games to Friedman's, one difference that stands out is the frequency of joint maximum games' (p. 410). This, he feels, is a result of the experimental design whereby his participants play in several game series each, so learning more about the technique of play. He finds that the more players there are, the less likely is joint profit maximisation to be reached.

Hoggatt's experiments are somewhat novel in that the participants were not paid and they competed in duopoly against a robot. Despite this element of unreality, the robot opponent permits greater control and his (second) experimental series brings the interesting result that the more cooperative the robot, the more cooperative the human player. Further experiments along these lines have been performed by Wolf and Shubik (1975).

Dolbear *et al*. use a similar basic model to that of Friedman, but include both states of information. They find that the equilibrium market price tends to be between the Cournot and joint profit maximisation positions while being inversely related to the number of firms. The other hypotheses they propose do not reach full statistical significance, though there is a presumption that full information raises profits and the dispersion of equilibrium profits. Thus 'Information seems to induce bargaining attempts that tend to result in price war or collusion' (p. 259).

Lowes and Pass introduced asymmetry in the demand or cost relation facing the two firms in their duopoly experiments. Whilst all their games were of the incomplete information variety, they informed players of an asymmetry when this was so. When there was symmetry, prices near to the non-cooperative equilibrium were obtained, whilst the stronger firm in the asymmetric case was often able (particularly when something about the asymmetry was known) to move the industry towards the cooperative solution point, a result they suggest parallels 'price leadership'.

Friedman and Hoggatt's recent work is essentially concerned with complete information games. They introduce the possibility of inventories (and costs associated with them) and firms have to choose both price and quantity, but we shall concentrate our brief remarks on pricing policy. In their three, four and six person asymmetric games the results 'show a fairly strong central tendency to Cournot behaviour; however it is also clear that the Cournot prices themselves are not chosen a high percentage of the time' (p. 10). In the two person asymmetric case, prices nearer to equal profits than Cournot or joint profit maximisation would imply are generally observed. These results contrast rather with the (simpler, but incomplete information) games of Lowes and Pass. In their symmetric games, prices substantially above the Cournot level were observed with two, three, four and six player games. There is some evidence that cooperation is easier to achieve with smaller numbers of players, though this is occluded by the effects on the subjects of experience in playing.

Broadly summarising the conclusions of the experiments mentioned above, we find the range of outcomes tends to be between Cournot and joint profit maximisation and that while 'the Cournot solution characterises behaviour in incomplete information situations' (Friedman, 1969, p. 414) with complete information there is a greater diversity of outcome, partly because a remarkably long time is needed to get the feel for the game and partly because this information state provides more opportunity for individual preferences to be revealed in play. One interesting insight is that, despite the lack of formal communication, players in at least some of the complete information games appear to be acting *as if* they were playing in infinite period games by choosing 'collusive', or cooperative, strategies even though they must know the game will end. On the diversity of outcomes in complete information games, Sherman (1971) considers that the evidence of simple prisoner's dilemma experiments (one example is Lave, 1962) which attempt to control for such personality factors as sex, isolation and risk attitude is potentially relevant, although unfortunately the results here are not clear cut.

Notes on the literature

There are several introductory treatments of the theory of games available, in intermediate microeconomics texts and elsewhere. One of the most relevant for present purposes is Bacharach (1976). Of the more rigorous treatments, Friedman (1977) is probably best as each chapter ends with remarks on the intuition behind the models presented. Bishop (1963) surveys the value approach to collusion, among other things. Yamey (1972) makes a great many points on the 'secret price cutting' literature. Two useful surveys of experimental oligopoly games are Friedman (1969) and Sherman (1971). A comprehensive recent exposition of oligopoly and game theory is provided in the early chapters of Shubik (1980).

4

A consideration of the effects of potential entry

In the previous two chapters we adopted very naive assumptions about entry, normally assuming the number of firms in the industry was fixed, so that no entry or exit was allowed. Our purpose in the present chapter is to explore the implications of relaxing this assumption.

To see the drastic impact entry conditions can have, consider initially allowing perfectly free entry to and exit from an industry, so effectively moving to a general equilibrium framework. Specifically, let us take the case where one industry is monopolised and all others contain a very large number of firms, so that they can be considered as perfectly competitive industries and the marginal firm in each earns zero or 'normal' profits. The monopolist earns above-normal profits so that there is an incentive for firms from other industries to enter his industry until returns to the marginal firm in that industry are zero in common with the rest of the economy. Thus, if the monopolist wishes to retain his position as sole supplier of his particular product under perfectly free entry he also must price so as to obtain only normal profits.

Further, Fama and Laffer (1972) have shown that even if there are only two firms in each industry, and perfectly free entry and exit for each industry, then each firm is in effect a perfect competitor in that she earns solely normal profits and her output decisions have no effect on price. They illustrate this by supposing that one firm expands output. Then, since they assume constant returns to scale in each industry, the other must contract output to *exactly the same extent* as this expansion, for otherwise returns in the industry are below normal and exit occurs (after which presumably the survivor produces output sufficient to ensure normal returns). Similarly, if one firm were to contract output, the other must expand to make up the deficit or entry will occur. Thus output decisions do not affect price. In terms of our notation of chapter 2 the result is that $dQ_i/dq_i = -1$ for each industry. This is of course very different from the situation where entry is not allowed, for as we saw in chapter 2, with a small fixed number of firms in each industry, positive profits may be earned.

Thus we may say that a necessary (but not sufficient) condition for the number of firms in an industry to affect the level of profits in that industry is that entry is not completely free, costless and quick. In the remainder of

56

this chapter we consider cases where entry conditions affect the established firms decision processes (i.e. conduct) to a greater or lesser extent. Exit conditions will receive a more perfunctory treatment, but crop up again in chapter 9.

1. Basic concepts

Those factors which prevent entry being perfectly free are known as *Barriers to Entry* and Bain (1962) has discussed the types of barriers which may exist in an industry in some detail. Basically he considered that there are three major categories of barriers (apart from legal exclusions) which are: absolute cost advantages, product differentiation advantages and economies of scale. We leave further consideration of the different types of barriers to entry until we have pursued some theoretical development, and in fact product differentiation (the effects of economic distance between products) and product differentiation advantages are largely left for separate discussion in chapters 6 and 7.

However the way that Bain has defined and detailed barriers to entry does give rise to one problem which we ought to discuss before proceeding further. This is the problem of the time interval we are considering. It is fairly obviously not the theoretical short run, for in that case there would not be any possibility of entry. It cannot easily be the theoretical long run either, for that would mean no firm having, for example, any product differentiation advantage over another, and all firms both potential and actual would have access to capital on the same terms. Nevertheless, Bain feels that such structural features as entry barriers are not ephemeral short-lived advantages, which leads Williamson (1963) to consider that we are talking about an 'intermediate-run' situation (see, for example, his p. 113, n. 6), some time period long enough for society to be concerned about.

Bain then defines the *Condition of Entry* to be the extent to which the established firms may raise price over costs over such a period without inducing entry, and categorises four general areas in which the barriers to entry may place an industry:

(i) Blockaded entry, where barriers are such that established firms could price even at the monopoly level yet still not incur entry.

(ii) Easy entry, where barriers are so small that pricing even very slightly above costs allows entry.

(iii) Ineffectively impeded entry, where pricing at a level at which no entry will occur is less profitable than maximising short run profits and allowing entry.

(iv) Effectively impeded entry; pricing at the level at which no entry will occur is more profitable than maximising short run profit and allowing entry.

The level of price below which no firm, even the most favourably placed, will find it profitable to enter is called the *limit price*.

In the next section, we consider the analysis of the 'theory of limit pricing' based upon a synthesis produced by Modigliani. This is extended to incorporate the four conditions of entry recognized by Bain in section 3. We then turn to further possible factors to be brought into the Modigliani type of static analysis in order to mirror reality more closely – for example the behaviour of established firms and the case of a number of potential entrants. Modifications to the theory brought about by assuming reactions by potential entrants to established firms alternative to that taken by Modigliani are considered in section 5. We then survey some work done on dynamic behaviour towards entrants. Finally in section 7 we go on to make a few comments of a welfare economic nature which necessitates modifying our definition of barriers.

2. The formulation of limit price

In formulating the limit price, we straightaway run into consideration of the expected reaction by the established firms to a potential entrant. In fact, the problem from the established firms' point of view is that of deciding what the entrant thinks they will do regarding their output if he decides to enter. In order to develop ideas we, like many others, make extensive use of a particularly straightforward assumption known as the *Sylos postulate* after Paulo Sylos-Labini (1962) who used it extensively in his work: The entrant assumes that the established firms will maintain their output in the face of potential entry, and the established firms know this to be the case. Making this assumption fixes the portion of the industry demand curve along which the entrant may operate. A further common assumption made for simplicity is that the established industry consists of a monopolist (firm 1) or a tightly knit group of collusive oligopolists.

These assumptions are crucially limiting, and we later have to relax them. The general point is that two forces interact in creating entry barriers: structural features and behavioural ones. Thus conduct becomes of central importance, but in order to examine the influence of structure we initially hold it constant. Hence we start with models assuming the Sylos postulate, one established firm (firm 1), and also one potential entrant (firm 2).

Within this framework, the simplest case to analyse is an *absolute cost difference* (advantage), where the potential entrant has a horizontal average cost curve some distance above that of the established firms. Here the limit price is simply set at the level of the entrant's costs and the price–cost margin obtainable without entry is the difference between the cost levels divided by the entrant's average cost. In a similar way, factors effecting an absolute advantage in demand for the established firm (say a product differentiation advantage) may be brought into consideration.

The case of scale economies is more complex and we concentrate on these to a greater extent in this chapter. The classic article in this area is

Modigliani's (1958); his arguments may be briefly summarised by discussion of the comparative statics of his simple case.

Here both the established and potential entrant firms have cost curves which are sharply discontinuous at minimum optimal scale, so that outputs lower than that are infinitely costly to produce. Thus we may say that the entry limiting output is given by $q_{1L} = q_c - \bar{q}$, where q_c is 'competitive' output, i.e. that output at which price is equal to marginal (and average) cost for all firms, and $\bar{q}$ is the minimum optimal scale. Defining the size of the market as $s = q_c/\bar{q}$ then we may write:

$$q_{1L} = q_c \left(1 - \frac{1}{s}\right) \tag{4.1}$$

We want to say something about limit price in relation to costs, thus we have to transform the above equation into one in terms of prices. This in general will involve knowing the form of the demand curve, in order to solve the equation for the limit price (p_L) explicitly, since in general:

$$p_L = f(q_{1L}) = f\left[q_c\left(1 - \frac{1}{s}\right)\right]$$

To take a particularly simple example, where the demand curve is of linear form, $p = \alpha - \beta q$ then:

$$q_{1L} = \frac{\alpha - p_L}{\beta}, \qquad q_c = \frac{\alpha - p_c}{\beta}$$

where p_c is 'competitive' price. Thus from (4.1):

$$p_L = \alpha - (\alpha - p_c)\left(1 - \frac{1}{s}\right) = p_c\left(1 + \frac{1}{\eta_c s}\right) \tag{4.2}$$

where

$$\eta_c = -(p_c/q_c) \cdot (dq_c/dp_c),$$

the modulus of the industry elasticity of demand at q_c.

For other demand curves, equation (4.2) gives the limit price to a linear approximation. Modigliani therefore writes (4.2) as an approximate equality. Following from this, it is easy to show that the price–cost margin corresponding to limit price is:

$$(\Pi/R)_L \equiv \frac{p_L - p_c}{p_L} = \frac{1}{\eta_c s + 1} \tag{4.3}$$

This of course implies that:

$$\frac{\partial(\Pi/R)_L}{\partial \eta_c} < 0, \qquad \frac{\partial(\Pi/R)_L}{\partial s} < 0$$

and if we choose to define the importance of economies of scale[1] as $\bar{q}/q_c$ or $1/s$ then:

$$\frac{\partial (\Pi/R)_{\mathrm{L}}}{\partial (\bar{q}/q_{\mathrm{c}})} > 0$$

In the words of his famous quotation:

'Under Sylos' postulate there is a well-defined maximum premium that the oligopolists can command over the competitive price, and this premium tends to increase with the importance of economies of scale and to decrease with the size of the market and the elasticity of demand' (p. 220).

More generally, economies of scale cannot be completely characterised by a minimum optimal scale, and we should also bring absolute cost and product differentiation advantages into account. For the present though, we treat a product differentiation advantage essentially as if it were an absolute demand or cost advantage and leave more explicit attention to it until chapter 6. Also, as we shall see, many writers of analytical papers choose simplified functional forms to capture the essence of scale economies.

However, there are really three *features of a scale curve* which are important in determining limit price, and we ought to discuss them generally before resorting to more specific cases in later sections. First, and most closely related to Modigliani's 'size of the market', there is the output level in which scale economies are exhausted. Another facet of obvious importance is the extent to which a firm is disadvantaged if it produces only a small fraction (say one quarter, or one hundredth) of the output at which full scale economies are attainable. We might call this the 'drop' of the scale curve. A third is the curvature, or bowedness which determines the extent of disadvantage at points other than the one specified for 'drop'. Since we have already seen algebraically the effect of market size, we concentrate in figure 4.1 on the drop and bowedness.

Here, given the Sylos postulate, output for the entrant is measured from $q_{1\mathrm{L}}$ and the established firm's decision is the placing of $q_{1\mathrm{L}}$ to render a potential entrant's optimal output level unprofitable. (Thus the industry demand curve in all cases is the same; it is the output level $0q_{1\mathrm{L}}$ which varies in our figure and so determines the height of the curve measured from $q_{1\mathrm{L}}$, the origin for firm 2). In general, limit price will be between the value of average costs for the potential entrant at zero output and at an output exhausting scale economies. Cost curve c_1 illustrates the point that, if the average cost curve has a slope closer to horizontal than the demand curve, it is the former quantity which is relevant to the determination of limit price. Cost curves c_2 and c_3, giving rise to limit prices $P_{\mathrm{L}2}$ and $P_{\mathrm{L}3}$, show that the degree of bowedness is important for a given amount (E_1 to E_3) of drop (measured between very small and minimum optimal points). Comparing c_2 with c_4 illustrates the point that a lesser amount of drop (E_2 to E_3) in general leads to a lower limit price, $P_{\mathrm{L}4}$. There are interactions between these features though, for the extremely bowed curve c_5 gives a lower price, $P_{\mathrm{L}5}$ than the less bowed curve c_4 which exhibits substantially smaller 'drop'.

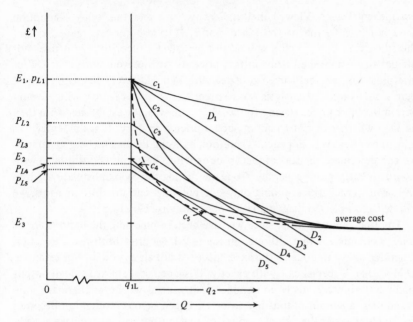

Figure 4.1

In addition both these facets of a scale curve will interact with the 'size of the market' effect. Finally notice that the established firm's margin of limit price above costs will vary directly with the absolute level of limit price assuming the established firm is able to exhaust scale economies at his level of output $0q_{1L}$, but need not do so if this is not the case since each of the values P_{L1} to P_{L5} correspond to differing outputs for the established firm.

It is easily seen that cases where there exist scale economies together with an absolute cost advantage may straightforwardly be analysed as a combination of the two factors. In general, elements determining all of these features will come into play in determining the level of the limit price. Nevertheless, there is theoretically rather a gap between saying something creates a barrier to entry (even under Bain's definition and the Sylos postulate) and knowing how to measure this in the most relevant manner. Empirical approaches to the topic are covered in section 10.1.

3. Alternative equilibria under the Sylos postulate

As Fisher (1959) and Osborne (1973) have pointed out, the Sylos postulate essentially gives rise to a Stackleberg equilibrium (which we discussed in chapters 2 and 3). The potential entrant believes the established firm will maintain output, and so acts as a Stackleberg follower, while the established firm knows this to be the potential entrant's belief, and so is able to act as a

Stackleberg leader. Viewed in this light, we see that the Sylos assumption need not lead to the prevention of entry. Thus Osborne has suggested that the 'theory of limit pricing' should not be called a theory, since it does not predict that established firms in fact price so as to prevent entry. On a strict interpretation, we feel forced to agree with him. However, the main point of Bain's discussion and analysis was to point to the sort of factors which would determine limit price. Having found where this was, the established firm then decided whether or not to adopt such a pricing strategy. If it did, entry was said to be effectively impeded. Therefore, by using the Stackleberg apparatus, we can determine the sort of factors upon which decisions about pricing with regard to entry more generally are made, taking the Sylos postulate as given and again (crucially) assuming only one potential entrant. In doing this, we follow Dixit's (1979) diagrammatic approach fairly closely.

The first point to note, since we have been emphasising the importance of scale economies, is that although in figure 2.1 we drew both firms' reaction functions as continuous to the axes, this need not always be so. For example, in Modigliani's special case with exactly 'L' shaped cost curves, a small output might be infinitely costly to produce.[2] In general whenever there are scale economies, a certain output has to be envisaged before production becomes profitable, though the actual amount of that output can, as we have already said, be difficult to ascertain. In Dixit's model this is relatively easy since costs are made up of a constant marginal cost plus a fixed component. Relating this to a graph of the established firm's and potential entrant's reaction functions we see that, since a firm might well rather produce nothing than a small output involving permanent losses, in the presence of substantial scale economies the reaction functions will become discontinuous at a certain output level.

We are now in a position to examine Bain's categorisation under the assumption there is only one firm contemplating entry.[3] The case of *blockaded entry* is illustrated in figure 4.2. (In all the figures of this section, we plot the established firm's output q_1 on the 'X' axis with the potential entrant's output q_2 on the 'Y' axis). Firm 1 has a reaction function ϕ_1 while that for firm 2 is ϕ_2. Firm 1's optimal output is at the point M_1 where his reaction function cuts the q_1 axis, and he is selling the monopoly level of output. His reaction function is assumed to become discontinuous at an output level B_1 due to the presence of scale economies. It is thus the line $M_1B_1B_1'T_1$. Similarly we have the line $M_2B_2B_2'T_2$ for the potential entrant. Now, as we have drawn the figure, scale economies are so large that the potential entrant's reaction function becomes discontinuous at a point representing an output level for firm 1 *below* the monopoly output. The established firm can thus happily produce the monopoly output, selling at a monopoly price, without attracting entry. In other words, entry is blockaded.[4]

The *easy entry* case is not easy to represent in our present diagram, partly because we assume one potential entrant. Let us pass over this and move on

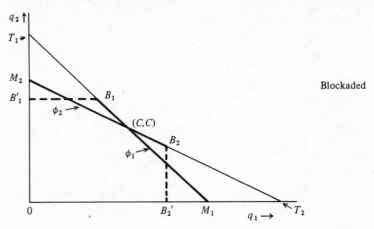

Figure 4.2

to *ineffectively impeded entry*. This is illustrated in figure 4.3. Here we have introduced isoprofit functions for firm 1 (those for firm 2 are omitted for clarity). Recall that successively higher isoprofit functions involve successively lower levels of profit. Thus the established firm, acting as a Stackleberg leader, wishes to set an output given by the isoprofit curve tangent to firm 2's reaction function. Previously, this occurred at point M_1; now, because scale economies are not as extensive, it occurs at point (S, C), with profits to firm 1 of Π_{14}. Firm 2 is thus expected to enter with an output of q_2 (and both will make profits after entry). This is more profitable for the established

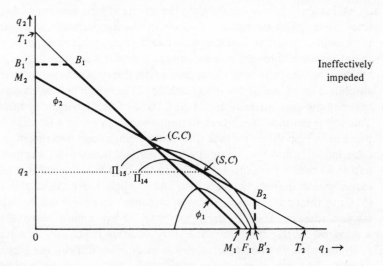

Figure 4.3

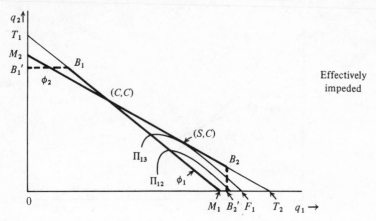

Figure 4.4

firm than producing an output, say slightly above the level B_2', which will prevent entry while involving profits represented by Π_{15}.

Finally in figure 4.4, we illustrate *effectively impeded entry*. Here the established firm could produce output corresponding to point (S, C) but chooses not to do so since that would involve a profit level Π_{13} whereas he could set an output level slightly above B_2' and attain a profit level Π_{12} while preventing entry. The important distinguishing feature between figures 4.3 and 4.4 is that in the former the isoprofit curve which is tangent to the potential entrant's reaction function cuts the q_1 axis at a level of output F_1 less than the minimum level which will stop entry by firm 2 (i.e. B_2'), whereas in figure 4.4, the reverse occurs.

We have so far been emphasising the effects of scale economies, treated as fixed costs, acting through the position of the discontinuity, in determining the classification of an industry with regard to entry. Other types of barriers to entry may be brought into account in a similar way, though this is much less easy to illustrate with the apparatus developed. Consider the case of an absolute cost advantage for the established firm, which may be thought of as lowering the cost curves of firm 1 with those of firm 2 remaining unchanged. This will mean that firm 2's reaction function stays where it is, while firm 1's point of monopoly output will shift to the right, since a lowering of marginal costs increases monopoly output *ceteris paribus*. Then, if M_1 was just to the left of B_2' before the shift, in moving to the right in figure 4.3, the isoprofit curves would shift to the right also and so might move the tangency point (S, C) to the right. Since B_2' remains unchanged and the point F_1 where the tangent isoprofit curve cuts the q_1 axis may, we have argued, move rightward, a previously ineffectively impeded entry situation might now become effectively impeded. It thus appears entry is made more difficult the bigger is the absolute cost advantage of the established firm, though to establish this

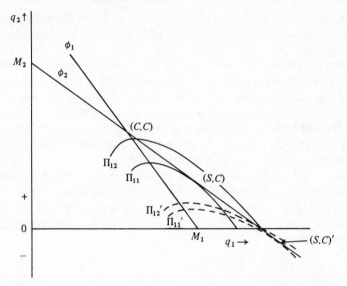

Figure 4.5

properly would require a formal model. Notice that an absolute advantage in demand, an upward shift in firm 1's demand curve all else remaining constant, would similarly shift M_1 to the right and so give rise to a similar conclusion.[5] Product differentiation *advantages* may be dealt with in like manner; Dixit also considers product differentiation *per se*, as we mention in chapter 6.

It is worth showing also that a discontinuity caused by scale economies is not necessary for the potential entrant to be effectively impeded. Consider figure 4.5 where firm 2's reaction function extends to an output of zero (perhaps due to a cost situation like that represented by c_1 in figure 4.1). Two alternative sets of isoprofit curves for firm 1 are drawn. With the set represented by solid lines, it is more profitable for the established firm to achieve the point (S, C), so earning profits of Π_{11}, than to block entry and earn Π_{12}. With the set represented by dashed lines the Stackleberg point is not achievable since it would require non-positive output for the potential entrant. The highest obtainable profit for the established firm in the face of entry is that point where the potential entrant's reaction function cuts the q_1 axis yielding profits Π'_{12} for the established firm. These are the cases Osborne (1973) analyses.

4. Some extensions to the basic model

As Stigler (1968) has said, the Bain–Sylos–Modigliani analysis raises a great many questions. He notes four he considers particularly troublesome. The first is whether or not it would be more profitable to retard the rate of entry, rather than either preventing or freely allowing it. In his second point, he essentially asks whether the Sylos postulate is the only sensible belief regarding post-entry outcomes. Thirdly, he speculates as to the role of projected industry growth. Lastly, as he puts it: 'The theory of oligopoly is solved by murder' (p. 21) – the established firms have simply been supposed to collude in setting industry price. A further question is that of the effects on the model of assuming there are a number of potential entrants rather than one. We will look at these points in the remaining sections of the chapter, except for growth, which we leave until our discussion of empirical work in chapter 10 as the arguments are more broadly based.

First a red herring. It might be supposed that we could accommodate Stigler's second and fourth points by extending the model of the early sections of chapter 2. This turns out not to be possible in general, but it is important to see why. Consider the (inverse) demand function facing the industry to be:

$$p = f(Q) = f(Q_1 + Q_2)$$

where Q_1 is the output of the established firms and Q_2 that of the potential entrants (which is zero). The important behavioural term for an individual established firm attempting to maximise profits is, in our current notation, the conjectural variation term dQ/dq_{1i}. In the model extended to include potential entry, this becomes:

$$\frac{dQ}{dq_{1i}} = \frac{dQ_1}{dq_{1i}} + \frac{dQ_2}{dQ_1} \cdot \frac{dQ_1}{dq_{1i}} = \left(1 + \frac{dQ_{1i}}{dq_{1i}}\right)\left(1 + \frac{dQ_2}{dQ_1}\right) \qquad (4.4)$$

– reactions both by other established firms and by potential competitors are important. We called the former λ_i in chapter 2. If we made an attempt to specify how potential entrants reacted in sum to established firms' changes in output, we could possibly derive an expression relating (say) the price–cost margin to various potentially observable elasticities and measures of concentration.

The difficulty is that the last term in equation (4.4) above essentially incorporates beliefs about the entrants' reaction function. But, as we have seen, in the presence of scale economies this is likely to be discontinuous. Thus the value of the last term may well vary depending upon which part of the reaction function is chosen and a differential calculus approach to the problem is not really appropriate.[6] The remainder of this section and parts of the next are devoted to analysing these questions by alternative methods.

The effect of increasing numbers of established firms and potential entrants

Since in the preceding two chapters we have discussed the possible reactions of established firms to each other in some detail, the concepts involved in integrating the analysis of a number of established firms together with the threat of potential entry can be dealt with relatively briefly. Until now, we have been following much of the relevant literature in assuming the established firms collude together regarding their own output. The question is what to put in place of this assumption.

For example, extending the earlier Cournot–Nash model to the case of N established firms, we see that if entrants are treated in like manner to established firms, each established firm will assume a potential entrant will keep his output unchanged, at zero. Thus there is no attempt to halt entry and so entry proceeds freely until it is blockaded by lack of profitable opportunity in the industry, as Fisher (1959) pointed out. The outcome is essentially similar to the equilibrium under monopolistic competition, except that indivisibilities (scale economies) may allow some profit for all, given that the number of firms has to be an integer.

Alternatively we might suppose that despite established firms acting non-cooperatively towards each other, they collude in adopting (say) a leadership strategy towards potential entrants. If this be accepted, how do outcomes differ from those analysed in figures 4.2 to 4.4? Assuming for simplicity only one potential entrant, there seems no reason why the reaction function it represents to the established firms should differ depending upon the number of established firms. However the established firms' reaction function will be moved rightwards since industry output (in the absence of an entry threat) will be above that with collusion, and this is what determines the positioning of M_1. Thus the equivalent to blockaded entry with price and output at the Cournot level is more likely than it would be at the monopoly level with joint profit maximisation. Also if the isoprofit curves (measuring profits which accrue in some fixed proportions to the established firms) move rightwards in a regular manner, it will become more likely that entry is effectively impeded in the same sense. The indication is that an increase in the number of (non-cooperative) established firms, by reducing profitability, makes entry less likely in this model. This leaves aside the question of how the established firms manage to agree on any necessary output restrictions to dissuade entry.

Assume now that there are two potential entrants and, for simplicity, one established firm. Suppose, with Sherman and Willett (1967), that the basic framework of the Bain–Sylos–Modigliani model is unchanged. They then find that, if anything, the entry-preventing price is raised rather than lowered by there being two (or indeed n) potential entrants rather than one.

They employ a game-theoretic analysis to demonstrate this point; however it may as easily be grasped on an intuitive level, an approach which enables us to relate their analysis to later comments. To take an example, suppose in a group of neighbourhood shops there is one greengrocer. Two other firms consider opening similar shops. If each has no knowledge of the other potential entrants, then the level of prices which would prevent entry by one will prevent entry when there are two. Alternatively, if each recognises the other firm had designs on entry then each will be dissuaded by the thought of

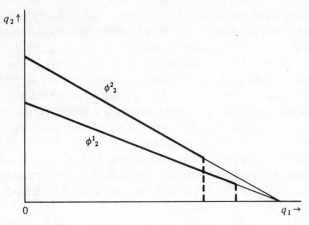

Figure 4.6

incurring losses if in fact both enter. Thus limit price will be no lower than the level which would just dissuade one firm. One particular intermediate case would be where each potential entrant entertains Cournot-type beliefs about the other. This gives rise to a collective potential entrant reaction function ϕ_2^2 above the one potential entrant reaction function ϕ_2^1 on the lines illustrated on figure 4.6. As the reader will discover upon trying various possibilities along the lines of figures 4.2 and 4.4, entry is more likely to be blockaded and more likely to be effectively impeded when there are two potential entrants than when there is only one. Thus 'potential entrants discourage entry'. In fact, Omori and Yarrow (1982) have shown that entry prevention is always optimal with an unlimited number of potential entrants and identical cost functions.

Comments on Sherman and Willett's result (especially Kalish *et al.*, 1978) have more often utilised a probabilistic approach to the question of entry. Specifically, Sherman and Willett's model can be interpreted as saying that, above the limit price emanating from the Sylos-type analysis, the probability of entry by one firm is unity, below this price it is zero. This may be replaced by a set of assumptions relating pre-entry prices to probabilities of one firm entry; to take but one example, probability might decline linearly with price from Sylos-type limit price down to long-run average cost, so at a given price, the probability of one firm entering might be 0.4.

When there are two potential entrants, the probability that one enters, given the other also does, naturally takes on a lower value than the probability that one enters, given the other does not, at a given pre-entry price. It is then straightforward to show that the overall probability of a particular firm entering, at a given price, is lower than the probability of entry when there is only one potential entrant. However, and this is the important point, this tells us little about the overall probability of entry of *at least one* firm into the industry. It turns out that an increase in the number of potential entrants from one to two (or more) may, depending upon the relevant parameters, either raise or lower the overall probability of entry.[7]

The important conclusion stemming from such analyses is that we are not in fact assured that an increase in the numbers of potential entrants will make entry easier and so improve resource allocation; case by case study is required. This wasteful competition in the field should be contrasted with efficient competition *for* the field, which is discussed in section 7.

5. Alternative beliefs and first mover advantages

Though theoretically the most favoured assumption regarding the entrant's and established firm's beliefs has probably been the Sylos postulate, there have in fact been several alternative suggestions. One which actually predates Sylos has its origins in work by Andrews (1949). This has received its most unequivocal exposition in Bhagwati (1970). As he states it: 'the demand for the entrant's output is restricted to [at most an equal] share in the *marginal* increment in aggregate (industry) demand when price falls below the pre-entry level' (p. 302), (with the qualification that, if the pre-entry price turns out to have been excessively high, buyers will transfer more custom to the entrant). Using these assumptions he derives a formula for limit price along the lines of equation (4.2) obtained from Modigliani.

However, before we broaden this range of exogenously-derived beliefs by a potential entrant further, we should ask a fundamental question: is there any reason for a potential entrant to relate pre-entry price by the established firm to what happens after entry takes place? (We again return to the single incumbent single entrant framework here, for simplicity.) It is the entrant's belief regarding the *post*-entry outcome which will determine her attitude to entry and if the established firm's implied threat regarding entry is unrealistic in that it will be altered if entry occurs, then we do not have a very firm basis for theorising.

This line of reasoning was probably first raised effectively by Wenders (1971*b*), but the implications have been succinctly put by Eaton and Lipsey (1981): 'Bain observed that *we cannot meaningfully analyse oligopoly problems without explicit attention to the possibility of entry.* [However it is now clear that] *we cannot analyse entry deterrence without an underlying model of oligopoly*' (p. 594, italics in original). Thus a threat is most likely to be believed when the potential entrant sees it will be in the interests of the established firm to maintain the position in the face of entry given his views about the post-entry outcome, that is when it becomes a *commitment*.

This viewpoint has an influence on the way we look at entry barriers. To take an example without, for the moment, going into details, suppose the installation by the established firm of a long-lived process gives him access to a particular 'U' shaped cost curve. The fact that money is sunk in the venture may be taken by a potential entrant as a sign of commitment, whereas the threat by the established firm to maintain output in the face of entry at a certain level may well not be believable, if it would lead to losses for the established firm after entry. Hence the paradox that the established firm's threat is made the stronger through the weakness of being committed himself.

Looking back at the previous section, we see the Sylos postulate implied a belief that the post-entry outcome would have the established firm being the leader. It may well be that two rather more plausible equilibrium 'rules' or solution concepts would be for the established firm and the potential entrant to co-operate if entry were to occur, or for them to reach a Cournot–Nash equilibrium.[8] In these cases, it might be thought that, except for *post-entry* absolute advantages such as superior products, entry barriers do not exist, since the firms will find themselves in identical positions after entry. In fact this is not so, as we shall see; there can still be what Salop (1979b) calls *pre-entry asymmetry* (otherwise called first-mover) advantages, because of commitment. We choose to develop the points below using a Cournot–Nash equilibrium.

To facilitate continuity, we follow Dixit's (1980) framework in adopting assumptions proposed in a model due to Spence (1977), that long run variable costs are a function both of output and capacity, but that capacity once installed does not influence marginal costs.[9] Therefore, in the short run, variable costs up to the level of installed capacity are purely a function of output by the established firm. His total cost function is:

$$C_1(q_1, k) = c_1(q_1) + r\bar{k}_1 \qquad (4.5)$$

where k, capacity, is measured in output units and r, its cost, is chosen to allow this. Hence, marginal costs experience a sudden jump as output corresponding to installed capacity is reached (see figure 4.7). For any given marginal revenue curve, like MR_1, involving profitable opportunities, there will be two potentially optimal output levels, the larger corresponding to the point where marginal revenue is equated with $c_1'(q_1)$, the smaller with $c_1'(q_1) + r$. Therefore there are two *potential* reaction functions like M_1M_2 and N_1N_2 in figure 4.8 and, corresponding to any given level of capacity, there will be a particular combination like the bold line $\phi_1(\bar{k}_{11})$, or $\phi_1(\bar{k}_{12})$.

Then, when we include firm 2's reaction function in figure 4.8 we see that there is not one, but a large number of potential Cournot–Nash equilibria along the portion GH of ϕ_2. (Because firm 2 is the entrant she has no installed capacity so only one potential reaction function.) Thus, the established firm can have some influence on the (profitability of) equilibrium by choosing his capacity level and may behave to a limited extent as a Stackleberg leader.

Again as in figures 4.2–4.4 there are various possibilities, and we refer back to the notation used there where relevant to describe the various cases. Entry may be *blockaded* because the point B_2' (where firm 2's reaction

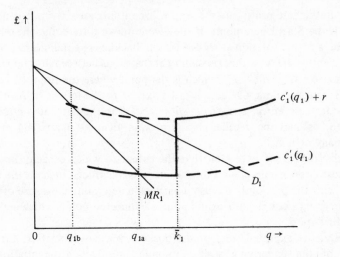

Figure 4.7

function becomes discontinuous) is to the left of M_1, as in figure 4.2, in which case the industry is a natural monopoly. Alternatively, entry can be *easy* in the sense that it cannot be impeded by choosing a credible amount of capacity. This occurs when B_2 is to the right of H, and is the case illustrated in figure 4.8. Consequently the established firm will want to choose a level of capacity giving the two-firm equilibrium in the region GH which

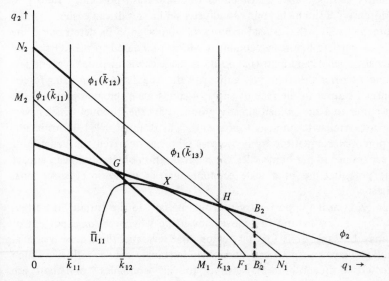

Figure 4.8

yields the highest profit. As the isoprofit contours are drawn, it is point X which is the Stackleberg point. If they were drawn differently, the outcome could be a corner solution at H because the Stackleberg equilibrium would be to the right of H. A further possibility is that B_2 is between M_1 and H. Then what matters is whether F_1, which is the point where the isoprofit contour which is tangent along GH cuts firm 1's axis, is to the left or right of B_2'. In the former case entry is *ineffectively impeded*, in the latter it is *effectively impeded*, as may be recalled by inspecting figures 4.3 and 4.4 and the accompanying text.

In this model we have seen that the extent to which capacity may be a sunk cost (irreversible commitment) interacts via things such as the length of GH with the previously-discussed barriers in determining the ease of entry. The foregoing example also exhibits three connected points which are worth expanding upon.

Firstly, the expected rules of the post-entry game do matter: for given values of the underlying scale economies, product differentiation etc. parameters, if the entrant believes the established firm will be forced to reduce output in the face of entry then the established firm will be able to command a lower premium of price above costs while deterring entry than if the potential entrant believes the established firm will maintain output. This is clouded somewhat in our analysis since between figures 4.2–4.4 and figure 4.8 more than one thing has changed. To see this, assume that, as in the original analysis, marginal costs cannot be lowered by preinvestment in capacity (so H moves to G). Then in an industry in which B_2 involves an output for firm 1 between those corresponding to G and M_1, under the Sylos rules entry is blockaded, whilst under Cournot–Nash post-entry rules it is not. Moreover, H can be beyond G and yet a similar result can ensue.

More generally, the crucial factors of importance in determining the impact of barriers like scale economies which are related to market size are the entrant's beliefs and industrial position. Scale economies look less and less daunting a barrier the more you anticipate the established firm being forced to contract output in the face of entry. Again, scale economies provide little threat either to a firm which already produces another product which never-theless uses similar technology ('cross entry', as Brunner, 1961, terms it) nor to a potential competitor from overseas who has achieved the benefits of scale economies in her home sales. Such a realisation obviously has an impact on the potential use of a scale economy barrier proxy in cross-sectional empirical work.

Thirdly, even if the post-entry outcome is 'fair' to the entrant, the estab-lished firm has a natural first-mover advantage whenever some portion of costs may be sunk. It is for this reason that several authors draw a crucial distinction between sunk costs and other seemingly similar influences such as fixed costs, though both may give rise to scale economies.[10] *Sunk costs* are those which involve purchases of plant and equipment etc. which will last for a period of years. Until the reinvestment decision comes up, these costs cannot be eliminated, even by ceasing production, so they are not part of the opportunity cost of production to an established firm though they are to an entrant. Thus, if a production process is capital intensive and the established firm already has sunk the costs of a plant, there is a capital barrier to entry.

Such costs should be contrasted carefully with *fixed costs*, which are necessary for production but do not vary with the output level; they may be eliminated if a firm decides not to produce. To draw the distinction more clearly, consider for example a man deciding to use an empty shed he has in order to set up a car repair business. He will want a hydraulic ramp costing $£K_0$ installed, for which he will need to borrow the money (or sink his own capital) but its salvage value is only $£K_1$ because of the difficulty of removing it. Hence, in entering this trade he has sunk a cost of $£(K_0 - K_1)$.[11] An example of something which is essentially a fixed cost would be the ladder which most of the various types of property maintenance men require; the resale value is virtually the same as the initial cost.

Returning to our previous analysis, both sunk and fixed costs may give rise to scale economies. However, in terms of figure 4.7, the sunk cost is akin to the capacity which allows the established firm, in the short run, onto a lower marginal (and also average variable) cost curve than the potential entrant, so effectively bending the rules in favour of the incumbent. The fixed cost is a determinant of the point at which the reaction function becomes discontinuous. Its impact as an entry barrier is therefore dependent upon the 'rules' adopted.

This matters particularly in the polar case where the post-entry game is played according to Bertrand's rules. The point was first forcibly made in writings by Brozen (1969), but Baumol, Panzar and Willig (1982) have developed and refined the view.[12] *If* all potential producers have access to the same technical and productive characteristics and consumers will respond quickly to price changes, yet the established firm(s) cannot respond swiftly enough when a potential entrant sets up for business at cheaper prices, then *in the absence of sunk costs*, there will be no barriers to entry and price will fall to average cost. Such a market structure has been called *perfectly contestable*. The presence of sunk costs is sufficient to prevent this desirable outcome, since the potential entrant is required on entry to make a commitment which has already been made by the established firm. Thus, unless the potential entrant is relatively more efficient, the cards are stacked against her. In effect, the barrier to entry is caused by there being a *barrier to exit*.

This viewpoint also leads to the belief, particularly amongst those of an Austrian persuasion, that many of the most important entry barriers are legal restrictions imposed by regulation authorities, such as the requirement to obtain licences to operate in certain industries, rather than creations (or results) of the established firms themselves (see Demsetz, 1982).

One implication of these points is that economists attempting to look at capital as a barrier to entry must be careful to distinguish between perpetual sunk costs, costs sunk only for a period, capital deteriorating over time and so on, as Eaton and Lipsey (1980) point out. This is particularly so since the presence of sunk costs is a sufficient condition for some other barriers like pure fixed costs and scale economies to be of any importance. Notice also that sunk costs need not only be embodied in physical capital, but instead perhaps in an innovation or in advertising goodwill. For a variety of reasons, an established firm can therefore find itself in a favourable position *vis a vis* a potential entrant without *necessarily* having contrived to do so; merely being first may entail a premium of price above cost.

An overview

The decision problem facing a firm contemplating entry is essentially an investment decision under uncertainty. It is thus influenced by structural features of the industry but, as we hope to have shown in this section, not by those alone.

To illustrate the point, at current prices, and given the size of investment required, suppose the potential entrant would break even with sales greater than x units. Therefore she has to assess whether such a sales level is realistic given the characteristics of the other firms' products, but in addition to consider how good a signal to post-entry price is pre-entry price. What is also crucially important is how much is recoverable if the investment should go wrong, and this depends upon the commitment established firms have made.

This investment decision is not just one made when moving from zero output in an industry to a positive output. All the essential features are present when a firm considers moving from, say, producing goods for others to brand to production of its own range as, for example Zanussi has done for the U.K. market. Thus in a similar way one can consider there being *barriers to mobility* (Caves and Porter, 1977).

Hence such decisions are both frequent and difficult. They depend upon an interaction of structural, technical and expectational factors, but they are elementally important in determining established industry profitability and its distribution between groups within an industry. They are also important for public policy, and this 'outsider's view' is extended in the final section, after we have considered some dynamics.

6. Long-run profit maximisation

As explained in section 3, it might not be profitable for an established firm, one it has decided what limit price is, actually to set that price. If it is not then, we assume, a firm may freely enter and the decision process commences afresh. In all this, only two policies presented themselves: to price to stop entry or to price to achieve the best possible solution while allowing it.

This was softened somewhat by the extensions of section 4, particularly the probabilistic viewpoint adopted towards the end of the section. But, as Hicks (1954) pointed out, why should not the established firm find it better to set a price between the two levels given above? That is, he suggested setting a price:

$$p^* = ap_m + (1-a)p_L, \qquad 1 \geqslant a \geqslant 0$$

where p_m is the price which maximises profits before entry occurs and p_L the price which would prevent entry. He called people who set the weights $(1-a)$ high, and a low, so choosing a price near to p_L, 'stickers', and those who chose the reverse course, a price near to p_m, 'snatchers' — the terminology is fairly obvious. In each case, entry will not be prevented, but may be retarded to some extent by such a compromise policy. Alternatively, why should not the established firm, as Pashigian (1968) suggests, initially price to allow entry and then, after a certain amount has occurred, price to prevent more?

Both these points occur as features of models designed to explain optimal long run strategies of established firms faced with the threat of entry. A large number of such models have been developed. Among them are papers by Gaskins (1971), Kamien and Schwartz (1971, 1975), Pyatt (1971), Ireland (1972a, 1972b), Jacquemin and Thisse (1972), Schupack (1972), Baron (1973), Wenders (1971a), de Bondt (1978), Encaoua, Jacquemin, and Michel (1979), and Reynolds (1982). After a brief outline, what we intend to do here is to discuss in some detail the first two contributions listed, since these reveal different aspects of the work in the area, while making occasional references to other papers.

The general approach of these papers is first to postulate a fixed entry limiting price, below which no new firms will enter. As Jacquemin and Thisse, overstating the determinacy of static entry-barrier theory, put it: 'The work of Bain, Sylos-Labini and Modigliani allows us to determine the exact size of the discrepancy between the limit price and the competitive price' (p. 69). To the extent that this assumption is simplistic, the models lack economic content. Secondly, the established industry (which is normally a monopolist or collusive group, possibly with a competitive fringe), is considered to maximise long run profits (at some relevant rate of discount) using a particular control variable, usually price. Thirdly, entrants are normally seen either as a flow into a competitive fringe or a once-for-all lump of entry. The assumption which makes these models novel is the reaction that potential entrants are assumed to take with respect to some industry performance characteristic (prices, profits or 'profit opportunities'), known as the state equation. The inherently dynamic problem posed in this manner is then solved using calculus of variations or control theory. Attention naturally focuses on the path followed by industry price over time, the eventual position of the initial incumbent and any comparative static predictions which can be gleaned from the models.

In general the established firm wishes to maximise long run profits using price as the control variable; future profits are discounted at a (continuous) discount rate r. Thus, a sensible maximand is the function:

$$V = \int_0^\infty \Pi(t)\, e^{-rt} \cdot dt$$

Gaskins' model is one of price leadership by a dominant firm whose profits are simply price minus a constant cost level multiplied by the difference between industry output and fringe output, viz:

$$\Pi(t) = [p(t) - c][Q(p(t)) - q_2(t)]$$

Thus, everything essentially hinges on the assumption about entry, which is presumed to occur at a rate:

$$q_2'(t) = k[p(t) - p_L]; \qquad p_L \geqslant c, \; k > 0 \tag{4.6}$$

proportional to the difference between price and limit price. The established firm in the dominant firm model chooses a price path, bearing in mind that higher prices now raise present profits at the expense of future ones, via (4.6).

The solution which results, typically has price falling over time from a level some way below p_m asymptotically to p_L, as illustrated by p_G^* in figure 4.9. Whilst this is going on, the established firm is losing shares to the market fringe (who nevertheless, continue to be price takers in his model). If the initially dominant firm has no cost advantage, in the long run his market share tends to zero. However, this is not a feature of Jacquemin and Thisse's amended version in which the dominant firm is allowed to take over

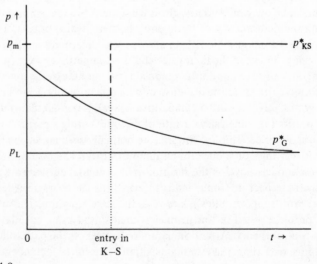

Figure 4.9

rivals, nor of Encaoua *et al.*'s more general model which is also based upon Gaskins' framework.[13]

Kamien and Schwartz (1971) build a model rather different from these. Their purpose is not to derive an optimal path as entry proceeds, but rather to discover the pricing policy prevailing until a lump of entry occurs, with the help of a simple two-period analysis. An interesting departure is that they view entry probabilistically.

In their first period (until entry occurs) the profits of the established firm naturally depend on the price it sets. The timing of entry is stochastically governed by the established firm's price, though. After entry has occurred, period II commences, the possibility of further entry (somewhat artificially) ends, and the established and entrant firms collude. Again, therefore, there is an obvious trade-off, because a higher price now increases the probability that entry will occur soon, whence industry profits have to be shared (not necessarily equally).

Kamien and Schwartz find it optimal for the firm to set price between p_m and p_L and hold it fixed until entry occurs, as p_{KS}^* in figure 4.9. Obviously such a model has little specific to say about terminal market share. However, Baron builds a model essentially similar to that of Kamien and Schwartz (except that the established firm maximises the expected *utility* of profit, which allows Baron to comment upon the effects of risk preference). His model has many periods, and potential entrants react to industry price. At the end of each period, an optimal price is chosen for the next. He shows this price to be less than the price which maximises pre-entry profit, also less than the price which makes the probability of entry equal to one, but in general, greater than average cost. Thus, over time, the established firm would be expected to lose market share.

Actually, in such relatively simple models it is fairly easy to see why the dominant firm loses market share: there are no economies of scale and little scope for strategic action such as pre-emption (which we discuss in chapter 6). Changing either of these assumptions can give rise to first-mover advantages which allow the dominant firm to take some initiative (see e.g. Encaoua *et al.*, 1979, and Worcester, 1957, as an early example).

Apart from what happens in the long run to the dominant firm, the predictions of such models with regard to parameter changes are also of potential interest. In Gaskins' model there are predictions both about the influence of various parameters on the final equilibrium (comparative static predictions) and in addition, predictions on optimal price movements. One prediction which arises in both frameworks is that an increase in the discount rate increases optimal price. This is fairly obvious, given the types of trade-offs which are involved between present and future· profits. Some of the other predictions turn out to be rather uninteresting.[14]

Nevertheless, one prediction which is of extreme interest is the effect of an increase in 'barriers to entry' on optimal price. Kamien and Schwartz do not have barriers or limit price explicitly in their model, but when they modify it by assuming that an increase in barriers reduces the 'hazard rate' of entry, they obtain the seemingly intuitive result that an increase in barriers increases p^*. Baron points out that theirs is not the only way to conceptualise an increase in barriers. This is because the 'hazard rate', and so the direction of the effect on optimal price, depends in general on the relationship between the rise in the profitability of no entry due to an increase in barriers and the rise in the rate at which the probability of entry increases as price rises.

Similar considerations govern Gaskins' results in this area. He shows that the more probable entry is at a given price (as represented by a larger parameter k in (4.6)), the lower is optimal price. However he also finds that the higher is limit price above costs, the *lower* is optimal price for a selection of simple demand laws he tries. This seems counter-intuitive, but may be understood better with the aid of figure 4.10 depicting his reaction function.[15] At the *same* price p^* before and after rise in limit price from p_L to p'_L, both the benefit, in terms of extra profit, of maintaining p^* rather than limit price, and the cost, in terms of future entry, fall.[16] It is not intuitively obvious that one will definitely change more than the other; this will depend upon the shape of the profit function (and the reaction function if we allowed it to vary) as his limited result implies. De Bondt also develops a model in which price may increase as barriers to entry fall when there is a lag before entry occurs.

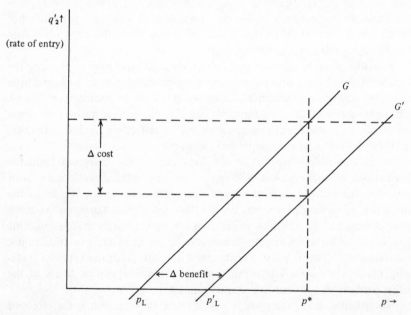

Figure 4.10

Thus, we are not assured that an increase in measured entry barriers will necessarily raise price and so the price–cost margin in the short run. Consequently, it is possible that cross-sectional empirical work implicitly relying upon equilibrium relationships may pick up a 'perverse' dynamic reaction to differing barrier heights. It seems the most we can confidently glean from the work surveyed which is of use in *cross-sectional* empirical studies, is that, as we would expect, actual price tends to be between the short run profit maximising and limit prices. Thus, factors affecting both are likely to be of importance in explaining industry performance in terms of profits.[17]

7. Some comments on welfare

So far, we have essentially been concerned with the use of barriers to entry as variables explaining the distribution of profitability within an industry or between industries. But as Bain (1954) pointed out, we may wish also to use the concept of barriers to entry in a societal welfare context as things to be removed to improve welfare. In that case, our existing definitional framework may no longer be adequate: Bain's 'condition of entry' is firmly embedded in a profitability interpretation.

Actually, some consensus seems to have emerged recently[18] in favour of a definition along the lines of Stigler's (1968, p. 67): 'A barrier to entry may be defined as a cost of producing ... which must be borne by a firm which seeks to enter an industry but is not borne by firms already in the industry'. However, recent views have limited barriers from the welfare point of view still further by excluding at least those differential costs which are essentially efficiency rents. Let us pursue some limited re-examination of barriers with this new definition in mind.

The first and most straightforward point relates to absolute cost/demand advantages. An established firm may have an absolute cost advantage which allows it to make higher than average profits. But these profits may contain an element of rent accruing to a scarce resource in the possession of the established firm. For example we may suppose (along the lines of Ferguson, 1974) that entrants jointly present a horizontal supply curve for the industry product. Assume the established firm has marginal and average costs, at some output rates, below this supply curve. Then if the established firm's marginal and average cost curves eventually rise, and do so in such a manner that the marginal cost curve cuts the supply curve before it cuts the industry demand curve, then the established firm wishing to prevent entry will be setting price equal to marginal cost. Here there is an economic rent (price is greater than average cost) due to the established firm's superior ability. On the other hand, if the rising marginal cost schedule cuts the demand curve before it cuts the potential entrant's supply curve, price can be above marginal cost without entry taking place. The difference between price and average cost here is partly rent and partly monopoly profit and only the latter can be considered as a barrier to entry in the welfare sense.

Secondly there are product differentiation advantages. Here a welfare interpretation is more difficult. Again an asymmetry between established firm and potential entrant is required for there to be a difference in profitability, but the question is how that asymmetry comes about. It could arise from the way consumers behave, from first-mover advantages or from deliberate actions of the firms concerned. These matters require more extensive discussion which is best postponed until chapter 7.

We also have the question of scale economies. One obvious difficulty here is that perfect competition cannot provide a benchmark for socially efficient performance. Prices set equal to marginal costs will lead to losses if there are diminishing returns at that point, so what we require (in the absence of lump-sum subsidies or efficient price discrimination) are prices creating the minimal distortions from marginal cost. Formally then, in the absence of income effects (for simplicity) for socially optimal subsidy-free prices we want those prices (p) to:

$$\text{maximise } CS(p) + \Pi(p) \text{ subject to } \Pi(p) \geqslant 0$$

where CS and Π refer to industry consumer surplus and profit. Prices with these properties are known as *Ramsey prices* (see Baumol, 1977, pp. 513–6 for discussion). Such prices will emerge in markets which are *perfectly contestable*, a property discussed in section 5. Perfect contestability thus provides a benchmark for socially efficient performance in naturally oligopolistic markets.

As we have seen, the importance of scale economies is very much wrapped up with the belief of the potential entrants. If they entertain essentially Bertrand-type conjectures, then fixed cost elements in scale economies need not constitute entry barriers in the welfare sense. That is, though only a small number of firms may serve a market in which there are high fixed costs, they can under some circumstances produce at optimal prices and so bring about a desirable result. One way to ensure this is to have an efficiently run competition *for* the field, where firms submit bids for the right to produce for a given period.

On the other hand, if there are sunk costs or if established firms can (deliberately or otherwise) sustain threats which potential entrants find compelling but which allow above-normal profits, then there is a barrier in a welfare sense. This may be 'innocent' (a characteristic of the technology or of potential entrants) or alternatively 'deliberate' (arranged by the established firm); it makes little difference to the fact there is a market failure. However, von Weizsäcker (1980*a*) points out this does not necessarily mean more firms should be persuaded to enter. To take a simple example, if average costs are continually declining, the optimal structure is naturally monopolistic. However a market outcome with scale economy barriers would often involve more than one firm producing profitability (von Weizsäcker assumes, for the purpose of illustration, a Cournot model). In order to improve welfare, more incumbents are definitely not required. Rather, more output should be produced by fewer firms. Thus the barrier is not a barrier to entry of new firms, but to entry of output, and any policy proposal should take this into consideration. Discovering remedies to natural monopoly problems as these is an important task for regulatory agencies. Hence the analytics of this chapter are relevant well beyond our present concerns (see e.g. Sharkey, 1982).

Notes on the literature

On the basic ideas and analysis of the barriers to entry question, Modigliani's (1958) synthesis is one of the more important pieces, as we have already implied. A succinct exposition of Bain's views and methods is available in Bain (1954). Dixit's (1979) analysis of the alternative equilibrium is also fairly accessible to the general reader. A survey of many points found in our discussion of alternative reactions to potential entry is provided by Caves and Porter (1977), particularly the first section. Their second section extends the analysis to 'barriers to mobility', that is intra-industry barriers. On the more recently expressed views regarding barriers, Salop's (1979*b*) short survey is very useful, also Encaoua, Geroski and Jacquemin's (1982) more extensive one. In addition, Dixit's (1982) game-theoretic treatment of the possibilities regarding strategic behaviour and credible threats and Eaton and Lipsey's (1981) discussion of the importance of different types of capital as commitments provide many insights. The literature on dynamic or long run behaviour with regard to potential entry is mostly rather difficult; the best explanatory study is probably Jacquemin and Thisse (1972). Baumol (1982) and Demsetz (1982) cover some welfare economic issues, among other things. Lastly, von Weizsäcker's thoughtful book (1980*b*) will give the reader many ideas in most of the areas discussed.

5

Monopoly power in
vertically related markets

Monopolists and oligopolists do not exist in isolation. As we have seen in earlier chapters, an oligopolist's market power is tempered both by the other firms in the same industry and by those who have a potential for entering the industry. But, apart from these constraints, a monopoly or an oligopoly can be affected by related industries, if these industries also possess market power.

To be sure, some industries purchase raw materials in competitive markets from which they fabricate a finished product which is sold to final consumers with little or no market power — the tobacco industry is probably the nearest example. But many others, for example the lead-acid battery makers, purchase (in their case) a substantial fraction of the total supply of lead in the U.K., a supply which comes from relatively few firms. They then sell their product to the retail trade but also to motor car assemblers who may possess both substantial selling and purchasing power. The market power of lead producers, motor car manufacturers, and possibly even suppliers of other important inputs into car assembly such as tyres, may have an impact on the market power which can be exercised by battery producers. It is the purpose of this chapter to examine the effects of such related market power and to consider the question of vertical integration (merger) between two successive stages of production. However, as is probably fairly obvious, we cannot hope to model in any detail the rich inter-relationships between industries.[1] This is particularly difficult given that industrial economists have not pursued the area theoretically with anything like the vigour they have expended on the oligopoly problem. Rather we wish simply to provide some pointers on the more important types of relationships which can exist between industries with market power.

Our plan is to start discussion at a fairly basic level in talking about successive market power, that is selling, but not buying, power at two or more stages of production, then mutually related market power, where powerful firms producing complementary products sell to the same industry. We turn in section 2 to vertical integration. After explaining the concept, we use the model of successive monopoly to obtain results assuming fixed proportions between inputs and outputs and go on to discuss contractual motives for integration. The results are modified in section 3 in moving to variable

82

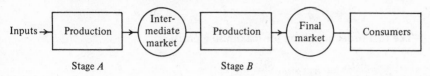

Figure 5.1

proportions models and in discussing uncertainty. Bilateral power – monopoly versus monopsony – is discussed and extensions developed in section 4, which also considers Galbraith's 'countervailing power' thesis. In this chapter, welfare economic points are somewhat more intermingled with positive analysis than is the case in most other chapters.

1. Successive and mutually related market power

Successive market power
Consider a production process involving more than one stage, like that illustrated in figure 5.1. We look first at the situation which is conceptually the simplest. Suppose a monopolist (in Stage A) sells his product to a further monopolist (Stage B) who utilises it in a fixed proportional manner (say, for ease, one to one) to manufacture his own product. Assume the Stage A monopolist faces constant marginal production costs of an amount c. B's other costs, apart from those of purchasing A's product, are constant at a level k per unit of output produced. Thus, developing the situation mathematically, profit for firm B may be written:

$$\Pi_B = p_B q - p_A q - kq,$$

where q is the level of output produced by B, and so also by A, under our assumption. B treats A's price as parametric.

Maximising profits with respect to output, realising that the final demand curve slopes downwards, but assuming the price of A's input, p_A, constant gives:

$$\frac{d\Pi_B}{dq} = p_B + q \cdot \frac{dp_B}{dq} - p_A - k = 0 \tag{5.1}$$

as firm B's first-order condition – marginal revenue equals marginal cost.[2] This may be written:

$$p_B \left(1 - \frac{1}{\eta_B}\right) - p_A - k = MR_B - p_A - k = 0 \tag{5.2}$$

where η_B is the modulus of the own-price elasticity of demand and MR_B is B's marginal revenue. From this we obtain the derived demand for A's product as the net marginal revenue product: $p_A = MR_B - k$. A's profit function is:

$$\Pi_A = p_A q - c \cdot q$$

The first order condition for maximising profit is:

$$\frac{d\Pi_A}{dq} = p_A + q \cdot \frac{dp_A}{dq} - c = 0$$

or

$$p_A \left(1 - \frac{1}{\eta_A}\right) = c, \tag{5.3}$$

η_A being the elasticity of the derived demand curve. Thus A also sets marginal revenue, as he perceives it, equal to marginal cost.

Diagrammatic exposition will be made slightly easier if we note that, from (5.2), we may also write:

$$\Pi_A = MR_B \cdot q - (c + k) \cdot q, \qquad \text{so that,}$$

$d(MR_B \cdot q)/dq = c + k$ is an alternative way of writing A's first-order profit-maximising condition. Thus firm A can be considered to be maximising profit by setting the curve 'marginal' (by which we shall mean the curve which bears the same relationship to the marginal revenue curve as the marginal revenue curve does to the demand curve) to B's marginal revenue curve, equal to the sum of the basic marginal costs. We denote this curve *MD* in figure 5.2, which assumes a linear final demand curve for simplicity. Output is therefore at a level q_B in that figure. Tracing up to the curve MR_B, which is k units *above* A's derived demand curve, gives a price p_I; thus the intermediate product A is exchanged at a price p_A. Firm B in turn adds his margin onto his perceived costs, p_I and so charges the market p_B.

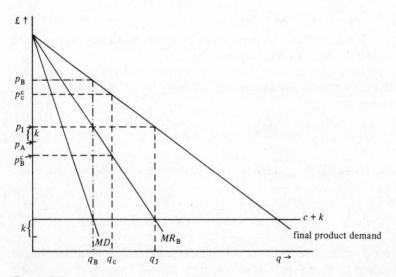

Figure 5.2

If instead there was only one stage of production, the monopoly occupant would set $MR_B = c + k$, producing output q_J for sale at a price of only p_I. Conversely, adding a further stage has the consequence of raising price further above original marginal costs, reducing output still further. But notice that, however many stages there are, each monopolist sets marginal revenue equal to marginal cost as he perceives it, so that the price–cost margin for each successive monopolist is the reciprocal of the elasticity of derived demand facing him at the relevant price. This may be verified mathematically in our two-stage model simply by rearranging (5.2) and (5.3) to read:

$$\frac{p_B - p_A - k}{p_B} = \frac{1}{\eta_B}$$

$$\frac{p_A - c}{p_A} = \frac{1}{\eta_A}$$

respectively. It arises because of the myopic way in which prices are accepted by following stages of production.

Thus, in this simple case, though the profit *amount* received by monopolist A is affected by dint of the two-stage organisation of production, the profit *margin* is still determined in the way a single monopolist's would be. Furthermore, it is conceptually fairly straightforward to extend the analysis to cover the cases of a monopolist selling to an oligopoly, of oligopoly selling to monopoly and of oligopoly selling to oligopoly — as long as the assumptions about interrelationships among the oligopolists at a particular stage are known. (They might, for example, act as Cournot firms). In every case the profit-margin would be equal to the reciprocal of the derived elasticity of demand.

Now our two-stage monopolists (or oligopolists) are not interested in the profit *margin* for its own sake, rather they are intent on maximising profit. Therefore if, instead of A presenting his opposite number B with a price which the latter takes as given, they were to enter into negotiation on a price–quantity contract, then both would have a potential for making more profits. Formally, they would jointly maximise:

$$\Pi_{B+A} = p_B q - (c + k)q, \tag{5.4}$$

yielding as the first-order condition:

$$p_B \left(1 - \frac{1}{\eta_B}\right) = c + k \tag{5.5}$$

Thus B's marginal revenue is set equal to $c + k$ and the traded quantity which would maximise joint profits is q_J in figure 5.2. Consumers pay a final price p_I for this quantity — as far as they are concerned the result is equivalent to that which would obtain if there were only one stage of production.[3] The more problematic aspect of the model to establish is the transfer price of A's product from A to B. We leave discussion of this until section 4. However, all we wish to establish for the present is that it is not necessarily in the interests of a monopolist at one stage of production to accept the price of a monopolist at a previous stage as given.[4]

This accepted, the corollary is that the price–cost margin (or profit margin on sales) need not be the same in a situation where there are two or more successive stages of production, as it is in the case where there is only one stage. For in our joint profit maximising model, it is clear that when the *total* margin between initial costs and final market price is equal to the elasticity of demand at that price (as can be seen by rearranging (5.5) to read $(p_B - c - k)/p_B = 1/\eta_B$), then the margin for B between final market price and the prices he pays (his costs k and his payment per unit to A) is less than the elasticity of demand at that point. Moreover, it becomes difficult to relate the price–cost margin A receives to the demand elasticity when the transfer price and quantity agreed upon are not on A's normal derived demand curve.

A further question arises. We initially looked at the case where B accepted A's price as given. We then turned our attention to the situation where B and A joined forces to the extent of a mutual agreement on the quantity of input to be traded, by maximising profits jointly, while bargaining over the transfer price in some way yet to be discussed. Are there possible intermediate positions between these? In providing a partial answer to this question by demonstrating an example of such an intermediate position, we initially digress in looking at the case of mutually related market power.

Mutually related market power

We mean by mutually related market power the situation such as we mentioned in the introduction where there is a potential constraint upon the exercise of market power by the battery industry because there is market power in the tyre industry and these products are jointly demanded by a third industry — motor cars. Why should there be any relationship here at all? To see this, suppose that the tyre industry raises its prices very substantially. If the motor industry has no alternative source, it must continue to purchase tyres, but is forced to pay more for them. This rise in costs will raise price in the normal manner, the quantity of cars sold will fall, so cutting the demand for batteries by motor manufacturers.

To take a simple version of this case, susceptible to fairly straightforward analysis, consider a model in which a tyre monopolist and a battery monopolist sell to a motor assembly industry having no market power either in sales or purchases. Assume in addition there is no replacement market for tyres or batteries, so sales can only be made to the motor industry which, fairly naturally given our example, uses fixed proportions of their inputs in making the final product. A final assumption, made purely to simplify the analysis, is that other inputs into a car, and their assembly, are costless.[5] The price of a car (p_c) is then simply the price of a battery (p_B) and a set of tyres (p_T).

One possible, though rather artificial, solution to the problem of pricing in this situation would be for the battery and tyre firms to combine in offering a package deal to the car makers which maximised their joint profit. That is, they would set $(p_B + p_T)$, so effectively p_c, at a level indicated by setting the curve marginal to the demand curve for cars equal to the sum of their marginal costs. However, we wish to focus on an alternative solution proposed by Cournot (1927).

Cournot's suggestion (in his chapter 9) is that each monopolist would maximise profits independently with respect to price, treating the price of the other as given. In this sense it is the analogue of his duopoly model, with price the appropriate decision variable here as the quantities traded have to be identical.

Treating this case formally, let the battery monopolist's profit function be given by:

$$\Pi_B = p_B q - c \cdot q,$$

where q is the common quantity and c the level of his marginal (and average) costs. Maximising with respect to p_B gives the first-order condition

$$\frac{d\Pi_B}{dp_B} = q + p_B \frac{dq}{dp_B} - c \cdot \frac{dq}{dp_B} = 0 \tag{5.6}$$

Now since $q = q(p_c) = q(p_B + p_T)$ is the demand for cars, then:

$$\frac{dq}{dp_B} = \frac{dq}{dp_c} \cdot \frac{dp_c}{dp_B} = \frac{dq}{dp_c} \left(1 + \frac{dp_T}{dp_B}\right) \tag{5.7}$$

But Cournot's battery seller's assumption is that his price changes have no effect on the tyre-monopolist's prices, i.e. $dp_T/dp_B = 0$. Therefore from (5.6):

$$(p_B - c)\frac{dq}{dp_c} = -q. \tag{5.8}$$

A similar assumption for the tyre seller yields:

$$(p_T - k)\frac{dq}{dp_c} = -q, \tag{5.9}$$

where k is the constant level of his marginal costs.

Recalling that $p_c = p_B + p_T$, we can sum (5.8) and (5.9) and rearrange to read:

$$\frac{p_c - c - k}{p_c} = -2\frac{q}{p_c} \cdot \frac{dp_c}{dq} = \frac{2}{\eta_c},$$

where η_c is the modulus of the demand elasticity for cars.

This solution may be slightly altered to form another solution within the *successive power* framework discussed in the previous subsection. Suppose now that the *monopoly* car producer makes his own tyres, and purchases batteries alone from outside. The car manufacturer's assumption is now the equivalent of the assumption made above: $dp_B/dp_c = 0$, that is a rise in the price charged for cars has no effect on the price paid for batteries. However as far as the battery monopolist is concerned, $dp_c/dp_B = 1$, a rise in the price of cars is equal to the rise in the price of batteries which engendered it. This is the equivalent of the earlier assumption of this subsection since there the battery manufacturer effectively considered that a rise in battery prices would raise car prices by an equivalent amount (see equation (5.7)).

When this variant is developed along similar lines to the mutually related power model of equations (5.6)–(5.9), we find that the *car* monopolist obtains the margin he would expect were he purchasing from suppliers with no market power in their sales. The battery monopolist's margin is:

$$\frac{p_B - c}{p_B} = -\frac{q}{p_B} \cdot \frac{dp_c}{dq} = \frac{1}{\eta_c} \cdot \frac{p_c}{p_B}$$

In the particular case we are using diagrammatically, involving linear demand and cost curves, this can be rewritten in terms of the elasticity facing B as:

$$\frac{p_B - c}{p_B} = -\frac{q}{p_B} \cdot \frac{1}{2} \cdot \frac{dp_B}{dq} = \frac{1}{2\eta_B},$$

since the slope of the demand curve facing him is twice as steep as that facing c. However the reader should be aware that with different demand and cost formulations, the result can look very different. In general though, the margin B obtains will *not* be what he would expect were he selling to industries with no market power. (Waterson, 1980, develops a more complex version of this model.)

The Cournot-type solution is drawn, for comparative purposes, on figure 5.2. The output, q_c is exchanged at a price $p_B^c - k$ and final market price is p_c^c. The figure brings out the essential symmetry of Cournot's model to his duopoly model – the profit areas look like those of the duopoly model found in most microeconomics textbooks except that they are placed on top of one another rather than side by side. This is because his model for the situation we are at present discussing is one of perfect complementarity between the two firms, whereas his duopoly model represents perfect substitutability. We can similarly generalise his present model – if there were three stages of production, each with a monopolist in residence, there would be three profit areas corresponding to a Cournot triopoly. Notice also that Cournot's solution is between the myopic profit maximising and joint-profit maximising solutions discussed in the previous subsection; it is thus indicative of a range of possible solutions between these values for the successive power situation. Unfortunately, unlike the oligopoly case, it is not a straightforward matter to derive a simple framework linking solutions within this range in terms of the relationship between price–cost margins and elasticities of demand, and we shall not explore the possibility of doing so here.

2. Vertical integration: concepts and motives

A firm is said to be vertically integrated if two or more successive stages of production are organised within the same firm. This immediately brings about the question of how one defines successive stages, that is how to define the industry. For example, if we consider there is an industry called motor vehicle assembly, then we would call vehicle assemblers who manufactured their own engines, gearboxes, and possibly even those who pressed their own steel body panels[6] vertically integrated. A change of definition to call the industry motor vehicle manufacture would alter our view on the extent of vertical integration radically. Thus, designing an acceptable measure of the extent of vertical integration is problematic.

This definitional problem is probably not as important (so long as definitions are fixed) when we consider *changes* in the extent of vertical integration.[7] We can legitimately enquire into the effects of a firm, however much or little integrated at the moment, deciding to integrate further for example. Such moves come into two categories: backward or 'upstream' vertical integration – producing more basic inputs than before, and forward or 'downstream' vertical integration – producing a more nearly finished product than before. The analogy is of a firm as being at a particular point on a stream which is a flow from the spring (the primary inputs) to the river (the final consumers). In our discussion we largely assume that the motive for downstream integration is the same as for the equivalent upstream integration.

Vertical integration with fixed proportions

For the purpose of this subsection, we assume that vertical integration at two successive stages of production does not affect the cost conditions at either stage and, further, that the input from the first stage (A) is utilised in a fixed proportion to final output at stage B, the later stage. For example, a motor engine manufacturer supplies one unit of his product to a motor assembler for every unit the assembler produces. In order to avoid problems of mutually related market power, we shall also assume that if the input A (say) is in the hands of a monopoly, no other inputs to B are monopolised.

It is fairly obvious that vertical integration between two firms in perfectly competitive industries, and also between a perfectly competitive supply industry and a monopolist final product seller, has no consequence within our framework. Further (but less obvious), vertical integration between a monopolist at stage A and a perfectly competitive industry at stage B does not change output, prices or welfare.

Here, the derived demand for the monopolist's product is given by the demand curve for the final product, shifted down by an amount representing the supply prices of the other factors (see Friedman, 1962 ch. 7, for example, for a diagrammatic exposition). Thus for firms in the competitive downstream industry, who do not realise the demand curve facing them is downward sloping, we have, instead of (5.1):

$$\frac{d\Pi_{Bi}}{dq_i} = p_B - p_A - k = 0$$

whence the derived demand for A's product is $p_A = p_B - k$. Monopolist A's profit function is therefore:

$$\Pi_A = p_A q - cq = p_B q - (c + k)q$$

This is identical to (5.4), which is the profit function under joint profit maximisation, or equally for an integrated monopolist. Accordingly the outcome is also the same: consumers pay a price p_I for output q_J.

Thus whether downstream costs k are added on before or after the monopoly profit has been taken is of no consequence: the monopolist can take his profit only once in the production process. As a corollary to this key point, the monopolist might integrate with just one firm in the perfectly competitive industry and use his favourable position to drive the other firms in that industry out, say by quoting higher prices for his inputs. However there would again be no welfare consequence in the sense normally used in industrial economics, though there would of course be a consequence for the entrepreneurs driven out.

Let us now consider the consequences of a vertical merger between a monopolist at stage A and a monopolist at stage B. We assume that, prior to the merger, the monopolist at stage B considered A's price as a parameter. In that case, as we saw in section 1, A could be said to face the final product marginal revenue curve as his demand curve and would set the curve 'marginal' to that equal to the sum of marginal costs. The pre-merger outcome is depicted in figure 5.2 – output is low, and final product price high, at p_B, because of the cumulative effect of successive markups. When they merge, they will obviously maximise joint profits. Thus output becomes larger, at q_J, and a final price p_I will be charged. Moreover, the profit area is greater than the sum of profits together made prior to the merger. When there are two monopolists in successive stages, there is therefore an incentive, in terms of increased profits, for their vertical integration. In addition, consumers benefit from lower prices, so consumers' surplus increases. Since both consumers' and producers' surplus increases, there is a welfare gain.

Some generalisations on the result regarding the merged successive monopolists have been provided by Greenhut and Ohta (1976). For example, they show that for a wide class of demand functions – more particularly those where the elasticity of the marginal revenue curve is the same as that of the demand curve at any price – the price the monopolist charges the final product seller(s) is constant whatever their market structure. They further demonstrate that, if the final market sector B consists of a number of Cournot oligopolists, vertical integration of the stage A monopolist with some or all of them always lowers final price and increases output, at the same time increasing profits to the merged firms. They have recently (1979) extended this to the case of two industries of Cournot oligopolists amongst which a sub-group of downstream and upstream firms merge vertically. Again, final price falls and output rises. The same happens if the merged group act as a Stackleberg leader to the remaining unintegrated firms.

Thus far, it appears that if it is in two firms' private interest to integrate vertically, this will also be socially desirable. However this is not always the case, as we shall see.

Contractual motives

So far, the suggested reason for vertical integration has been extremely mechanistic, and the conclusions clear-cut. But, as Williamson (1971) pointed out, there are a wide range of considerations involved. We survey these briefly below, then explore some of them more extensively in the following section.

Williamson suggested that the basic question is a comparative institutional one.[8] Most economists believe a market with a large number of buyers and sellers to be a useful impersonal device for coordinating actions. More complex bilateral contracts within a market framework may be more feasible in some other cases. Vertical integration deliberately suppresses these market mechanisms, presumably because in some cases the market is a (comparative) failure.

The market fails to coordinate vertical relationships where there are externalities or interdependencies which are difficult (and occasionally impossible) to capture contractually. In a frictionless world, vertical integration would simply be an alternative to the optimal contract. The sort of factors which make contractual arrangements difficult, and so make vertical integration more likely, include the following: (i) how to design contracts which cater for technological interdependency (such as where iron which is hot when produced is hot-rolled in fabricating bars); (ii) how to decide on the contingent supply relations when the product is complex and requires periodic revision or, more generally, if not every contingency can be foreseen; (iii) how to allocate risk-bearing and to avoid risk allocation influencing decisions, (for example if the market for a particular product line falls below expectations, to what extent should component manufacturers suffer?); (iv) how to coordinate information gathering to achieve economies without jeopardising commercial secrecy; (v) how to avoid substitution away from factors priced at above marginal cost (which may be necessary to make their production profitable); and (vi) how to monitor and police contractual arrangements to ensure what was agreed is being carried out.

It is not claimed that these factors make contractual solutions impossible, or vertical integration inevitable, simply that they might explain vertical integration as a phenomenon. Williamson's view is that vertical integration can reduce many of these contractual costs by altering the claims structure from a between to a within firm framework. Fiats by the overall management are more likely to be accepted when the rewards are to be shared than if they are likely to go to someone else. A good example is where, in the absence of vertical integration, haggling over the transfer price for an input is likely to be extensive since there is a considerable incentive: it is privately profitable. Within the integrated firm though, haggling is a zero sum game and management should therefore be able to impose a transfer price unilaterally. Williamson also emphasises that monitoring and policing activities may be easier within the firm than through an external contract because states of the world and decisions are more easily distinguished.

On the other hand, when two or more successive operations are vertically integrated, there is a natural bias towards internal procurement of components even if the division concerned is relatively inefficient. Also, bounded rationality means that the greater the extent of the firm, the more hierarchical layers of control are required to retain equivalent surveillance. For these and other reasons, there may be diseconomies in internalising transactions through vertical integration.

Thus, the general presumption of the contractual viewpoint is that vertical integration will take place where it is mutually beneficial and not occur where use of the market would be cheaper. What is not clear is whether vertical integration is always in society's best interest. Certain aspects of this question receive attention in the next section.

3. Vertical integration: some important considerations

Just as in the case of a horizontal merger, there might be circumstances in vertical integration where the gains to the firms involved are more than outweighed by losses to consumers. Five areas where this problem potentially arises are discussed below. They are: where the proportions in which the input from the A industry is used in the B industry may be varied, where there are substantial upstream scale economies, where uncertainties or random factors are present and where entry barriers may be created, or price discrimination facilitated.

Variable proportions

Suppose a monopolist at level A sells her product to a perfectly competitive industry at level B, but that there are many possible ways of combining this input with others to produce the final product. The higher the monopolist prices factor A, the less it will be used and so the more intensive in other factors will production be. There are then two connected consequences of her integration with all or part of industry B – for the most part we will simply take the case where A considers taking over the whole of industry B.

The first consequence has been analysed diagrammatically by Vernon and Graham (1971), but a verbal argument is equally compelling.[9] Prior to integration, input A will have been priced some way above marginal cost. After integration, the integrated firm will value it at only marginal cost. Thus, *assuming the same level of final output is produced before and after integration*, more of the input A will be used in production since its cost has fallen. With the simplifying assumption that there are only two factors, available at constant supply prices, this can be represented simply as a move around a production isoquant until a new point of tangency between the new isocost line and the isoquant is achieved. Now, using the old factor proportions at the new relative prices (their relative marginal costs) will involve higher total costs of production than using the new factor proportions at the new relative prices. There is thus a welfare gain on integration. To put it another way, the firms in the competitive industry would previously have been better off if they had been able to persuade (sign a contract with) the monopolist to accept a lump sum from them equivalent to her monopoly profit, in exchange for her charging them marginal cost for input A.

There is thus an incentive for a monopolist to indulge in vertical integration and so far, it would seem, a welfare gain involved. But after integration the monopolist has extended the monopoly power previously contained by the substitution possibilities. She may therefore be able to increase price of the final product to take advantage of this, meanwhile cutting back on output.[10] This gives rise to the possibility of a welfare loss, to be balanced against the gain previously under discussion.

Schmalensee (1973) has examined mathematically a fairly general case along these lines.[11] He assumes a downward sloping demand function, constant factor prices (in the case of factor A, a constant marginal, and so average, cost of production), and a constant returns to scale production function. He allows the monopolist to integrate only partially into the competitive industry, rather than constraining it to make an all-or-nothing decision, but in intermediate cases the monopolist is forced (by assumption) to sell the final product at the same price as the remainder of industry B. He finds, as we would expect given our earlier verbal discussion, that the monopolist always has an incentive for further forward integration, whether or not she previously owned some of the final product industry. (Alternatively, any one of the final product firms has an incentive to integrate backward and monopolise the industry.) Also, average (and marginal) cost decreases as vertical integration increases, being lowest when the monopolist sells directly. The most important effect, that of vertical integration on the price of input A (and so on the price of the final product B) appears impossible to sign. As a consequence, the overall welfare effect cannot be determined if the product price increases.

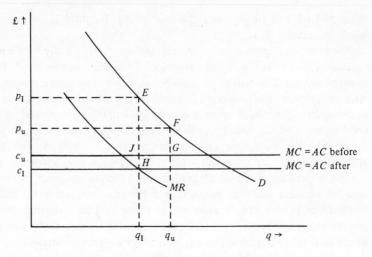

Figure 5.3

In certain particular cases, the relevant magnitudes can be calculated. Schmalensee, Warren-Boulton (1974) and Hay (1973) all show analytically that with constant elasticity of final demand and a Cobb–Douglas production function, vertical integration by the monopolist increases price. Thus the situation is as represented in figure 5.3, drawn for the final product market, before and after complete vertical integration. Profit from the monopolist prior to vertical integration is given by the area $p_u FGc_u$, being the difference between final product price (p_u) and costs (c_u) of producing this output – valuing these at marginal costs using the old factor proportions – multiplied by the output q_u.[12] Profit after vertical integration is the larger area $p_I EHc_I$, the difference between final price after integration and costs c_I (lower than c_u since more optimal proportions are used, as explained earlier). The consequent net change in welfare is the area $EFGJ$, which is lost, minus the rectangle $c_u c_I HJ$, which is gained, and is negative in this particular case.

Additional analytical results in this area appear very difficult to obtain, though a promising approach has recently been made by Westfield (1981). In order to gain some insights into the problem consider the elasticity of derived demand for A, which may be written (see e.g. Allen, 1938, pp. 372–3).

$$E_A = k_A \eta + (1 - k_A)\sigma \qquad (5.10)$$

where η, σ and k_A are final demand elasticity, elasticity of substitution in production and the share of A in factor payments respectively. The difficulty is that in general η, σ and k_A are all determined endogenously along with the price of A. The earlier Cobb–Douglas case with constant elasticity of demand in addition has k_A fixed so E_A may be calculated explicitly from (5.10). Even with constant elasticity of substitution, k_A is endogenous; this is the case analysed by Warren-Boulton (1974), who has recourse to simulation techniques to obtain results. He finds that product price usually rises on integration.

Warren-Boulton's analysis has been extended by Waterson (1982b) to the situation of a group of oligopolistic downstream firms. Notice that in the Greenhut–Ohta (1976) type of models discussed in section 2, vertical integration does not increase the integrator's monopoly power, but does eliminate the intermediate distortion caused by cumulative markups. In models like Warren-Boulton's and Westfield's, monopoly power is increased since substitution possibilities are removed and there are no cumulative markups to be eliminated. In the former case, price falls to a degree dependent on downstream monopoly power while in the latter it commonly rises, particularly if substitution possibilities are extensive. In oligopoly, one would expect both these effects, which suggests a trade-off between downstream monopoly power (as measured, for example, by the number of downstream firms) and elasticity of substitution, regarding the effect of price on vertical integration. The existence of this trade-off, together with a similar one on welfare outcomes, is demonstrated by Waterson.

Recently also, Dixit (1983) has looked at vertical integration in the context of a monopolistically competitive industry (using a product differentiation framework to be discussed in the following chapter). Within his model, vertical integration is far more benign than would be suggested by analogy with perfect competition. It removes the problem of cumulative markups and also improves the provision of product variety.

Upstream scale economies

It is quite often the case that upstream activities are subject to substantial scale economies. (Downstream activities may be also, but unless there are also upstream scale economies, they may be analysed as an oligopoly problem.) For example, both the glass and the gearboxes which go into a motor car probably come from processes involving substantial scale economies, but while engines are commonly produced by the car assemblers, glass usually is not.

Here it is likely that a counterbalance of forces is involved. Because the demand offered by any one downstream firm may fail to exhaust all available scale economies, it would be efficient for there to be a separate upstream stage producing the input. In extreme cases (say, to take a simple example, when the upstream cost function for input A is $c(A) = c_o A + F$) efficiency may involve monopoly production of the immediate product. However, this market organisation requires input price above marginal cost (in order to cover the fixed costs) and may allow quite a substantial monopoly profit to be earned. This would encourage the downstream users to economise on the input in question if substitution is possible. Alternatively, downstream firms could sacrifice scale economies by producing the input themselves, but at the same time gain the benefit of being able to value (shadow-price) additional units of the input at marginal cost.[13] They simultaneously make it difficult for the upstream firm(s) who remain unintegrated as their market thins out.

Within this simple framework, if we assume the absence of income effects and that output of the other firms remains unchanged[14] then benefits may be evaluated as the appropriate amount of consumer surplus accruing to the downstream producer. Taking the cost function for input (A) production used in the example above:

$$C(A) = c_o A + F$$

and derived demand for the input $D(p_A)$, p_A being the price charged, then the firms will integrate if the benefits of doing so in the form of a lower price outweigh the costs of in-house production, that is if:

$$\int_{c_o}^{p_u} D(p_A) \cdot dp_A - F > 0$$

where p_u is the price charged for the input prior to integration.

It is clear that the sign of this expression will depend on the parameters of the model, but that in general some integration will take place. Notice however that from society's point of view, the optimal solution is for monopoly production of the input at marginal cost together, presumably, with some means of paying for the lump sum element; that is for a two-part tariff involving a fixed and a variable component. Thus, whatever integration has taken place is socially non-optimal.

Porter and Spence (1977) develop a more complex model along these lines where the upstream product is a standardised one and downstream producers have the choice between using that and a specialised input they develop for their own use. Consequently, their model has some interesting parallels with models of optimal product differentiation discussed in chapter 6 below. The upshot is that some integration is socially desirable. However, it still transpires that more integration takes place than is optimal. As we have said before, socially desirable results potentially are achievable here, by means of contracts which permit flexibility in input design yet gain the advantages of scale economies (and, hopefully, avoid the temptation of downstream collusion). One *possible* example is the cooperative engine design and production some European car manufacturers participate in.

In the case where both upstream and downstream scale economies exist up to very high output levels, it is quite likely that vertical integration will occur for contractual reasons, because such a situation of bilateral monopoly is likely to lead to excessive haggling, as we see in the final section.

Uncertainty

In a typical model involving two successive markets like that illustrated in figure 5.1, randomness or uncertainty may be introduced at one or more stages in the production process. For example, there may be a given industry demand schedule, but uncertainty about the allocation of demand between downstream firms. There may be uncertainty about the way downstream firms allocate demand between upstream producers. Or there may be uncertainty about the total supply of the upstream product, say because it is a product like oil for which supply depends on the vagaries of success in exploration.

However, uncertainty only becomes relevant to the analysis of vertical integration decisions when time (or price rigidity) is important. If, when demands are known, downstream producers can have recourse to factor markets and these factor suppliers can produce such inputs as are called forth all within the payment period, then markets cannot be bettered (privately or socially). But, if some irreversible decisions have to be made before the true state of the world is revealed, this can be costly to the firms involved.

Vertical integration may be able to reduce these costs by improving information over the set of states of the world (less variance), or by in effect allowing time to be bought. For example, an integrated firm may know more about the likely production of inputs, or demand for them, earlier than an unintegrated firm. Various authors have introduced time and uncertainty at different stages of the process represented in figure 5.1 and so developed different models of the same underlying problem. Let us consider some of these, adopting their assumptions of constant returns to scale at both upstream and downstream stages and so allowing potentially large numbers of firms at both levels.

One very relevant consideration is whether an integrated firm may nevertheless enter the intermediate market as buyer and seller as necessary. If this is the case, the integrated firm is subject to no more rigidities than the unintegrated but can gain some advantages through reduced uncertainty. Therefore in equilibrium all firms are likely to be integrated. Such a model is constructed by Arrow (1975), who introduces uncertainty at the upstream production stage. An integrating firm gains a time advantage in the form of some knowledge about the likely production level of the input, so integration proves advantageous to the firm. As far as society is concerned, the more upstream firms that are banded together, the less uncertainty there is, and consequently the less likely are precommitments which turn out with hindsight to be wrong.

Hence it would *seem* to be socially optimal for complete horizontal and vertical merger to take place, resulting in one giant firm. However this is obviously absurd, since it is conditional upon monopolistic pricing problems not being encountered. Such results, which are not unique to Arrow's model, arise because of the rather simple framework into which uncertainty is introduced.

Vertical integration is more commonly modelled as a situation in which the integrated firm does not indulge in sales on the intermediate goods market (though it may purchase there). While this is probably a relevant feature of reality to incorporate, it is nevertheless difficult to explain why the firm constrains itself in this way; possibly the answer is to be found in contractual difficulties. For whatever reason it arises, introducing this rigidity means the case for vertical integration is no longer clear-cut.[15] The firm now has to counterbalance two forces: the inflexibility of vertical integration against possibly lower costs.

To see this, let us suppose, with Bernhardt (1977) and Carlton (1979), that uncertainty arises through random sourcing policies of downstream producers (and, though it is not particularly important, randomness in final demands), and that prices in the factor markets are set prior to derived demands being known so that these markets do not clear. Because there is a risk, in every period, for every upstream firm of being left with unsold stock then the trading price must be greater than production costs. Hence the incentive to integrate is provided by the chance of obtaining the input at cost or, to look at it from the supplier's side, the reduction in the variability of demand for the input. The disincentive comes from the chance of being left with unwanted inputs (which are assumed to be wasted) or, in the supplier's eyes, an increase in variability arising from demand being tied to the particular downstream firm's product. Without going into details, it seems intuitively sensible that there will be private incentives for at least some vertical integration to take place as there is still some possibility of outside sourcing in periods of high demand.

Upon integration, risk is transferred downstream. Now, Carlton assumes there are more downstream than upstream firms in the integrated world. Hence, integration is socially undesirable since the downstream firms, being greater in number, cannot absorb risk as efficiently as the upstream.[16] Consequently we see again that privately profitable vertical integration is not necessarily socially desirable.

Entry barriers and price discrimination

Two further possible anticompetitive impacts of vertical integration discussed in the literature are entry barriers and price discrimination; the former goes back to Marshall (1920, pp. 409–10). In both cases, the claim that there are anticompetitive consequences has been disputed.

It is fairly clear that if entry at one level alone is feasible, then the fact that *some* firms are integrated is not of itself important, and does not constitute a barrier to entry. However if, for whatever reason, all firms currently in an industry are integrated then entry can normally only be contemplated at both stages. The durability of the combined monopoly power becomes the durability of the stronger stage. Moreover, more capital would be required to enter than at one stage alone. Therefore the argument regarding vertical integration as a barrier *of itself* turns on whether large capital requirements constitute a barrier to entry. Williamson's view (1971, 1979) is that they may;

Bork's position (as quoted in Williamson) is that they do not. Now, if, as is normally thought, the capital market requires that larger projects should attract differentially higher interest rates because the risks are greater, then larger capital requirements could be a barrier to entry.

To reformulate the arguments in terms of concepts used in the previous chapter, vertical integration by established firms which necessitates entry at both stages means the market is less likely to be *contestable*. It is less likely that a potential entrant will have access to the same know-how at *both* stages of production as the established firm has. It is also less plausible that customers will respond quickly to a potential entrant's price signal, because fulfilment of the contract is likely to take longer. There are also more likely to be sunk costs. For any of these reasons, the potential entrant may be on less than fair terms with the established firm, so entry barriers will be raised by vertical integration. There is also the point that, whereas threats to cut price do not scare an intending entrant from upstream, this mode of entry is removed when the upstream belongs to the same firm.

As far as price discrimination is concerned, there is general agreement that this may be facilitated by vertical integration (see Williamson, 1979). The argument is as follows: The ability to discriminate hinges on being able to identify groups of customers having different demand elasticities, then being able to prevent those charged a low price from reselling to people willing to pay higher prices. With some goods, resales can be prevented automatically (e.g. telephone call rates for different times of day), with others it is less easily arranged. Nevertheless, vertical integration can undoubtedly help to prevent leakage between markets if the monopoly (or collusively oligopolistic) upstream firm integrates into one or more of the downstream markets, while still possibly allowing sales of the upstream product to unintegrated firms for specific uses. What is not clear is whether this is anticompetitive. The usual argument is that price discrimination, by increasing total output, *improves* societal welfare but, as we pointed out in chapter 1, this is not necessarily the case.

4. Bilateral monopoly

Thus far outcomes have, on the whole, been straightforward to analyse and predict, at least with the simple assumptions we have been making. Matters become more complex when monopsony power enters the picture; in fact it is often said that the case of bilateral monopoly is 'indeterminate'. Monopsony power properly arises only when supply curves are upward sloping (though see our caveat in note 4, p. 216). In our analysis we start with a simple example; this time of a monopolist in the sale of A's product and a monopsonist in its purchase at stage B. The latter may have to compete with a large number of others in selling her product, or she may be a monopolist in addition, for which case the name monemporist has been coined. We

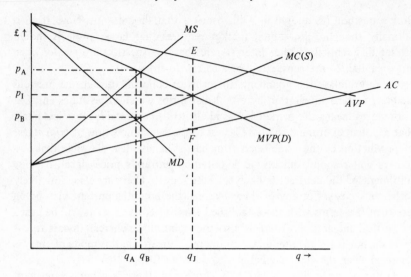

Figure 5.4

start by assuming she has no selling power. Her demand for the produce of A
is then given by the (net) marginal value product of the factor, a curve we
label $MVP(D)$ in figure 5.4. The monopolist A has in turn a rising marginal
cost of producing A. If (artificially) we assume she is unable to exercise her
market power, then this would appear to the monopsonist to be a supply
curve; we label it $MC(S)$.

In figure 5.4, if A were able to exercise her market power in selling,
and B were unable to exercise her monopsony power, A would realise the
demand curve is downward sloping and would wish to set the curve 'marginal'
to it (MD) equal to marginal cost $MC(S)$. Thus she would set output q_A
and price p_A.

Conversely, if B could exercise monopsony power, A being unable to
utilise her monopoly power, B would wish to set the curve 'marginal' to
$MC(S)$, that is MS, equal to $MVP(D)$, purchasing q_B at a price p_B.[17] Thus A
and B agree neither upon the most desirable price nor, except by accident,
on the quantity to be traded.

On the other hand, if A and B were to agree jointly to maximise profits,
then they would set marginal cost equal to (net) marginal value product
to determine output q_J. But then price is NOT determined as p_I. Rather,
it is the subject of bargaining where the upper limit of exchange price is
average (net) value product, B making no profit, and the lower limit average
cost, where A is on the margin of indifference as to whether to trade;
price is indeterminate within the range EF in theoretical terms unless we
are willing to make additional assumptions. This range exists in the joint
profit maximising successive monopoly model of section 1 also. Some

suggestions on possible additional assumptions to solve the indeterminacy problem come shortly.

We can easily alter the diagram to cater for the case where B is a monemporist rather than merely a monopsonist. All this involves is redefining the curve D to be (net) marginal *revenue* product, with an appropriate associated adjustment to MD (which then becomes equivalent to MD in figure 5.2). The analysis proceeds unchanged. Secondly, it might appear (particularly given the labels S and D) that output under joint profit maximisation is identical to the output traded were sectors A and B to have no market power at all. However this would be *untrue* in the long run since supernormal profits (rents) are being carried by one or both parties when the traded quantity is q_J. Thus if entry (at both stages) were completely free, it would ensue until output increased to a point where marginal cost again equals (net) marginal product, but in addition average cost equals average net value product, and zero economic profits were earned; the normal long run competitive case.[18]

Approaches to solutions of the indeterminacy problem

Many other authors have been eager to solve the previously noted indeterminacy problem by splitting the proceeds of bilateral monopoly power between the participants. Several had as their prime concern the union–management bargaining process. Because of this they tend to be mainly concerned about institutional factors. While we shall touch obliquely upon such studies, our main concern will be the more analytical studies with somewhat wider relevance. Most of the work in this (narrower) field has been concerned with solving the indeterminacy under joint-profit maximisation bilateral monopoly, often using game-theoretic concepts.

In the language of the theory of games, bilateral monopoly is normally considered to be a two-person cooperative non-zero sum game, with fixed threat bargaining. It is non-zero sum because there are gains from trade and is fixed threat since the most obvious and compelling threat is to refuse trade. As von Neumann and Morgernstern (1953) analyse the game, there is a solution given by the contract curve, or the line EF in figure 5.4. This is of course not a unique solution since any point on the contract curve will do as well as any other, so that we have come no further than orthodox theory will take us. However, many other game theorists are willing to add extra assumptions in order to prescribe a unique outcome. This is the *value* approach, mentioned in chapter 3.

The most famous of solutions is undoubtedly that of Nash (1950). At the joint profit maximising output we may define an objective-payoff frontier in profit space; a straight line of unit downward slope defines each player's profit. From this we map into utility space to derive the utility frontier using the player's utility of profit functions. Discussion then proceeds on the basis of choosing a point on this utility frontier (drawn for a special case

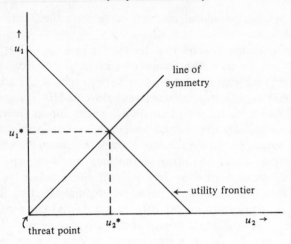

Figure 5.5

in Figure 5.5), which is scaled to set the threat point at the origin for both players. Besides assuming efficiency, Nash uses three other assumptions to provide a solution, now known as the symmetry, transformation invariance and independence of irrelevant alternatives axioms. The first asserts that if the utility frontier is symmetrical with respect to the players' utilities u_1 and u_2, so that we can change the axes without altering the functional form, then the solution gives equal utility (measured from the threat point) to both players. Transformation invariance allows for order-preserving linear transformations of utility to occur without altering the solution. If the utility frontier is now unfavourably altered at any but the above given solution point, this does not alter the outcome by the final axiom. These axioms are sufficient to establish the Nash solution $(u_1{}^*, u_2{}^*)$, which involves maximising the *product* of the two players' utilities, measured from the threat point.

Now if we are willing to restrict ourselves to utility functions which are linear in profit for both parties, we may dispense with the final axiom, since the utility frontier is always a straight line as drawn in figure 5.5. In fact, in the present context, it makes sense to think of utility as transferable between the two players and so effectively a pseudonym for profits, since if the firms are pure profit maximisers, each additional unit of profit, from whatever source, is equally worthwhile.[19] In this case, the first two axioms are sufficient to establish the solution: namely that an equal share of profits is received by each player.

There have been other axiomatic approaches in this area. Examples are provided by Raiffa (1957), Shapley (1953), Zeuthen (1930, ch. IV) and Harsanyi (1963). The last of these degenerates to Shapley's value *and* to Nash in the simple situation here, as do Zeuthen and most of Raiffa's solutions.

Foldes (1964) has a rather different approach. His model has as its analytical basis a Hicksian-type theory of bargaining where determinacy is obtained by taking into account time preferences, or threats of delay before trade can take place. Such threats can be used to extract concessions. Thus, his bargainers have utility functions, with arguments of profit share obtained and time before agreement is reached. However if the time preferences (discount rates) of the two actors involved do not differ systematically (and there seems no particular reason why they should unless there is a possibility of entry) then his model leads to a result identical to the half-way rule obtained from the simple Nash case considered earlier.

Spindler (1974) also reaches the conclusion that joint profit maximisation with each firm taking half the profit available is the most reasonable outcome. His argument is that the bargaining power of each firm can be directly measured by the degree of economic dependence on the other firm, which dependence is linearly related to the amount of profit to be received, since each extra unit of profit has the same value. Both firms are in a position to offer a share of the same total profit area initially, thus both start with equal bargaining power. Whenever one or the other firm has a greater relative bargaining power, it is less dependent on the other firm and so should be able to extract concessions. The natural outcome of such a process is that bargaining power and economic dependence are equalised when both firms receive a half share of the profits available.[20]

We could of course offer criticisms of the assumptions underlying the above models; Bishop (1963) has an extensive critique along these lines. It is probably more useful though, to accept that, despite the widely differing starting points of the theories of determinacy, the conclusion that two monopoly firms facing one another should share equally the profits accruing by joint maximisation would find widespread approval. This solution appears eminently reasonable unless we accept that there are systematic factors which would tend to make either one or the other party predominant in any bargain.

Having said this, we should note that such a solution could be considered as either normative or positive. Thus, while the axiomatic approach implies some positive theoretic value in the solution, Raiffa for example believes that his solutions are normative in the sense that they are alternatives which a 'fair arbitrator' might suggest. To the extent that such a fair arbitrator seems to occupy a similar post to that of the Walrasian auctioneer, we may well, even then, consider that the solution outlined has positive content.

Possible extensions to the 'half-shares' solution

Any extensions to the conclusion of the previous subsection that, in the absence of any additional information, two opposing monopoly bargainers shall share profits equally, must if anything, be more *ad hoc* than that argument. For once we move to considering the effects of having more than one firm on either 'side' of the bargain we have to solve what is effectively an oligopoly problem. Also, the various authors mentioned so far have not considered these extensions to any great extent.

With this caveat in mind, we can nevertheless suggest possible solutions in more complex cases. For example, if there are an equal number of parties on both sides of the bargain, shares might again be equal. Further, it seems sensible that, when numbers are unequal, the industry with more (equally sized) firms would have a smaller share. In addition though, firm size inequalities on both sides of the bargain should be brought into account. Thus one *possible* formula for determining the profit share of the B sector would be for it to obtain the proportion $n_A/(n_A + n_B)$ of the total profit, where n_A is a measure of the 'numbers equivalent' in industry A, and likewise for B. (See chapter 9 for discussion of 'numbers equivalent'.)

An important point is that, if there is more than one firm selling the final product, a monopoly price may well not be enforceable on the final consumers. Thus, if concentration increases (numbers equivalent fall) in the final product (B) sector it is quite likely that a final price nearer the monopoly price will result, so increasing the total price-cost margin available. The share of this margin going to the B industry will also increase, given our formula, and so the *share* of the margin for A decreases. However, depending upon the extent of the increase in the total margin relative to the increase in the margin going to those in B, the *margin* for the firms in A may either increase or decrease consequent upon B's increase in concentration. In other words, there are two opposing effects on A's margin instituted by a change in B's structure and we cannot immediately predict the net outcome.[21]

Mutually related market power provides a further complication. In the situation where B is supplied by two monopolists providing products which are perfect complements in the production of B's product (say labour and capital used in fixed proportions, for example) any of the three parties can threaten to halt the operations of the other, assuming no other sources of factors or outlets. Thus the only effective coalition involves all three parties and under the Nashian scheme the product of their utilities becomes the effective maximand. By symmetry the solution involves each player obtaining a third of the profit maximising surplus even if, for example, one input is a relatively unimportant part of the product. Incidentally in extending the model in this manner, we run into one of Bishop's criticisms. He notes (p. 579) that if a previous monopoly union were to split itself into n constituent skill unions then the Nashian arbitrator would award each party $1/(n + 1)$ of the total profit, whereas previously Labour as a whole obtained only one half of this surplus. The most obvious, though not fully satisfactory, answer to this point is to say that if indeed each of the separate skills is indispensable then the monopoly union obtaining initially was not an optimal structure for that particular industry.

At the other end of the spectrum, if the two factors are perfect substitutes then of course the bargaining power of the input sellers is only that of duopoly. Thus with variable proportions in production, some solution between these polar extremes should be achieved, though it must be admitted that the limits are potentially extremely wide. Finally, sellers of factors normally supply several sectors of industry with intermediate products, rather than just supplying sector B. Hence these various sales should be weighted in determining the margin for a particular industry. Possibly, weighting by (some function of) proportions sold to the various sectors is relevant, and empirical treatments (considered in chapter 10) commonly adopt this approach.

Countervailing power

Situations of bilateral oligopoly were claimed by Galbraith, in his book *American Capitalism* (1952), to be not only widespread but also to have important welfare properties:

'To begin with a broad and somewhat too dogmatically stated position, private economic power is held in check by the countervailing power of those who are subject to it . . . The long trend towards concentration of industrial enterprise into the hands of relatively few firms has brought into existence not only strong sellers . . . but also strong buyers . . . The two develop together . . . the one is in response to the other' (p. 118). Others, for example Stigler (1954) and Miller (1954), have been more sceptical.

Essentially, there are two strands to the argument, one of which is primarily an empirical question: Do strong sellers tend to be faced by strong buyers? Galbraith claimed they were, not only in labour markets (unions developing as a response to powerful management) but also in final goods markets (powerful retailers extracting concessions from manufacturers of consumer goods) and to some extent in intermediate goods markets. Stigler claimed there were many exceptions and that those cases which did fit Galbraith's view were not necessarily spontaneous developments.[22] Notice incidentally, that Galbraith's scheme is not necessarily meant to apply to European countries, though one might ask why not.

In any event, given that there are some situations where strong buyers and sellers face each other, we should enquire into the second aspect: the consequences. Does the restraining influence of strong buyers on strong sellers benefit the community? Galbraith claims countervailing power stands up well in a test of consumer welfare maximisation (though it is not clear this is always what he has in mind as something to be maximised; he is also interested in absence of social tension). For example, he places the outcome (pricing) of the advent of large chain food stores in the U.S., arguably arising from countervailing power, on a par with the outcome of the British Co-operative movement. However, he also looks favourably on the per-formance of labour unions and agricultural selling groups, gaining benefits for themselves. In short, it is not clear whether countervailing power is presumed to eliminate, to oppose, or merely to redistribute margins between prices and costs.

Now, in some cases margins may be eliminated and everyone made better off. We have for example the situation in section 1 where joint determination of profits means myopic markups are eliminated. One of Galbraith's examples (the building industry) appears to fit this pattern. Generalising from earlier work concerned with successive market power or bilateral power, we can say that if greater countervailing power encourages bargaining to mutual advantage rather than myopic margin-setting, then societal welfare can be improved, though not increased to a maximum. One difficulty with this interpretation is that vertical integration would encourage such bargaining in our view, whereas Galbraith believes forward vertical integration can actually circumvent countervailing power.

More critically, though, it is only likely that margins will be eliminated, and a quasi-competitive situation develop, if entry into the final (retailing) stage is easy[23] or 'contestable'. To this extent, Galbraith's view is no different from standard positions, as he admits (1954, p. 4). If powerful retailers are able to force price bargaining onto manufacturers, but are themselves constrained by competition, countervailing power is indeed efficacious in maximising social welfare. But why are manufacturers willing to concede cost-based prices to powerful retailers? It must surely be only if entry into manufacturing is also easy, so that Galbraith's suggested sanction (p. 126) of retailers developing their own supply sources would not be much of a threat. Hence it would seem that the strongest version of Galbraith's view — that margins are eliminated, depends upon entry barriers into manufacturing being low. In a sense, it is an early version of the 'perfectly contestable' argument put in chapter 4.

Notes on the literature

One of the best discussions and sources of references on the general area covered in this chapter, particularly the earlier sections, is Machlup and Taber (1960). On the material of vertical pricing relationships, Hicks (1935) and Morgan (1949) are also good; the latter is particularly careful to set out the relevant assumptions in his treatment of bilateral monopoly. A thorough investigation of several models is provided by Zeuthen (1930), though his analytics may prove difficult for students versed in more modern techniques. Kaserman (1978) provides an extensive review of all but the most recent work on vertical integration, while Warren-Boulton's (1978) chapter 6 extends his contribution into the area of union-management processes. A lively discussion of cooperative games in general may be found in Bacharach (1976), and Bishop (1963) provides an extensive analysis and critique, accessible to the general reader, of game theoretic solutions to the 'indeterminacy problem'. Lastly, Reisman (1980, chapter 4) provides a review of Galbraith's thesis.

6

Models of product differentiation

Apart from some general comments in chapters 2 and 4, we have largely been proceeding on the assumption that the firms in an industry produce substantially the same product. This, however, is patently not the case for most industries and in this chapter we discuss theoretical approaches to the problem of industries in which the firms' products are differentiated from one another.

We start in section 1 with the simplest possible case of product differentiation: what has been called vertical product differentiation, where products differ only in the amount of quality embedded in them. We provide some insights into the debate on the effects of market structure on a product's quality. In section 2 we move to horizontal product differentiation and explain Lancaster's 'goods-characteristics' approach to the demand for differentiated products in which goods are conceived of as packages of characteristics. Section 3 reviews and extends Hotelling's spatial competition model and explains its relevance to the question of product differentiation. Using these two models, particularly the latter, we are able in section 4 to derive some important predictions regarding the effects of product differentiation *per se* on profits, barriers to entry and brand proliferation. Section 5 extends and then offers a comparison between the Lancaster and spatial competition models and Chamberlin's model. Section 6 covers some important welfare results arising from the introduction of product differentiation.

1. Product quality

The simplest possible way in which products may be differentiated from one another is by their having more or less of a given characteristic. To take a particular case, goods might differ solely in durability, for example the length of time a lightbulb[1] or razor lasts. One obviously important question, and that which will be our concern in the present section, is whether monopolists might supply less durable goods than similar competitive industries. We might then hope to see what is likely to be the outcome in intermediate (oligopolistic) market structures.

The debate in this area has normally compared the two industry structures by means of one of the following simple devices enabling the monopolist's marginal cost curve to be synonymous with the competitive industry's supply curve (implicitly assuming competition to be optimal): either by equating the case of competition with a situation in which the monopolist acts so as to maximise social benefit (setting price equal to marginal cost), or by assuming the monopoly to be a cartel of a large number of firms, which act independently in the case of competition.

To gain the essence of the debate, let us consider a model due to Kihlstrom and Levhari (1977). They make three basic assumptions. The first is that there is a 'linear service technology'. In this, the quantity of services (z) is related to the quantity of goods (q) by the formula:

$$z = s \cdot q, \tag{6.1}$$

s being the amount of service provided by a unit of the commodity. In terms of our first example, z is the amount of light hours and q the number of light-bulbs. People naturally demand lightbulbs (or whatever) not for intrinsic reasons but rather for the service they provide. Thus we may suppose the demand curve for services, z, to be $r(z)$, where r is the per unit price of the service, so the per unit price of goods of quality s is $p = r \cdot s$. The demand curve for goods of quality s may then be written as:

$$p(s, q) = r(s \cdot q) \cdot s \tag{6.2}$$

Assumptions also have to be made on the cost side. One of the most straightforward is that the cost function according to which *goods* are produced is separable and of the form:

$$c(s, q) = \gamma(s) \cdot q^\beta, \qquad \beta \geqslant 1 \tag{6.3}$$

Since we wish to talk about the market for services, it is natural to think of the firm producing these via the production of goods of various qualities. It is useful to redefine a cost curve for *services* as the minimum cost way of producing any given quantity of services, z, from the inputs quality and quantity of goods. Once this is done, the marginal cost of producing services can be equated in (r, z) space with the marginal revenue curve associated with the demand for services, to yield the monopoly service output level and, by reading up to the demand curve, the monopoly price. Similarly, given our initial assumptions, we can take the marginal cost curve as a supply curve under 'competitition' so that supply may be equated with demand. As is normal in analyses of this type, the monopoly output is smaller, and price higher, than under competition. We omit a diagram since this part of the analysis is so standard.

The important question is: will the quality embodied in the services supplied by the monopolist be lower than in those supplied by the 'competitive' industry, or does the monopolist supply equivalent quality goods, albeit not as many of them. To answer this, notice that the cost curve for services is obtained by minimising (6.3) subject to (6.1). The Lagrangean function is:

$$L(s, q, \lambda) = \gamma(s) \cdot q^{\beta} - \lambda(sq - z)$$

First-order conditions for minimisation with respect to s and y are:

$$\frac{\partial L}{\partial q} = \beta \cdot \gamma(s) \cdot q^{\beta - 1} - \lambda s = 0$$

$$\frac{\partial L}{\partial s} = \gamma'(s) \cdot q^{\beta} - \lambda q = 0$$

From these we obtain by rearrangement and division:

$$\frac{\gamma'(s) \cdot s}{\gamma(s)} = \beta$$

This gives us a value for s, say s^*, which is independent of q and z. Thus, the conditions for cost minimisation (assuming the second order conditions are satisfied[2]) state that the level of quality per unit is independent of market structure, so the lightbulbs last the same time under monopoly and competition.

However, the result arises strictly because of the particular form taken by the cost function in (6.3). A more general separable (or a non-separable) cost function would not have the property that the amount of quality in each unit is independent of the number of units produced. Nevertheless, Saving (1982) points out that additional restrictions may be imposed upon the cost function by introducing the requirement that the industry is a 'constant cost' one (see, e.g. Koutsoyiannis, 1979, p. 165). These, together with (6.1), will guarantee the quality invariance result.

More generally, Kihlstrom and Levhari show that, as long as there is a 'linear service technology' (i.e. (6.1) holds) then, regardless of cost conditions, competition is efficient in the normal welfare sense. Hence, monopolists will produce a lower than optimal supply of services in total at too high a price, (in the same way that they normally supply too few goods) whether the services are packaged in goods of equal or unequal quality. Intuitively, if the good is divisible (any quantity can be bought) then it is as if the service is being bought directly rather than the good, and we can expect normal results to hold.

So far, we have been discussing a case where there is a constant demand for services. But changing quality can have more complex effects. Quality might be a form of durability which raises the demand function but in turn affects future stocks consumers hold. As an example, improving the life of fluorescent light tubes from five times the life of incandescent bulbs to ten times might raise demand now but reduce replacement demand. A more complex case, discussed by Levhari and Peles (1973), is colour versus black and white television. Here, quality is not a direct substitute for quantity. In both cases, results depend crucially upon the cost assumption utilised.

The general theoretical difficulty is in finding a complete set of necessary conditions for the invariant quality result. Thus in general monopolists may produce goods more, less or equally durable compared with those of competitive industries; having already indicated the basic ideas involved, we do not intend to discuss the variants in detail.[3] Instead we move on to consider the more general case where there is no established rank order: horizontal product differentiation.

2. The demand for characteristics

In the previous section, we supposed consumers to demand the services or characteristics of a good rather than the good itself, as in (6.1). More generally, Lancaster (1966, 1971, 1975, and 1979) has suggested that a consumer's preference ordering is defined on bundles of characteristics rather than bundles of goods. In matrix formulation we might define the relationship as:

$$z = Bq \tag{6.4}$$

where z is now an $m \times 1$ vector of characteristics, q an $n \times 1$ vector of goods and B an $m \times n$ matrix of constant coefficients relating the two. In order for this to simplify analysis, we presume that $n > m$. If we could now assert that the matrix B were block-diagonal, that is of the form:

$$B = \begin{bmatrix} \beta_1 & 0 & 0 & 0 \\ 0 & \beta_2 & 0 & 0 \\ 0 & 0 & \beta_3 & 0 \\ 0 & 0 & 0 & \beta_4 \end{bmatrix}$$

it would seem natural to define four (in our example) industries by the coefficients in β_1, β_2, β_3 and β_4 relating specific characteristics to specific products. For example if β_1 were a 2×5 submatrix, then the first five goods would involve various combinations of two characteristics which no other goods possess. This set of five goods is very like a Chamberlinian group.[4] In fact, a slight relaxation of block-diagonality is allowable while still retaining the group concept.

To illustrate the approach, assume the only two characteristics a (rather boring) consumer looks for in food are protein and vitamins (each assumed to be one-dimensional characteristics). Four goods, each produced by a different firm, can provide him with these in various proportions; particular cases may be meat, green vegetables, milk and brown rice, though we simply use names A, B, C and D. Each gives him a certain proportion of the two characteristics, as indicated by rays $0A$ to $0D$ in figure 6.1. A unit of resource (e.g. £1) will call forth an amount of good A represented by point a, giving the consumer an amount a_p of protein, a_v of vitamins; points b, c and

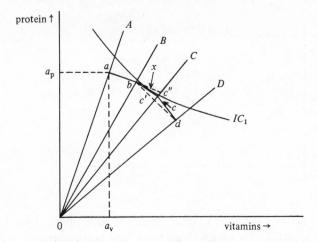

Figure 6.1

d are similarly constructed. This provides us with the bare bones of the technical side of Lancaster's model.

At this stage, the analysis can essentially follow one of two paths. In the first of these, the consumer need not spend all his money on any one good, but can combine goods in any proportions. Given this, he has the choice of buying anywhere on the locus a, b, c, d known as the *market opportunities frontier* or *representative efficiency frontier.*[5] The point he actually chooses is revealed by superimposing his indifference map defined on the two characteristics and finding the tangency point, here x, where he buys some B and some C. These two goods are known as *neighbours*, since they are in close competition with each other at the prevailing prices in a way A and C are not, for some combination of the latter will not rationally be chosen. In fact the consumer will never choose more than two goods in a two-characteristics situation.

Continuing to apply this apparatus, notice that a fall in the price of C (say) has the effect of moving point c away from the origin; it means more proteins and vitamins per £. Once we have made an assumption about other firms' prices, we can construct the demand curve facing C. Let us assume others' prices remain unchanged, a hypothesis equivalent to a Cournot-type assumption, but on prices (so leading to a Nash equilibrium), which is usually called zero conjectural variations (ZCV) in the present context. Now, as the price of C falls, the tangency point will move so that our representative consumer will buy more C at the expense of B. Beyond a price represented by point c'' no one will buy B since a combination of A and C is cheaper. Similarly as C's price rises, less of the good will be bought, until point c' is reached, after which all consumers will be better off buying a combination of B and D (now neighbours) along the dotted line $bc'd$. This suggests a general shape for the

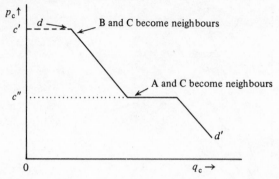

Figure 6.2

individual's demand for good *C*, under the ZCV assumption, along the lines of *dd'* in figure 6.2, downward sloping portions being interspersed by discontinuous jumps as the neighbour relationship changes. This is essentially Chamberlin's *dd'* curve for the individual consumer, because it gives the demand for one good under the assumption that others' prices (and specifications) remain unchanged.

It is not always possible for a consumer to combine two goods to obtain her optimal package in this way: a half pint of beer plus a half of cider mixed does not provide a linear combination of the characteristics provided by a pint of one or a pint of the other. The alternative route to the demand function (Lancaster 1975, 1979) is to start from a product differentiation curve (PDC) as exemplified in figure 6.3 by PDC_1 rather than a series of line segments. This is akin to a production possibility frontier, indicating all the

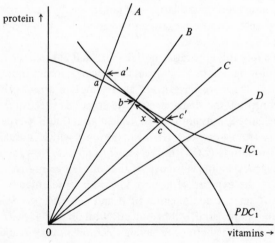

Figure 6.3

potential (and not just the actual) products combining the two characteristics under best practice production techniques. Like it (but unlike the first method), PDC_1 has a physical unit rather than money value connotation. More resources would call forth a PDC further from the origin. Normally not all the products represented on the PDC are available, only say, A, C and D. Our representative consumer has an indifference map exemplified by IC_1 and so would be keenest on a product with specification B. In order to feel as well off as when receiving an amount $0b$ of B, she would have to be given an amount $0c'$ of its nearest available neighbour C. A natural resource-based measure of the ratio of compensation for accepting that is $0c'/0c$ ($= h$, say). This *compensating ratio*, h, is a function of the arc distance, x, along the PDC between the available and preferred good. Thus the *compensating function* may be written:

$$h = h(c - b) = h(x) \tag{6.5}$$

The functional relationship depends, in general, on both the shape of the PDC and the consumer's indifference curve and may be expected to look something like the curve $h(x)$ drawn in figure 6.4 given the shape of PDC_1 and IC_1.

In this example with two characteristics, the consumer faces a choice between two possibilities a and c, neither of which is ideal given her taste structure. If their prices were equal, the one with the smaller compensating ratio would be purchased,[6] in this case C. However as the other (A) became cheaper, there would be a point at which its low price compensated sufficiently for its poorer specification (higher compensating ratio) and our consumer would switch her custom. Given a range of consumers with varying tastes, together with the assumption of zero conjectural variations, each good should face a smooth market demand curve over some range of prices, though the derivation of the exact shape is not as straightforward as in the previous approach.

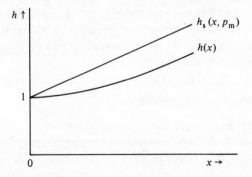

Figure 6.4

To recap briefly then, in Lancaster's second model only one of the goods in the range will be bought at the prevailing set of prices, and as prices vary, custom will abruptly switch from one to the other. In his first model, compensation takes place through goods, since the customer can buy linear combinations of them, and so the individual's demand for a particular good will vary smoothly with its price over a restricted range. In both models, the relationship between individual purchases and price over the range for which the good in question is the 'best buy' is not specified. Also, in order to have smooth demand curves over a wide range of prices, it is necessary to move to the market demand curve and to assume there are a number of consumers with a variety of tastes.

Actually, as Archibald and Rosenbluth (1975) pointed out, the ZCV assumption common to both models is rather peculiar in the Lancastrian context for, as we saw, although the group is large, each good has only two neighbours. With such a small number, it is unlikely for a firm to believe others will not react to her price changes. This will not matter particularly for our later purposes, as we use the assumption merely for expository reasons, but does throw into doubt Chamberlin's analysis of the 'large group'. One way out of these difficulties is to investigate whether, when more characteristics are of importance, the number of neighbours becomes larger. Archibald and Rosenbluth find that, with three relevant characteristics, some, though not all, goods can have a large number of neighbours. With four or more characteristics it is definitely *possible* for each firm to have a large number of effective competitors[7] and so for Chamberlin's dd' curve sensibly to be constructed.

Notice that in this type of model, consumers are essentially placing valuations on characteristics rather than goods. Each good can be regarded as a 'package' of characteristics. Thus the demand for a car is the demand for a vehicle exhibiting various characteristics, for example, speed, convenience, capacity, comfort and style. If competition prevails, the product market's behaviour will implicitly reveal the function relating the price of the final good to its various characteristics and so average implicit or 'hedonic' prices for the characteristics. This technique has been developed in several empirical studies of such goods, (e.g. Cowling and Cubbin, 1971), but is not strictly valid when there are fixed costs in production, since not all locations on the characteristics space will be filled by production units (see Rosen, 1963). We now move to an alternative technique.

3. The relevance of spatial competition

Though Lancaster's approach to product differentiation has proved useful, insights can be gained in other ways. Argument by analogy from spatial competition models following upon Hotelling's (1929) pioneering work has been a very fruitful source of such insights. The purpose of this section is simply to develop those analogies.

Hotelling, in his studies of the economic influence of space, assumed customers were located evenly over space, as if along a straight finite line. Each one of the large number of such customers was assumed in the formal model to buy one unit of the good from the supplier quoting her the lowest price, thus demand is proportional to the length of the market served. But instead of talking about distance, Hotelling says, we could consider the line to represent, say, sweetness/sourness of cider. At one end are those customers who most appreciate the sourest ciders, at the other those with an exceptionally sweet tooth; the firms also are producing at various points on the line. Thus with care, predictions about spatial effects can be extended to cover product differentiation.

Returning to the formal spatial model, two assumptions are necessary to treat spatial effects seriously. The first is that 'transport' is supplied at a non-trivial cost t per unit distance (x). Thus delivered price, p_d, is related to mill price, p_m as follows:

$$p_d = p_m + xt \qquad (6.6)$$

Secondly, there are scale economies or increasing returns in the supply of the product, at least initially. The simplest relation with this property, and the one we use, is:

$$C = F + cq \qquad (6.7)$$

where C is total cost made up of a fixed (F) and a variable component. If we did not assume increasing returns, firms would produce at the points where consumers are located and discussion of space effects would become vacuous. Given (6.7), the number of firms will be limited by the necessity to remain profitable. Customers buy from the firm with the lowest delivered price.

Firms now have to choose both price and location, and one question which immediately arises is whether firms choose location once and for all, or whether they are allowed to relocate. Hotelling assumed the latter, and thus in his duopoly model the firms ended up next to each other in the centre of the market. In a triopoly, there is no equilibrium since all three firms cluster, the middle one then has no sales and so will move, and so on.[8]

However, it seems plausible that relocation is a costly exercise, so that for practical purposes firms can be regarded as fixed. Eaton and Lipsey (1978) have explored the question of fixed location and, after making some simplifications, they find it to be appropriate when more than half a firm's fixed costs are 'location specific' and quite plausible if over a quarter of costs are sunk in this manner rather than in other capital. Schmalensee (1978) argues that repositioning costs may be substantial in a product development context.

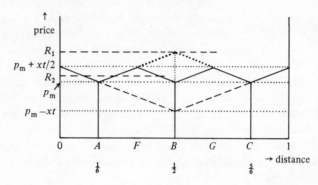

Figure 6.5

Now if location involves an irreversible decision, firms will locate in the realisation that those still to enter (assume their number is known) can take advantage of any gaps in the market. Therefore we may expect a symmetrical pattern in equilibrium, for much the same reason that someone cutting cake to share will attempt to make the slices equal if he is to be the last to choose one (see also Prescott and Visscher, 1977, for some mechanisms).

As far as pricing is concerned, we choose Hotelling's assumption of zero conjectural variations (ZCV). (Again though, since each firm has only two neighbours, the choice is not obvious.) We are now able to analyse the demand curve facing an individual firm.

Consider figure 6.5, where we have assumed for simplicity three firms A, B and C in the industry 1/6, 1/2 and 5/6 of the way along the market. Both A and C are taken to be setting a mill price p_m; actual prices to customers are given by (6.6). Thus if B also were to set p_m she would sell an amount proportional to the distance FG. As she raises mill price her sales diminish regularly until she sets it at $p_m + xt \ (= R_1)$ when she sells nothing. Similarly, at mill prices below p_m her sales will increase in a regular manner until $p_m - xt$ is reached. At and beyond this point, B sells also to customers to the left of A and to the right of C and her sales experience a sudden jump from being proportional to $2x$ to $3x$ as the other firms are undercut and leave the industry. With more firms, sudden jumps would be experienced. Under the rather unrealistic assumption of one customer per unit length whatever the price, the demand curve facing B would thus be of the form *RSTU* illustrated in figure 6.6 (ignore point Q for the moment). If each customer had a downward sloping demand curve, demand would fall off as prices rose, resulting in a somewhat modified curve facing B; one example is the dashed line $R'S'T'U'$. Notice the basic similarity of the demand curves facing the individual in figures 6.6 and 6.2; we comment on this in section 5.

Eaton and Lipsey (1978) have pointed out that, although the firm's demand curve in Hotelling's model is kinked, it may strongly be argued that even under the ZCV assumption the only relevant portion is the section *RS*.

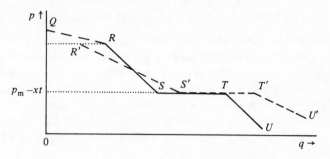

Figure 6.6

This is embodied in their 'no-mill-price-undercutting' restriction. Referring back to figure 6.5 and assuming that all firms have the same marginal production cost c (not shown), the argument is essentially that A (say) will wish to set a mill price, p_A, between marginal cost and the delivered price of B's product at A's location. That is:

$$c \leqslant p_A \leqslant p_B + xt \qquad (6.8)$$

However, in order for B to sell profitably at *A's location*:

$$p_A > p_B + xt \geqslant c. \qquad (6.9)$$

But A can prevent (6.9) from holding. Thus B will not want to force A out by undercutting his mill price and the only relevant part of her demand curve is the segment RS.

The key assumptions of our Hotelling-type model seem relevant when restated to accord with the product differentiation interpretation. These are: a range of increasing returns or some element of sunk costs once a particular product type is chosen, customers spread over a variety of preference positions and intermingled with firms and, lastly, costly alteration of products to precise tastes. However the last of these may not always be best specified in the precise form used in (6.6) within the product differentiation context. One example where that form *is* relevant is suggested by Stigler's (1964, appendix) case of a customer buying an 'off the peg' suit who is charged for alterations to make it fit. To give an example of an alternative, Schmalensee (1978), suggests a more appropriate demand function for brand i may be:

$$q_i(p, N) = f(p) \cdot g(N), \qquad (6.10)$$

where N is the number of established brands available (or the reciprocal of the 'distance' between them given that locational equilibration has already taken place) and p is the price charged by all firms. He proposes that $g(N)$ falls with N, though not enough to make total sales of the product range fall as N increases.

4. Predictions of the effects of product differentiation

Having spelt out the spatial competition approach, we are now able to use this apparatus to suggest some insights into the working of differentiated product markets. We are able to predict that supernormal profit can exist even in the face of an *apparently* competitive environment and that brand proliferation by established firms can be a barrier to entry. In doing so, we bring in the Lancastrian and other models where similar predictions occur. Some points on the analogy between models are gathered in section 5.

Product differentiation, profit and entry barriers

One of the most striking predictions of Hotelling-type models is that pure profit can exist in equilibrium given non-cooperative behaviour (ZCV) by established firms and free entry. To show this we take a simple example (from Schmalensee, 1978) where the cost function is given by (6.7) and the demand function by (6.10). With fixed locations, the N established brands are a distance $1/N$ apart on a line of unit length (or, to avoid any problem of the firms nearest to each end facing a different situation, around a circle of unit circumference). Profits for a typical established firm are therefore given by a function of price and distance served:

$$\Pi(p, N) = (p - c)f(p) \cdot g(N) - F; \qquad p > c \qquad (6.11)$$

Now, given the form of the demand function (6.10) and the level of price p^* maximising profits given an (arbitrary) assumption regarding rival behaviour, a certain value $\bar{N}$ will be the solution of $\Pi(p^*, \bar{N}) = 0$. Assume $\bar{N} > N$, so that all established firms are profitable or, if this happens not to be the case, lower F sufficiently to make it so. We are then assured that the potential for pure profit exists when there is no possibility of entry.

But what happens if entry is allowed? Assume the potential entrant also charges p^*.[9] He is forced to locate between two established firms, and will do best by choosing a point halfway between them. The position of such a potential entrant, E, in an industry of four established firms is depicted in figure 6.7. When E enters, he can expect to sell to half the customers between him and his neighbours, that is to a length $\frac{1}{4}N + \frac{1}{4}N = \frac{1}{2}N$, since they are assumed fixed in location. Thus his profits will be given by $\Pi(p^*, 2N)$. This value will be positive only if $\bar{N} > 2N$, so entry takes place if $\bar{N}/2 > N$. Combining this with the earlier condition, established firms will earn pure profits without attracting entry as long as $\bar{N}/2 < N < \bar{N}$.

Now the reader may not be entirely convinced by this simplified example. However, Eaton and Lipsey (1978) have shown that in a more general model the result persists, whatever the particular assumption made about rivals' reaction, as long as mill-price-undercutting is ruled out. This includes ZCV which seems, on the face of it, extremely conducive to price-cutting strategies.

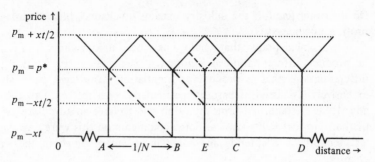

Figure 6.7

The other crucial assumption, which we have already discussed, is fixed location of established firms. Granted these assumptions, location combines with scale economies (indivisibilities) to provide a substantial entry barrier, by bringing about a localised crowding absent from spaceless models. Indeed, in the context of a simplified example, Eaton and Lipsey show established firms can earn up to twice the 'normal' rate of return on capital without attracting entry. Furthermore, the possibility of supernormal profit consistent with full equilibrium has been demonstrated in the Lancastrian context by Archibald and Rosenbluth (1975). Essentially, the fixed locations assumption turns what might be merely a fixed cost into a sunk cost, so effectively creating an entry barrier (see chapter 4).

Having said that product differentiation (or location) provides a barrier to entry, the point should be carefully qualified. The basic difficulty is the discontinuity noted above; a potentially wide range of packing of firms into the industry is consistent with pure profit equilibrium.[10] Now if we somehow increased the distance between firms, so increasing product differentiation, by lengthening the market but having the same density of customers, it would become more likely that a firm could enter between two existing firms and make profits. Thus, increasing product differentiation lowers the probability that entry will be blockaded and, in that sense, lowers entry barriers, as can be seen in Eaton and Lipsey's example (p. 462). However, if even after the increase entry were blockaded, the existing firms would become more profitable.

There are some interesting comparisons with results from Dixit's (1979) model which we discussed in chapter 4. He took a particularly straightforward special case where product differentiation was characterised by a parameter in the (linear) demand functions measuring the effect of the opponent's output on price. A fall in this parameter indicates a rise in product differentiation in the classical sense of distance from competitors. He shows that as the products become poorer substitutes (more highly differentiated) both blockaded entry and effectively impeded entry are less likely – entry is made easier.

On the other hand, if the industry remains blockaded, the established firm's profit is unchanged.

Notice, incidentally, that what we have been talking about here is horizontal product differentiation as a potential barrier to entry. Vertical product differentiation, that is product differentiation *advantages*, have also been extensively discussed as barriers, particularly with reference to the role of advertising. Established firms are often said to have an advantage as a result of their product being known. Some comments on this were provided in the last section of chapter 4, and some more are provided in the following chapter.

Brand proliferation and entry deterrence

When we relax the implicit assumption that each firm produces one product or brand, we find powerful arguments for the commonly observed phenomenon of established firms selling many brands in the same industry. The fundamental point is that since limit pricing is an unlikely strategy to pursue within a differentiated product market, other entry limiting strategies come into prominence; brand proliferation turns out to be an extremely attractive one.

To see this, suppose in figure 6.7 only firms A, C and D are at present in the industry, all setting a mill price of p_m. As it stands, there is a chance of a firm entering in position B and making profits. (We assume further entry at E would be unprofitable). How can this be stopped? Firms A and C could in fact price down to $(p_m - xt)$ in order to dissuade entry by limit pricing. However this would involve them making a loss on these sales and possibly even an overall loss if they were unable to price discriminate (e.g. customers to the left of A might purchase output from customers in the range A–B). Furthermore if B does decide to enter and so become relatively immobile, it will serve *all* firms if price is raised to p_m. Thus, pre-entry price is a poor signal of post-entry profit opportunities. If, instead, A or C or a cartel of all firms (whichever is the most alert) sets up a brand in position B before entry occurs, we are in the circumstances of the previous subsection. All the established firms make profits on their established brands while deterring entry, simply by the threat of maintaining position if it eventuates. Thus established firms will look to pre-emptive product proliferation to fill spaces where there could be sufficient custom to attract entry,[11] rather than limit pricing.

There is a further twist to the argument, explored by Eaton and Lipsey (1979). Suppose that in a particular market depicted in figure 6.8 only one firm A, may operate profitably and the optimal location is in the centre of the market at A_0. Yet it is widely foreseen that at some future date the density of customers will increase sufficiently for further plants or products to become a viable proposition and the optimal locations (to be discussed below) are B_1 and B_2. Thus there will be competition among potential sellers

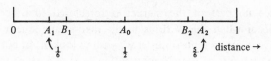

Figure 6.8

to gain the advantages of such future profits, that is a race to be next into the field. If the number of potential competitors is large, this will presumably push back the date of entry to the time when the present discounted value of profits to the winner is equal to the present discounted value of his losses in the early period before demand has grown sufficiently.[12]

Now, the firm which actually enters has the chance of choosing the location of B_1 and B_2. Under Hotelling's assumption of completely inelastic demand from each individual customer he would choose points just to the left and right of A_0. As Smithies (1940) points out, a relaxation of this assumption lessens but does not remove the centripetal tendency. However if A were choosing the position of the new plants, she would locate them further apart (in fact, $\frac{1}{6}$ and $\frac{5}{6}$ of the total distance along the line) in order to make larger total profits from the market. Moreover, if A were the builder she could probably price more optimally over the whole market than when in competition with B. In sum, A would expect larger future profits from building the new plants than any potential entrant and therefore would be willing to build them earlier than any potential entrant while still breaking even on this investment. Having established the new plants, A is at liberty to decide whether to operate them or to keep them as unused excess capacity as a pre-emptive strategy. Switching the argument to brands, product proliferation is likely to occur to a greater extent than is needed to serve the present market and some product types may not actually be marketed; brand names may be registered for future use.[13]

5. Extensions and comparisons

One important consideration in spatial competition models is the treatment of what are known as 'outside goods', that is the remainder of the economy. A straightforward treatment of this is provided by Salop (1979a), and we follow his paper quite closely here. The basic point is that we have assumed that all consumers in the market buy one or other of the available goods. When we modify this assumption, the demand curve facing the producer, as depicted in figure 6.6, is changed also.

Consider that consumers are spaced evenly around a circle of unit length, there being D consumers in all. Firms are free to enter, and to choose location and price. The fact that product space is a circle, imparts a stability to the costless locational equilibrium that Salop assumes which is missing from linear models, since no part of the market is foreclosed to other firms. Equilibrium will occur when the N firms in the market are equally spaced round the circle. There are two possibilities we wish to look at. In both, each consumer demands one unit of the cheapest inside good as long as the price does not exceed a fixed reservation price R common to all consumers, representing valuation relative to the outside good. All other money is spent on the outside good.

In the first case, which is essentially the same as those considered up to now, the reservation price is at a level such as R_1 in figure 6.5, meaning that everyone buys one of the goods. If the mill price of a neighbouring firm's good is fixed at $\bar{p}$ and transport costs are linear as in (6.6) then setting a mill price p will imply sales to those within a distance x_i such that:

$$p + x_i t \leqslant \bar{p} + t((1/N) - x_i)$$

Here $(1/N)$ is the distance between firms in locational equilibrium. Hence the marginal consumer is at a distance given by:

$$x_i = \frac{1}{2t}\left(\bar{p} + \frac{t}{N} - p\right)$$

and since each firm has both a left- and a right-hand neighbour, and density of customers is D, the firm's demand curve is:

$$q_i = 2Dx_i = \frac{D}{t}\left(\bar{p} + \frac{t}{N} - p\right) \tag{6.12}$$

In the second case, which will occur when prices are higher, the industry may find itself in a relationship to reservation price along the lines of R_2, such that not everyone is served. Salop calls this the monopoly case and calls the former one competitive. Sales will now be made to consumers in the interval:

$$p + x_i t \leqslant R$$

and the demand facing the firm in this case will be:

$$q_i = 2Dx_i = 2D(R - p)/t \tag{6.13}$$

Notice that in the 'competitive' case, $\partial p/\partial q_i = -t/D$ whereas in the monopoly case, $\partial p/\partial q_i = -t/2D$. The boundary between these occurs when the furthest consumers are paying R for an inside good, and thus at higher prices the slope becomes flatter in the (p, q) plane. Consequently, the introduction of outside goods causes a kink in the firm's demand curve to appear at R in figure 6.6 with a new branch QR having formed over which the good competes only with the outside good. Notice this kinked demand curve arises through a very different set of assumptions from those behind the kinked demand curve of chapter 2.

Actually, the behaviour of Salop's model in terms of equilibrium characteristics is perverse at the kink, though not elsewhere. Because he assumes

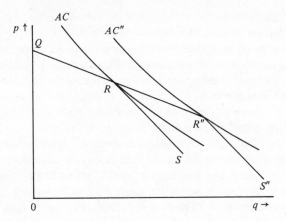

Figure 6.9

the equilibrium involves exactly zero profits to each firm (and remember, he assumes costless relocation, unlike the models of the previous section), when fixed costs rise the present configuration becomes unprofitable. A firm will drop out, the others will relocate and price eventually *falls* because the remaining firms are able to exploit scale economies to a greater extent. The point is illustrated in figure 6.9 (adapted from figure 6.6) where AC'' represents the new higher costs and $QR''S''$ is the demand facing each firm after one has left and others relocated. A similar analysis prevails for increases in marginal cost which lower price, also for decreases in the natural measure of the extent of product differentiation (t/D), which raise price. The responses along segments QR and RS are the reverse of these.

For many markets, this rather abrupt behaviour with respect to the outside good may be unrealistic. In principle though, the sudden kink would appear to be a product of the particular assumption about a fixed reservation price rather than an intrinsic property of the spatial competition model.

Comparisons

As Lancaster (1979) has suggested, it is possible to cast spatial competition analysis within a Lancastrian framework. The equivalent of Lancaster's compensating ratio is the value p_d/p_m from (6.6), representing the ratio of price paid for a precisely tailored product to what is paid for the available good. Hence we have:

$$h_s(x, p_m) = 1 + xt/p_m$$

as the spatial competition version of (6.5). This is drawn for a given p_m in figure 6.4.

Notice Lancaster's function is both smoother (at the outset) and nonlinear. However, though it is usual to analyse spatial models in which distance costs are linear, this is by no means necessary (or even desirable) within the product differentiation context. An alternative, for example, is Greenhut and Ohta's (1975) model of price discrimination over economic space, which is equivalent to a particular type of nonlinearity in distance costs. Logically therefore, 'distance' costs *could* take any form and could follow the path illustrated by Lancaster's $h(x)$ function in figure 6.4 within a sensible spatial competition model. In that case, the two approaches to pricing behaviour would be formally identical. The linear spatial model is purely an example, though a common one.

Lancaster claims additionally that smoother substitution for outside goods is a feature of his approach. In the model thus extended, consumers may be compensated for not receiving their most favoured goods either by other goods within the group or by the (for simplicity, single composite) outside good, or both. The relevant parameter is an elasticity of substitution, rather than a fixed reservation price, and a price change for one good has both inside and outside equivalents of the income and substitution effects; there is no kink.

Further points of comparison arise in the assumptions regarding locational fixity and pricing. As we have seen, there are some difficulties in Hotelling's model regarding location when changes in location are costless. Partly as a consequence, many spatial models involve fixed location, imposing a sunk cost which has widespread implications, as we have seen. In the circular version, Salop assumed flexible location while Schmalensee used fixed. Lancaster always assumes flexible location (or *costless* entry and exit, which is the same thing), and as a consequence equilibrium only exists for a limited range of parameter values. Particular circumstances may suggest which assumption to employ in any practical case. They may also suggest whether the common assumption of zero conjectural variations is the most relevant, or whether another should be used.

Finally, although no single model is appropriate in all circumstances to capture product differentiation, it remains true that, as with standard consumer theory, one can accept the demand curve as a concept without necessarily believing in a particular derivation. Indeed, Dixit and Stiglitz (1977) have suggested that standard consumer theory with its assumption of convex indifference surfaces defined over quantities of (potential as well as actual) commodities, already embodies sufficiently the concept of the desirability of variety.[14] This implies that a direct approach to product differentiation involving own and cross product terms, as covered already in chapter 2, may be countenanced. In order to make the approach operational they, like some others, adopt specific functional forms in deriving results, such as those which are mentioned in the following section.

6. Product differentiation and welfare

The standard welfare question is whether the socially optimal quantity of goods will be supplied at the socially optimal prices. When we turn to differentiated products we have to enquire more closely whether the correct number of goods is supplied, in the socially optimal quantities and whether the goods have the optimal amount of quality embedded in them through the characteristics they provide.

When markets are 'complete' in the sense that there are as many goods for sale as there are characteristics in the goods then (as Leland, 1977, shows), all consumers have the same implicit prices for characteristics, once having maximised utility over goods consumed. Firms, when in perfect competition, treat these implicit characteristics prices as parameters, so will set the marginal worth of each characteristic equal to its marginal cost. If constant or decreasing returns to scale exist in the production of all varieties of goods, it will be socially optimal for (at least) every consumer's most favoured goods to be produced, the market will be complete and such goods can each be priced at marginal cost within a market system by firms under perfect competition. Thus the perfectly competitive market solution will be Pareto-optimal.

Under constant returns to scale (for example) then, the only real question is whether forms of industrial organisation other than perfect competition may be optimal in at least some partial sense. The brief answer is: no, unless perfect price discrimination is feasible.[15]

As we have suggested though, the most interesting, important and problematic cases arise when producing differentiated products involves increasing returns and/or fixed costs associated with advertising, research or whatever. In those cases, marginal cost pricing will induce losses, so perfect competition is unfeasible. At the same time, because there are costs to allowing variety, it will not in general be optimal to supply products tailored to each consumer's needs. In fact if returns to scale are sufficiently great, producing a single variety of a good will be socially optimal. Comparisons between market and optimum become complex.

In order to obtain a feel for the issues involved, let us first examine the simplified framework of Salop's (1979a) model. We can note immediately that because consumers have inelastic demands up to the reservation price, distortions will come about solely through the numbers of products, not prices different from marginal costs.

The *market equilibrium* in Salop's model will involve equal prices as well as equal spacing, due to the symmetry of the products involved. These prices will be such as to maximise profits for each firm as well as being just sufficient to cover costs, given free entry and costless relocation (and forgetting about the integer problem on firm numbers). Thus, in the case where all points in the market are served ('competition'), utilising (6.7) regarding costs we have:

$$p + q_i \frac{\partial p}{\partial q_i} = c \Bigg\}$$

(6.14a)

$$p = c + F/q_i \Bigg\}$$

(6.14b)

where $\partial p/\partial q_i = -t/D$. Also, since $p = \bar{p}$, (6.12) yields:

$$q_i = D/N \tag{6.15}$$

It is easy to eliminate price in (6.14) to solve for q_i and thence for the equilibrium number of firms in competition (N_c) from (6.15):

$$N_c = \sqrt{tD/F} \tag{6.16}$$

Turning to *societal welfare*, as far as a typical consumer is concerned, the benefit gained from consuming the product is represented by the difference between price paid (including 'travelling cost' tx_i) and valuation R. Society benefits by the difference between valuation and resource costs: $R - tx_i - c$. Aggregating over consumers, there are $2N$ similar intervals where they may find themselves, each of length $1/2N$, and D consumers in all. Total surplus, not forgetting fixed costs, is therefore:

$$W = 2ND \int_0^{1/2N} (R - tx - c) \cdot \mathrm{d}x - NF$$

Integration yields:

$$W = D(R - \tfrac{1}{4}(t/N) - c) - NF$$

Finally then, maximising welfare by choosing the optimal number of firms and products, N (recalling that price is of no account here), upon rearranging, we have:

$$N^* = 0.5\sqrt{tD/F} < N_c \tag{6.17}$$

Monopolistic or spatial competition then, yields superabundant variety in this case, a conclusion in line with casual reasoning along 'excess capacity' lines. By a similar procedure, it is also possible to show that monopoly (in Salop's sense) yields too much variety.

However neither result is a general one, but both arise because of the particular assumption about how consumers evaluate products distant from their ideal. We should recall here that linear evaluation of distance is purely a simplifying assumption. To illustrate, it is possible to go through the analytics of the 'competition' case above, with one change. If, to take a specifically chosen and rather arbitrary case, (6.6) is replaced by:

$$p_d = p_m + (\sqrt{x}) \cdot t \tag{6.18}$$

and (tD/F) is given the value 32, the same procedure shows that $N_c = 2$, whereas N^* is almost double that, at about 3.85. Here, monopolistic competition gives too little variety.

The general point is that monopolistic competition, spatial competition, Lancaster's model, or whatever, can give either too many or too few products. It is not hard to see why, intuitively. An individual firm considering introducing a product will not take into account consumer surplus. It is the fact that profits do not represent all the social benefits to be obtained from its introduction, which is a force making for too little variety. On the other hand, the firm will not take into account either, the detrimental effects on demand for other firms' products of introducing a substitute, which is a force acting towards there being too many products. Hence, parameters such as the size of fixed costs, own and cross-price elasticities of demand, can push the outcome in either direction.

Interestingly, if we imposed a break-even constraint like (6.14b) on the welfare maximisation, then a second-best societal optimum involving 'Ramsey' prices (see chapter 4) might not be too bad. In the specific case where the social utility function is of constant elasticity form, Dixit and Stiglitz (1977) find that the second-best and market solutions coincide.[16] That is, prices and the numbers of products (firms) are the same. This is not, it should be emphasised, a general result.

We should also recall from section 1.3 that since some products are more likely to be produced than others, by the same token some product groups as a whole may be produced whilst others would add more to societal welfare. This caveat applies to all the above discussion.

Finally note that, throughout the chapter, we have implicitly been assuming that the attributes of a product were known to consumers as well as to producers. When consumers have *incomplete information* about quality, they will indulge in search behaviour. The interplay of this with producers' supply of information through advertising is discussed in section 7.4, but see also Akerlof (1970) for some potential problems regarding market equilibrium.

Notes on the literature

Two useful surveys of the product quality debate are provided by Schmalensee (1979) and Saving (1982). The basic ideas of the Lancastrian and Hotelling approaches to product differentiation are discussed quite well in Green (1976) and Vickrey (1964, ch. 8) respectively. On the applications to industrial organisation, Archibald and Rosenbluth (1975) is the key article as far as Lancaster's earlier work is concerned. Lancaster (1979, chs. 2 and 6) provides some comparisons between his and the spatial model. Eaton and Lipsey (1976) have produced a very readable survey of their work in the field of spatial competition, while Schmalensee (1978) is an interesting application of this type of analysis, as well as a useful summary. A survey paper by Spence (1976a) covers some of the issues involved in optimal product differentiation very succinctly.

In our discussion of the spatial model, we have relied very heavily on the Hotelling zero conjectural variation assumption. The relation between this and some other assumptions including the commonly used Löschian competition is discussed in Capozza and van Order (1978).

7

Advertising

The purpose of this chapter is to explore theoretically the role of advertising. If we could assume each firm in an industry produced the same product, there would be little point in a firm advertising except to identify itself as a point of supply and to provide information on its price. However once we allow a differentiated product industry, as we have in the previous chapter, advertising comes to have a much wider importance; it might even be used to imply differences or superiorities which do not in fact exist. Hence the necessity for widening the model. Advertising, throughout the chapter, is used as a convenient pseudonym for selling and promotional expense more generally.

This topic area has generated an extraordinary amount of debate and disagreement. Partly this arises through differences in beliefs on the basic role of advertising. Difficulties are also caused because it does not fit neatly into the structure–conduct–performance paradigm: it is not unequivocally in any of those categories. After introducing a basic framework in the first section, we review some of the arguments suggesting how market structure might affect advertising in section 2, then arguments implying the reverse association in section 3. In section 4 we link advertising more closely with information, and so move towards some insights into whether advertising is a 'good' or a 'bad' thing.

1. The Dorfman–Steiner condition and some extensions

Let us start our discussion with a basic result: the condition for optimal advertising for a firm (say a monopolist) under static conditions. This is known as the Dorfman–Steiner condition in honour of their seminal paper (1954).

Consider demand facing the firm to be a function of price and advertising:

$$q = q(p, A) \tag{7.1}$$

Here A is advertising expenditure, increases in which shift the demand curve to the right. Arguably it would be more realistic to assume that advertising messages do this, rather than expenditure. Essentially then, the implicit simplifying assumption here is that the price of an advertising message is fixed at unity, thus that the productivity of successive messages is constant.

The firm's costs consist of production cost, a function of output $C(q)$, and the cost of advertising, A. Therefore profit is:

$$\Pi(p, A) = p \cdot q(p, A) - C[q(p, A)] - A. \tag{7.2}$$

Maximising profit with respect to price and advertising, assuming the second order conditions hold, yields the first order conditions:

$$\frac{\partial \Pi}{\partial p} = q + p \cdot \frac{\partial q}{\partial p} - \frac{dC}{dq} \cdot \frac{\partial q}{\partial p} = 0 \tag{7.3}$$

$$\frac{\partial \Pi}{\partial A} = p \cdot \frac{\partial q}{\partial A} - \frac{dC}{dq} \cdot \frac{\partial q}{\partial A} - 1 = 0 \tag{7.4}$$

Re-arranging equation (7.3) slightly, we see it is merely the normal condition for optimal pricing, that is the price–cost margin is equal to the reciprocal of the price elasticity of demand, η_p:

$$\frac{(p - dC/dq)}{p} = -1 \Big/ \frac{p}{q} \cdot \frac{\partial q}{\partial p} = \frac{1}{\eta_p} \tag{7.5}$$

If we then arrange (7.4) to yield an expression for the price–cost margin and substitute for the elasticity of demand from (7.5), we have:

$$p \frac{\partial q}{\partial A} = \eta_p \tag{7.6}$$

advertising will be utilised up to the point at which its marginal value product is equal to the price elasticity of demand. A common and very suggestive reformulation of the Dorfman–Steiner condition is to define an advertising elasticity of demand $\eta_A = (A/q)(\partial q/\partial A)$. Inserting this in (7.6) easily yields the result:

$$\frac{A}{p \cdot q} \equiv \frac{A}{R} = \frac{\eta_A}{\eta_p} \tag{7.7}$$

the firm's optimal advertising/sales revenue ratio is equal to the ratio of its advertising elasticity of demand to the price elasticity of demand it faces.

One very important point should be apparent from this demonstration: the level of advertising is chosen simultaneously with the level of price. Thus, to imply a causal chain leading to advertising from some other variable, or vice versa, is hazardous. For example, the level of advertising might affect the *price* elasticity of demand and thus the price–cost margin. However such an effect will be muddled by the effect of price on the advertising elasticity of demand. In special cases though, predictions are more straightforward. If, for example, the demand function is Cobb–Douglas in form so that both elasticities are constant, this points to the simple rule of spending a constant proportion of sales revenue on advertising.

The model so far is extremely simple. Our next task is to suggest two generalisations and analyse their consequences. Firstly, advertising may have an impact also on future period sales by moulding consumers' attitudes or creating a bandwagon effect among other consumers. Secondly, we assume the firm is in an oligopolistic industry, since equation (7.7) relates easily to industry magnitudes only under the assumption that the firm is a monopolist.

Nerlove and Arrow (1962) have analysed the problem of determining the optimal stock of goodwill, G, created by advertising. In this, advertising acts as gross investment in a stock which depreciates at a rate of δ, i.e.:

$$dG/dt = A - \delta G$$

The monopolist maximises the discounted value of profits subject to this. They find the condition analogous to (7.7) to be:

$$\frac{G}{R} = \frac{\eta_a}{\eta_p(r + \delta)} \tag{7.8}$$

where η_a is the elasticity of demand with respect to goodwill $(\partial q/\partial G) \cdot (G/q)$ and r is the discount rate.

There are a number of problems with their formulation however. One is that while past advertising builds up a stock, past prices and consumers' stocks of the good (past purchases) do not. The treatment is thus asymmetric. Further, the stock of goodwill is related to the flow of sales in (7.8) so the flow of advertising is related to the change in the sales flow, an unlikely mechanism. Also, since G is unobservable, it is difficult to formulate a testable version of (7.8). Schmalensee (1972), who explains this in more detail, builds an alternative dynamic model in which a version of the original condition (7.7) appears. Specifically, the firm's advertising/sales ratio is equal to the ratio of its long run elasticities of demand with respect to advertising and price, i.e. the effects of these variables on equilibrium demand. Given this result, we feel we can discuss oligopoly without considering dynamics, since only the interpretation of the elasticities would differ.

In an oligopolistic situation, the established firms will settle upon prices and levels of advertising simultaneously, based upon their ideas about rival reactions. In order to focus upon the advertising decision, we will assume they all charge the same price, p. Thus we take the demand function facing an individual firm to be of the form:

$$q_i = q_i(p, A_i, A_r)$$

where A_r refers to rivals' advertising expenditure and A_i to the firm's own. Profits are thus:

$$\Pi_i = p \cdot q_i(p, A_i, A_r) - C_i[q_i(p, A_i, A_r)] - A_i$$

The firm maximises profits with respect to her own advertising (and also her own price in a full model),[1] producing the first-order condition:

$$\frac{\partial \Pi_i}{\partial A_i} = \left(p - \frac{\mathrm{d}C_i}{\mathrm{d}q_i}\right)\left[\frac{\partial q_i}{\partial A_i} + \frac{\partial q_i}{\partial A_\mathbf{r}} \cdot \frac{\mathrm{d}A_\mathbf{r}}{\mathrm{d}A_i}\right] - 1 = 0 \qquad (7.9)$$

Analogously with our oligopoly models of chapter 2, the term $\mathrm{d}A_\mathbf{r}/\mathrm{d}A_i$ is to be interpreted as representing firm i's conjecture about how rivals will respond to changes in her advertising expenditures. From this term we define a conjectural elasticity $(\mathrm{d}A_\mathbf{r}/\mathrm{d}A_i)(A_i/A_\mathbf{r}) = \eta_{ar}$, measuring the effect of own advertising on rivals' advertising behaviour. Two other important elasticities are $(\partial q_i/\partial A_i)(A_i/q_i) = \eta_{aq} (> 0)$ representing the direct effect of own advertising on own demand, and $(\partial q_i/\partial A_r)(A_\mathbf{r}/q_i) = \eta_{rq} (< 0?)$ the effect of rivals' advertising on own demand.

Expanding the term in square brackets in (7.9) and utilising the three definitions above we have:

$$\frac{\partial q_i}{\partial A_i} + \frac{\partial q_i}{\partial A_\mathbf{r}} \cdot \frac{\mathrm{d}A_\mathbf{r}}{\mathrm{d}A_i} = \frac{q_i}{A_i}[\eta_{aq} + \eta_{rq} \cdot \eta_{ar}]$$

Thus in (7.9), by re-arrangement:

$$\frac{A_i}{pq_i} \equiv \frac{A_i}{R_i} = \left(\frac{p - \mathrm{d}C_i/\mathrm{d}q_i}{p}\right) \cdot [\eta_{aq} + \eta_{rq} \cdot \eta_{ar}] \qquad (7.10)$$

the oligopolist's advertising/sales ratio depends upon the three elasticities defined in the previous paragraph and her price–cost margin. More generally, it depends upon buyer behaviour towards advertising and rivalrous behaviour with respect to price and advertising; if plausible hypotheses about these various effects could be developed[2] we would be in a position to explain the advertising/sales ratio.

In the three sections following, we first examine arguments suggesting a causal chain from advertising to market structure, then arguments suggesting the reverse causation. Finally we look at the role of the consumer more closely, and so formulate a welfare economic view of advertising.

2. Effects of market structure on advertising

One important question is whether as numbers in the industry increase firms advertise more or less intensively. Some people argue intensity will fall as the industry becomes less monopolistic, since the firm can capture a smaller proportion of the benefits of its own advertising: a beer advertisement might send consumers in search of a pint of the first brand they happen to encounter! On the other hand, if advertising is used as a weapon of rivalry, a large number of firms might mean increased potential gains at the expense of other firms from any particular campaign, and thus more advertising. Other people again, argue there is no direct relation. To look at all aspects of this question, we develop an extremely simple illustrative model[3] based upon (7.10) and so on the Dorfman–Steiner condition.

Assume for simplicity firms entertain Cournot-type beliefs about advertising so that η_{ar} in (7.10) is zero. Yet still there are two potential effects of a change in a firm's advertising, both bound up in η_{aq} – an effect upon market share and one on the level of total demand for the product. Notice that $q_i \equiv s_i Q$: i's output can be expressed as his share s_i of total output Q. Thus:

$$\frac{\partial q_i}{\partial A_i} \equiv \frac{\partial (Q \cdot s_i)}{\partial A_i} = s_i \frac{\partial Q}{\partial A_i} + Q \frac{\partial s_i}{\partial A_i}$$

so that, after slight rearrangement:

$$\eta_{aq} \equiv \frac{A_i}{q_i} \cdot \frac{\partial q_i}{\partial A_i} = \frac{A_i}{Q} \cdot \frac{\partial Q}{\partial A_i} + \frac{A_i}{s_i} \cdot \frac{\partial s_i}{\partial A_i} \tag{7.11}$$

Now concerning the first term:

$$\frac{A_i}{Q} \cdot \frac{\partial Q}{\partial A_i} = \left(\frac{A}{Q} \cdot \frac{\partial Q}{\partial A} \right) \frac{A_i}{A} = \eta_{AQ} \cdot a_i \tag{7.11a}$$

where a_i is i's share of total industry advertising and η_{AQ} is the industry advertising elasticity of demand.[4] Also, assume all firms set the same price and that all firms' advertising is equally effective, so shares of output depend upon relative advertising expenditures:

$$s_i = A_i \bigg/ \sum_{j=1}^{n} A_j.$$

In these circumstances:

$$\frac{A_i}{s_i} \cdot \frac{\partial s_i}{\partial A_i} = \frac{A_i}{s_i} \left[\frac{1}{\Sigma A_j} - \frac{A_i}{(\Sigma A_j)^2} \right] = 1 - s_i \tag{7.11b}$$

Substituting the relations (7.11a and b) back into (7.11) and thence into the version of equation (7.10) where the possibility of interaction is excluded ($\eta_{ar} = 0$) gives:

$$\frac{A_i}{R_i} = \left(\frac{p - dC_i/dq_i}{p} \right) [a_i \eta_{AQ} + (1 - s_i)] \tag{7.12}$$

If we assume all the firms have the same cost functions (and given their advertising is equally effective) they will all be of the same size. In that case $a_i = s_i = 1/N$, N being the number of firms. For concreteness we assume price is set as if the firms were Cournot quantity setting oligopolists,[5] so we can substitute $1/(N\eta_p)$ for the price–cost margin in (7.12), η_p being the industry price elasticity of demand.

Finally then, (7.12) becomes:

$$\frac{A_i}{R_i} = \frac{A}{R} = \frac{\eta_{AQ} + N - 1}{N^2 \eta_p} \tag{7.13}$$

Table 7.1.

$\eta_p = 2$	$N =$ 1	2	3	4	5	10
0.5	0.250	0.188	0.139	0.109	0.090	0.048
$\eta_{AQ} =$ 0.25	0.125	0.156	0.125	0.102	0.085	0.046
0.1	0.050	0.138	0.117	0.097	0.082	0.046

As expected, if $N = 1$ we get back to the monopoly result. However if there are more firms, the advertising/sales ratio can be either higher or lower than under monopoly. This point is clearly illustrated in table 7.1 which charts values for the advertising/sales ratio for varying numbers of firms and three representative advertising elasticities.[6] In the first row of the table we see that advertising intensity falls as numbers in the industry increase whereas in the other rows advertising intensity first rises then falls; in the last row advertising intensity is above the monopoly level even with five firms in the industry.

Of course we must stress that the numbers in the table are purely arbitrary given the concatenation of simplifying assumptions we used to reach them. However they do indicate that those who argue for a positive relationship and those who argue for a negative relationship between intensity and concentration can both be right over some range of values. Also, interestingly, Cable (1972) and Sutton (1974) have put forward verbal arguments for an inverted 'U' shaped relationship as demonstrated in the second and third rows of the table.

Another relationship between industry structure and advertising emanating from the Dorfman–Steiner condition is the extent of 'cost-fixity' and its effect on advertising. Rewriting (7.6) by replacing the price elasticity of demand, we have:

$$p \frac{\partial q}{\partial A} = \frac{p}{p - dC/dq}$$

Assuming, by analogy with production theory, that the marginal value product of advertising is decreasing in the neighbourhood of equilibrium, we can say that more expenditure on advertising will be associated with a lower value for the marginal product and so, in turn, with the right hand side of the above expression. This occurs when marginal cost is relatively small. In other words, when short run production costs are relatively fixed, advertising can make an important marginal contribution to profit and so be extensively used. Interestingly, stage-coach lines, whose production costs were obviously largely fixed, were among the first users of advertising.

The structure of manufacturing relative to retailing will also potentially have an influence on the amount of advertising, and how it is shared between manufacturers and retailers, also possibly on product differentiation strategies more generally. Such relationships and their effects on product promotion strategies are considered at length in Porter (1976). More broadly, many features of the type of product will have an influence on the amount and type of advertising due to differing degrees of 'advertisability'. One of the most important facets of a product is the extent to which it is bought by firms rather than private consumers, and this is thought to have a major influence on the amount and style of advertising. Empirical workers often enter variables to account for differing 'advertisability' alongside market structural variables in explaining advertising intensity, but we do not propose to give details or examples at present.

3. The effects of advertising on market power

As already indicated, a very popular empirical activity has been to relate the level of concentration to the ratio of advertising to sales. However the theoretical links from advertising to concentration are not particularly strong or direct. Perhaps the best argument for this direction of causation (suggested by Greer, 1971) is the idea that advertising creates diverse individual returns for individual firms, so those who run successful advertising campaigns grow relatively large and the industry's concentration increases.[7] Such determinants of concentration are discussed in chapter 9. We move on instead to look at the theoretical effects of advertising as a barrier to entry, which may then as a result lead to concentration and/or influence profit margins.

Advertising as a barrier to entry

Advertising might create or raise barriers to entry if there exist economies of scale in advertising[8] so resulting in a scale economy barrier, or if advertising can create durable preferences for established firms' products which are hard and expensive to recreate, so making for a product differentiation advantage barrier. We take the arguments in this order.

There are two intersecting strands to the argument on advertising scale economies, which can be thought of as corresponding to technical and pecuniary economies. Those who argue there are technical economies are saying that, if the number of messages doubles, the effect on sales is more than doubled. More advertising messages imply two things: an increase in the number of messages received by some consumers and an increase in the number of consumers who receive messages. Presumably, rational advertisers will seek first to inform those who are the most likely purchasers. In addition, after a certain number of messages have reached any particular consumer, the effect of additional messages is bound to be lessened. Thus technical economies, though they may exist, are likely to be limited in extent.

The second influence is through decreasing costs of advertising. We all know of the local newspaper offers of 'three insertions for the price of two' which presumably are based upon lower setting costs. But, it is asserted, large firms also benefit from discounts for quantity of advertising expenditure over a period and in addition there are fixed costs in producing, say, a T.V.

advertisement. Thus it is plausible to suggest that cost per message falls as expenditure increases. This will raise the output level at which minimum advertising costs are achieved above the point where diminishing returns to advertising *messages* set in.[9] If the underlying assertions are correct, there will be scale economies in advertising and these, possibly combined with production scale economies, may be effective in preventing or delaying entry, even when the established industry earns above normal profits, through mechanisms explained at length in chapter 4.

Actually, as Spence (1980) points out, what is relevant in determining economies of scale in a world with advertising, is whether costs per money unit of revenue decline as output increases. The argument in a nutshell is that, in an industry where products are differentiated, production of revenue units comes about through the combination of physical unit and advertising unit inputs.[10] Costs per revenue unit decline if the 'production function' exhibits scale economies. This can happen even if there are diminishing returns to each input taken separately, just as with a standard production function.

The analysis so far is based upon a static model. But as we said when discussing Nerlove and Arrow's model, it seems plausible to assume that advertising's effect might be longer lasting. Thus we may enquire into the effects of the brand loyalty thereby created, and so product differentiation advantages. Assume a situation in which a firm is considering entry. Suppose her equilibrium share of industry output depends upon her share of industry advertising expenditure, since a common price will be charged by all. However, because advertising only gradually has an effect upon goodwill, it takes time for her output to build up to its equilibrium level. This will mean losses in the early periods when heavy advertising expenditure are incurred. The more intensively the established firms are advertising, the heavier these earlier losses will be and the less likely they are to be outweighed by later profits, suitably discounted. Thus, assuming the established firms can advertise heavily enough to make entry unprofitable while still not spending sufficiently to cut their own profits to zero, entry can profitably be prevented.[11]

So goes one argument. On the other hand, even if the established industry were a monopolist, presumably it once had to incur large advertising expenditure to attract consumers away from alternative products. We neglected this point by talking of the established firm in long run equilibrium. Thus, as Schmalensee (1974) and Needham (1976) suggest, in the absence of increasing returns, what is really required in order for durable brand preferences to create a barrier to entry is that there is a basic asymmetry between potential and established firms in demand or costs. Otherwise, a properly expensed comparison of the established and potential entrant firms' advertising policies would show the former making losses also. Durability, it seems, would only be of importance here if there were increasing returns, when it could act as a sunk cost.

The asymmetry point is made, though in rather a different way, by Williamson (1963). Very briefly, in his model the limit price has a technically determined base level but may be raised above this by the use of advertising. The established firm wishes to maximise profits while preventing entry, which he does by maximising profit with respect to output and advertising,[12] subject to the ensuing price being less than limit price. Nevertheless it transpires that it may not be worthwhile to use advertising to prevent entry; the advantage of increasing advertising may be more than offset by the additional costs involved.

But in fact, as we indicated in section 4.5, most hypotheses regarding *behaviour* towards entrants do encompass asymmetries. If we allow this, advertising (with or without lagged effects) may be reinstated as a potential creator of entry barriers even if the post-entry demand and cost position of the indigenous and itinerant firms are the same.

To see this in its simplest form, assume the potential entrant holds a Sylos postulate on output and advertising, and suppose the profit function facing *both* established firm (firm 1) and potential entrant (2) is of the form:[13]

$$\Pi_i = p(q_i, q_j, A_i, A_j)q_i - C(q_i) - A_i \qquad i, j = 1, 2 \qquad (7.14)$$

Prior to entry, the established firm's profits are given by setting q_2 and A_2 equal to zero. However the potential entrant's profits are given by setting q_1 and A_1 to their pre-entry non-zero values (given the Sylos postulate). It is natural to assume that $\partial \Pi_i / \partial q_j < 0$ and $\partial \Pi_i / \partial A_j < 0$. Then it is perfectly possible, to take an example, for production at the monopoly level to be profitable, yet for those monopoly values for q_1 and A_1, when substituted into (7.14), not to allow the potential entrant to make profits even when she chooses the most favourable output for herself. Hence entry is, in this example, blockaded (more generally, entry barriers are raised) not because of an asymmetry in the profit function nor due to increasing returns but because of the 'rules of the game'. The point is elaborated upon in Cubbin (1981).

It has been suggested, to the contrary of the above arguments, that advertising is a bulwark of a competitive industry structure. This point is taken up in the next section.

4. Advertising, information and welfare

It is salutory to reflect that we have so far barely mentioned the intention behind a firm using advertising, nor its relationship to product differentiation (which is possibly via effects on the B matrix in equation (6.5)). Indeed, we are not alone in this; one of the foremost workers in the field was forced to admit in discussion (Mann, 1974, p. 156) that he had thought little about the implications of such a question.

If we were to assume that sovereign consumers had perfect information about all products, then advertising would be of no avail, so expenditure on it would be a social waste. However, we all know by experience that advertising seeks to inform, but also to persuade; it cannot be that so many washing powders produce whiter, cleaner results than the rest! Thus, in order to enquire more deeply about the intent of advertising, it is necessary to have some view regarding the way consumers use information in choosing brands, then to fit the (necessarily biased) information provided by advertising into this framework.

The introduction of information, or rather goodwill, of itself can lead to problems for our model of the market process. To see this, suppose consumers know the quality level of a particular product but not that of its rival. Trying the new brand then imposes a cost on the consumer so that, unless it promises to be superior and/or is priced more cheaply than the established brand, it will not be sampled. Nevertheless, if goodwill can be bought cheaply in small amounts and there are no production economies of scale, no problem arises. There will always be a few people who find the present product marginally too expensive but are willing to try an alternative which has some chance of proving equally good. Under those conditions just outlined, there will be firms willing to provide it.

On the other hand, the product may need to establish goodwill through durability, or by passing a test costly to the firm, like type approval for motor cars; that is, goodwill may have the nature of a sunk cost. There may be production scale economies which interact with the demand disadvantage (which amounts to a natural asymmetry in the 'rules' of the oligopoly game), again meaning goodwill acts like a barrier to entry. Models of this type are analysed by Schmalensee (1982) and von Weizsäcker (1980b). As the latter points out though, there is little one can do about such barriers;[14] he prefers to call them disadvantages due to externalities. Advertising then, must be viewed from the standpoint of how it affects this *status quo*.

The ways in which information is provided by advertising depends, among many other things, upon the type of good. Nelson (1970) distinguishes between 'search' and 'experience' goods. Search goods are those whose properties may substantially be verified prior to purchase. Advertising's role here is to get consumers to examine the products, and the provision of misleading information would lead to lost credibility, so predominantly straightforward advertising would be expected. With experience goods (e.g. a car), the characteristics cannot be appreciated without purchase, so there is an incentive to exaggerate them. This holds even in the long run, if the characteristics are not purely objective. Of course, most goods are mixtures of both types.

Nevertheless, with search goods (or experience goods whose claims may be quickly and directly evaluated, for example, a universal hangover cure) then there is a tendency for advertising to accord closely with the truth.[15] Thus, those with the most incentive to advertise are the firms which genuinely provide a good service and the mere fact that a firm advertises may provide the

138   *Economic theory of the industry*

consumer with favourable information (Nelson, 1970). Advertising then becomes a vehicle for arbitrage, so it is likely to increase demand elasticities (with respect to price) and improve competition. This is Brozen's (1974) view about the nature of advertising generally.

In Dixit and Norman's (1978) view, a firm advertises in order to change consumers' tastes in a direction profitable to the firm by shifting the demand curve facing the firm. The question of whether the pre- or post-advertising tastes are more in line with a consumer's true interests is not addressed since they make welfare comparison from both standpoints. The fundamental assumption they use is that advertising lowers the elasticity of demand for the product by making other goods seem a poorer substitute. Consequently, it raises the price–cost margin a firm with market power achieves on its sales.

Taking the case of a monopolist with constant marginal (and so, average variable) costs of production c, the demand curve she faces before increasing advertising by a small amount is D_1 and after, D_2. Thus, in figure 7.1, the old and new equilibria are A_1 and A_2 respectively. We assume A_2 involves a greater output, q_2, as well as a greater price, p_2, than A_1 (price p_1 output q_1); if this were not so, resources would not have been shifted into this relatively underproduced good and welfare would definitely have fallen.

By increasing her advertising, the monopolist has increased her gross profits by the shaded area. What has happened to welfare, measured without regard to distribution? To discuss this, Dixit and Norman argue we should use a consistent standard of reference regarding tastes, rather than measuring the areas under the demand curves between the price axis and the respective

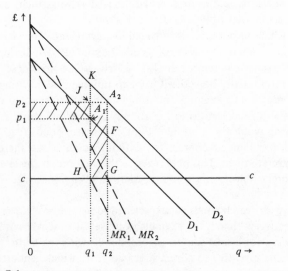

Figure 7.1

outputs. Thus, on a pre-advertising standard we forget about D_2 and find the welfare increase to be the area A_1FGH, the area under D_1 between the two outputs. Assuming the distance between D_1 and D_2 to be small, we may all but neglect areas of the '$\Delta p\Delta q$' type, for example A_1JA_2F. Thus we can write the change in welfare (change in profit[16] plus consumer surplus) as: $\Delta W_1 \leqslant \Delta\Pi - q_1\Delta p$. Similarly, on a post-advertising standard, we forget about D_1. The welfare increase is therefore $GHKA_2$ or, making the same type of approximation, $\Delta W_2 \geqslant \Delta\Pi - q_1\Delta p$. In general then, when the increase in advertising is very small, we have its welfare effect as:

$$\Delta W = \Delta\Pi - q\Delta p. \tag{7.15}$$

whatever the viewpoint adopted.

Notice that, because of the assumption that advertising raises price, an increase in advertising has two opposing effects, making firms better off by $\Delta\Pi$ and consumers worse off by the amount $q\Delta p$. Thus, from a position of no advertising, welfare can only be increased by a small amount of adveritising if it is profitable, but may not be increased even then − private profit is a necessary but not sufficient condition for welfare benefits. Even more importantly, if a firm is doing a profit-maximising amount of advertising then $\Delta\Pi = 0$. Thus, from (7.15) we see that welfare would be reduced by increasing advertising further or, to put it another way, welfare would be increased by reducing the level of advertising some way below that disseminated by a profit-maximising monopolist.

Dixit and Norman go on to develop a formal model of the monopoly case, in which an exact version of (7.15) is arrived at.[17] They then model a simple oligopoly situation and again produce a criterion for the evaluation of welfare effects. Here advertising may be excessive from a social point of view even if it does not increase price. The reason is not hard to discern intuitively. Suppose the firms set advertising at Cournot levels. Again from their individual points of view, $\Delta\Pi = 0$ at that level. But to the extent that the marginal profitability of a firm's own advertising is positive beyond the point at which it is marginally profitable to the group because such advertising has the effect simply of shifting demand amongst firms, it is socially wasteful. Thus there is in effect an extra term to subtract in arriving at the total welfare effect. They further generalise the model to allow for free entry − that is they consider the case of monopolistic competition. Here it turns out that the influence of advertising on price is of no importance; advertising always gives rise to deleterious social effects at market equilibrium levels. This is because entry always sends profits to zero, so an increase in advertising raises the natural price *index* of output in the industry in order to pay for it.

In Dixit and Norman's model, advertising may or may not be informative; an advertisement of price and address of a good is informative and may shift demand towards the advertiser in the way they assume. However, their model is restrictive in that the amount of advertising determines the extent to which demand is affected. In Kotowitz and Mathewson's (1979*b*) model, advertising is necessarily informative, but it informs (at least some) consumers of the existence of the product or of its characteristics (in an easily verifiable manner). This seemingly subtle contrast produces very different results.

The basic idea in Kotowitz and Mathewson is that advertising does not change tastes. Consumers who do not know of the product have a latent demand for it and advertising is one means by which this becomes realised, so buyer and seller are able to trade to their mutual advantage. Through time, as advertising proceeds, additional consumers are made aware of the product and choose whether to buy or not. This is an inherently dynamic process, yet we can bring out its main features in a simplified static manner.[18]

Because the newly informed consumers are assumed to have the same taste distribution as the old, when a further $x\%$ of consumers know about the product, demand at any price is $(100 + x)\%$ of what it was. Consequently, industry demand elasticity at any price remains constant. Thus the monopolist who (by assumption) is selling the product sets a constant markup of price over marginal cost (which we assume equals average variable cost). Therefore old consumers are unaffected in welfare terms by the advertising[19] and we may look solely at the position of new consumers.

Consider figure (7.2), which represents a set of newly-informed consumers with group demand D_n, corresponding to which is the marginal revenue curve MR_n. Marginal production costs are c. In advertising to these consumers, the monopolist will gain the monopoly profit labelled 'Π' but will be unable in general to extract the triangular area of inframarginal consumer surplus 'CS' above it. She will advertise in each period, up to the point at which the gain in monopoly profits is equal to the costs of advertising to these consumers. Thus, at the precisely optimal level of advertising, the social gain of the profit area is just cancelled by the resource costs of achieving it. However, there is

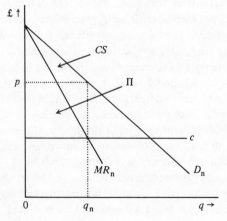

Figure 7.2

an additional social gain accruing to consumers, namely the triangular area already mentioned.[20] Therefore the monopolist, being unable to capture this, is advertising to *less* than a socially optimal extent when maximising profits. Under oligopoly though, we might conjecture, this result need no longer hold since some advertising might simply be counteracting that of rivals. (One might think of supermarkets advertising a few cut-price offers each.)

In general then, advertising has no clear impact on welfare. Advertising does provide information, but that information will normally be biased and consumers, if and when they realise this, may experience regret. Advertisements rarely give the whole truth nor (at least imply) nothing but the truth. The extent to which the information is useful is likely to vary greatly with the product and the consumer. To those who are new to it, advertising increases welfare;[21] to those who are extensively informed already, it is likely not to increase welfare, so being a social cost. To some people, of course, advertising may provide utility either in itself (as a superior alternative to the television programme) or when combined with the good to provide an image of the 'good life' (see Fisher and McGowan, 1979).

Notes on the literature

There are many sources on the basic theory of the effects of advertising. As we have indicated by our copious references, Schmalensee (1972, especially chapters 2 and 7) is one of the best. Lambin (1976, ch. 2) extends the Dorfman–Steiner model of section 1. A rigorous but non-mathematical (and fairly critical) discussion of the relationships in sections 2 and 3 is Ferguson (1974, ch. 2); Simon (1970 especially ch. 9) also reasons the arguments verbally. Butters (1976) provides a short summary of the arguments of section 3. Chapters 5 and 6 in von Weizsäcker's book (1980*b*) provide some useful insights into information and goodwill. Lastly, a recent book by Koutsoyiannis (1982) has a lengthy chapter on advertising including many of the points raised here and, among other things, dealing with the Dorfman–Steiner model and Williamson's model in great detail.

8

Technical change and market structure

In one sense, this chapter is fundamentally different from the others. Whilst they deal with equilibrium, this deals with innovation, which imposes change. Actually, the tools that have already been developed can be used here; we make rather a point of doing this in the next section. The trick is that if the change is subject to regular laws, its rate can be optimised in the same way that the level of another variable may be. Yet, the differences should not be underestimated. All technical change takes place as a result of extended knowledge, and knowledge is by no means an ordinary commodity; it has many of the characteristics of a public good, in that your use of it does not necessarily prevent anyone else's.

This area is also unusual in that it has been overwhelmingly influenced by the writings of one man, and in particular one short chapter 'The Process of Creative Destruction'. In *Capitalism, Socialism and Democracy*, Schumpeter (1943), the man in question, sketched an intriguing version of the new supplanting the old, of capitalism as an evolutionary process. In particular, the point which continually attracts the attention of theorists and empiricists alike is that a system which is efficient by the standards of its day may be inferior in the long run. To be more specific, even if perfect competition held the prize in all other static respects (which is not our claim), it need not do so over time. The entrepreneur invests in a new process or product because of the profit this entails. But if, given what we have said about knowledge, others can speedily copy, the reward for progress will be minimal. His suggestion is that some monopoly, some difficulty in entry, is required to allow entrepreneurs the necessary reward for foresight (and it is fairly clear in Schumpeter's writing that foresight rather than risk-taking is the relevant element here). The key question, which underlies nearly all the theory discussed here, is: how much monopoly?

The section which follows introduces the basic concepts and identifies a number of facets of the innovatory process which require discussion. These are the importance of appropriability in discrete innovations (section 2); the impact of uncertainty (section 3), particularly on firm size; diffusion (section 4) and rivalry (section 5), which involve truly dynamic models, the influences *on* market structure (section 6) and, finally, the optimal life for patent protection (section 7). Some of the most difficult dynamic analyses are treated in a rather cursory manner, but references, as always, are provided at the end.

1. Definitions and models

At the beginning of the chain, there is *basic research*, the seeking of knowledge for its own sake. More commonly, firms engage in *applied research*, research directed towards a specific area. Either one of these leads, in lucky cases, to an *invention*, that is discovery of a specific piece of knowledge, a means of doing or making something. Such an invention may be patented. Then comes *development*, the second and usually more expensive part of 'R & D'. Here there is a specific end in sight, showing that the basic idea is feasible and practical, turning the prototype into something of potential commercial (or social) use. For example, playing with a toy boat in a bath may convince someone he has invented the hydrofoil (it is not claimed that this is what actually happened), but the principle has to be demonstrated on a commercial sized boat.

At this stage, in the case of a product, a new production function has been formulated. In the case of a process, like a new way to obtain gold from its ore, an existing production function has been shifted, the isoquants being relabelled or changing in shape.[1] When commercial application takes place, we have *product or process innovation*. Sometimes a remarkably long time can elapse between invention and innovation, even for currently profitable ventures such as the fluorescent lamp and the float-glass process. This may reflect in part the requirement that relative prices are favourable (for example, energy-saving processes) but also indicates that a very substantial and risky act of entrepreneurship is often required to turn the basic idea into an innovation.

With product innovations, it is usual, though not inevitable, for the innovator to market the new good directly. Other firms may subsequently seek to imitate successful products. *Imitation* is often cheaper than innovation, because many blind alleys followed by the original innovator can be seen as such by imitators observing the initial success. In the case of a process innovation, like a new method of making beer, it is possible that the innovation arises in, say, the chemical industry, but is of use in the brewing industry. The imitative spread of such a process through the final product industry is often called *diffusion* in such cases. Vertical pricing relationships (see chapter 5) are involved. Naturally, many discoveries have aspects both of process and product innovation; new products at one stage may enable new processes downstream.

At the end of the chain then, we have technical change taking place; more services, or a greater variety of them, are available from a given level of inputs.[2] In some cases, the changes may have arisen naturally, in the same way that fitting all the pieces but one into a jigsaw then allows the picture to be completed. Such autonomous innovation cannot be influenced by economic factors, presumably. On the other hand, many innovative acts arise either through the force of technology pushing discoveries which are potentially marketable ('technology-push') or through the call from the market place for something new ('demand-pull'). Here, economic motives are clearly at work; economic policies, the nature of the firm and the structure of the market in which it finds itself are potential influences on the rate of technical change. To be sure, some industries seem (at any point in history) to be more naturally progressive than others, but there will also be factors susceptible to economic analysis. At the same time as economic factors are influencing the rate and direction of innovative activity, this activity is itself changing the economic environment: some firms succeed and others do not, some processes necessitate large plants for successful operation, and so on.

In starting to look at some aspects of all this, let us fix ideas by considering some simple models of the process, devoid of complications.

We start with a very simple model of product innovation by an established firm. We suppose that research improves the product in consumers' eyes by satisfying latent demands more efficiently (for example, by improving the sound quality of a stereo system). Hence more of the product will be demanded at any price, and demand facing the firm is a function of price and research:

$$q = q(p,x); \qquad q_p < 0, q_x > 0 \tag{8.1}$$

The firm's costs are direct production cost (assumed unaffected by research) plus research costs. Hence profit is:

$$\Pi(p,x) = p \cdot q(p,x) - C[q(p,x)] - x \tag{8.2}$$

The astute reader (that almost legendary figure) will have noticed we have effectively rewritten equations (7.1) and (7.2) as (8.1) and (8.2), though replacing A by x. Consequently, results can, with care, be read off by a similar transposition from chapter 7. Thus, the rule for optimal research expenditure allocation is, from (7.7):

$$\frac{x}{R} = \frac{\eta_x}{\eta_p} \tag{8.3}$$

where $\eta_x = (x/q) \cdot (\partial q/\partial x)$, the research (or product improvement) elasticity of demand. There will also in principle be an equivalent of (7.10) applicable to the oligopolistic situation, relating the oligopolist's research to sales ratio to elasticities measuring the effect of own research activities on rivals' research behaviour, the direct effect of research on own demand, the effect of rivals' product improvements on own demand, and the price–cost margin. Furthermore, and perhaps more interesting, we can suggest from (7.13) and table 7.1 that the research to sales ratio may, but need not, have a monotonic relationship with firm numbers: research intensity could either rise or fall with concentration, or may peak at an intermediate level (which is, incidentally, quite a popular view). However all this is predicated on research behaving in much the same way as advertising.

Similar suggestions could be made for process innovation. Of course the model would have to be modified somewhat: one possible specification for the profit function (for a monopolist) would be the following:

$$\Pi = p(q) \cdot q - C(q, x) - x \qquad (8.4)$$

Demand now depends only on price, since research leaves the product unchanged. It does, however, reduce the cost of producing any given output level, that is $\partial C/\partial x < 0$. We shall return to this framework again in section 6. For the moment we merely note two points. First, that although the cost curve is shifted downward rather than the demand curve outward as research proceeds, one might expect the same general kind of considerations as were suggested for the product model to be valid here in determining research intensity. Second, we note a point which warns that direct translation from the previous chapter may be misleading. Suppose that expenditure of an amount x reduces average costs from c to c' and twice the expenditure reduces them by twice as much to c''. The situation is depicted in figure 8.1 (much of the detail of which does not concern us at present). But output is increasing as average costs fall. Consequently, the second increment in research expenditure of x adds more to profit than the first[3] and an equilibrium level of spending would not be reached unless, in contradiction to the above, expenditures on research were subject to quite sharply diminishing returns in cost reduction. The problem arises because of the public good nature of information. Specifically, the same piece of knowledge can, in principle, be

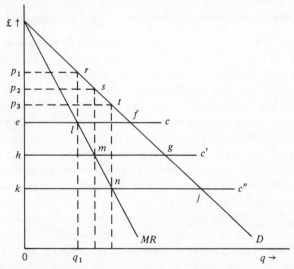

Figure 8.1

applied within the firm at any scale of operation. Further ramifications of this important property of information will be considered later.

Hence, although models such as those described above give some leads, they do not get to grips fully with the problem. For one thing, large amounts of research expenditure do not guarantee marketable results; there is uncertainty involved. Also, those results which are obtained may be of a 'lumpy' nature, that is a little extra research may produce nothing, but a certain amount may allow a discrete improvement. Thus, calculus methods may not always be appropriate. Getting results, in terms of a new product or commissioning a new process, can take an appreciable amount of time, and rivals may not be idle whilst this is going on, so dynamics can have an important role to play. In fact, they are essential in explaining the time difference between invention and innovation. To be sure, all these things could be said to be true of advertising. Really, the difference is a matter of degree, but it is surely right for the questions to be tackled here, whether or not the reader feels they should have been considered earlier. Much of the rest of the chapter is concerned with the implications of the points sketched out above.

There is one further important matter. The two models outlined earlier assume the knowledge gained by research is appropriable only by the firm doing that research. But as we said in the introduction, the publicness of research findings may extend outside the firm, to others who are capable of copying the ideas. Thus, more research by firm A may add to firm B's profits rather than detracting from them, as is generally assumed with advertising. In the next section we discuss models where the question of the appropriability of research is placed in sharp relief.

2. Discrete innovations, market structure and appropriability

Suppose an innovation capable of lowering per-unit production costs by a non-marginal amount (for example from c to c' in figure 8.2) is made. The innovation is best thought of here as a clever idea which took time and money to develop, but then costs virtually nothing to implement. We assume first that there is no control either over use of the innovation or over entry into the industry. Consequently, firms in the industry will reduce price to c' and/or firms will enter until price falls to c'. Since the equilibrium price embodies none of the costs of developing the new technology, then logically no one would have set out to do the development work. Thus, if knowledge is freely appropriable, some monopoly power or similar market imperfection is required to enable technical advance.

One possibility is that barriers to entry determine fixed industry numbers. For example, there may be only two firms, and no possibility of entry. Then, if the cost of innovating is less than the expected benefits to that firm, a firm will invest despite the fact that the other firm will benefit without incurring the costs. The argument is illustrated for a Cournot duopoly in figure 8.3,

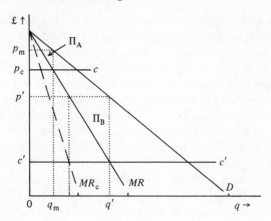

Figure 8.2

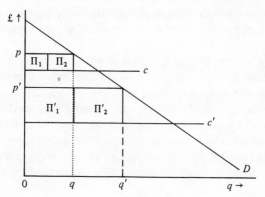

Figure 8.3

where primes denote post-innovation magnitudes. Assuming the way prices are set pre- and post- innovation is the same, the more concentrated the industry, the larger the increase in profit for a given cost reduction and so the larger the incentive to innovate, even assuming others copy.

An alternative is that there is a patents system. The pros and cons of long versus short patents are to be discussed in section 7. For the moment we take the polar opposite to the case above; patents are assumed to grant a perpetual monopoly to the inventor. As an immediate consequence, there is no (direct) competition between the *producer* of the innovation and anyone else; the competitive framework must arise in the using industry. In short, we are looking at the demand for the innovation keeping the supply side fixed.

Arrow (1962), who initiated this line of enquiry, looked into whether there would be more incentive for the inventor were she selling to a monopolistic or a competitive industry. In his conceptual experiment, both industries have the same demand curve and the same level of unit costs (so the competitive industry's supply curve is level with the monopolist's marginal cost curve) before innovation. Thus (see again figure 8.2) preinvention prices of p_m and p_c, under monopoly and competition respectively, are charged. The inventor has sole rights to a process which will lower unit costs to c' and wishes to take full advantage of this to extract the maximum return for her effort. In a competitive industry the inventor, realising the demand curve for the final product is downward sloping, would charge a per-unit output royalty $(p' - c')$ to maximise her return, that is she will act as a monopolist. She earns profit area Π_B per period.

Arrow's inventor uses a different tack when facing the monopolist, in order to circumvent a potential bilateral monopoly problem (see chapter 5). Setting a per-unit royalty would cut output sharply once the final product monopolist had also taken his margin. It is therefore best for inventor and monopolist to maximise joint profits and bargain over their share. This again gives a final post innovation price p' and total profits Π_B. The most the inventor can command is a lump-sum of $\Pi_B - \Pi_A$ per period; more than this will mean the monopolist would be worse off after having made the innovation.[4]

Thus in Arrow's scheme there is a greater incentive to invent for a competitive industry than a monopoly. This comparison may be extended to competition versus oligopoly by noting that the established firms in an oligopoly have pre-existing profits which again reduce the maximum the inventor can claim below the competitive level. We would therefore expect that more resources would be devoted by inventive people towards cost-reducing innovations aimed at competitive industries, and consequently, competition as a form of market organisation is certainly no bar to technical progress.

The conclusion may also be extended to the case of a *non-drastic* innovation. A non-drastic innovation is one where the cost reduction on innovation is not substantial enough for a monopoly margin added to post-innovation costs to result in a price below p_c. This case is illustrated in figure 8.4. Thus under competition, the most the inventor can earn is a per-unit royalty $(p_c - c')$ over an output q_c; more than this and the existing firms will not innovate. However earnings under monopoly organisation of the final market are again $\Pi_B - \Pi_A$, for $p'_m < p_m$ since $c' < c$. While it may not seem clear from the figure, Arrow demonstrates that the royalty earned from the competitive industry (and so the incentive) is greater than from the monopolist. To sketch the demonstration, note that $\Pi_A > (p'_m - c) \cdot q'_m$ or else the monopolist would have charged p'_m rather than p_m, pre-invention. Thus $\Pi_B - \Pi_A < (p_c - c') \cdot q'_m < (p_c - c') \cdot q_c$.

Demsetz (1969) points out that in Arrow's analysis, the monopolist starts off with substantially smaller output than the competitive industry. If we were instead to make the comparison between industries with the same

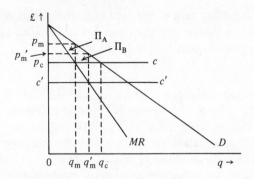

Figure 8.4

pre-innovation output, the results would change somewhat. We can do this in figure 8.2 by making MR the demand curve facing the competitive industry and adding MR_c, the associated marginal revenue curve. Then, at least for linear demand curves, Demsetz is able to show that the value $\Pi_B - \Pi_A$ is greater than the reward the inventor obtains from the competitive industry. Thus he does not accept Arrow's conclusion.[5]

There have been several contributions concerning demand conditions.[6] Rather than going into these ramifications, we prefer to point out that one particular definition of pre-invention industry 'sameness' may be more relevant for one situation, another for another. For example, when assessing a horizontal merger one criterion might be whether, as a consequence, there will be less technical progress. In this case, to the extent to which the debate is relevant, Arrow's definition of sameness applies, since the industry demand curve remains unchanged.

It is also relevant to enquire whether cost conditions are likely to be the same. Waterson (1982a) points out that technical change may be associated with a particular factor of production being introduced, a new machine or a new general facility like the microprocessor. In that case, the owner of the new process may have to recoup his reward through selling the input which is involved. This is much more likely to be the case when the innovation-using industry is competitive in structure, because there the large number of outputs are difficult to monitor and individual bargains are more awkward to make than under monopoly. The problem with an input royalty is that the user will attempt to economise on the input, so creating a distortion in costs (of the same general type as that featured in the vertical integration situation of figure 5.3). Thus, given otherwise Arrovian conditions, the incentive under competition will not always dominate that under monopoly, particularly, it turns out, when the input is relatively unimportant.

In conclusion, the lesson of these results is that, whilst some element of monopoly is required for process innovation to occur, the precise form and amount of the monopolistic influence required varies a great deal with the other conditions in the market such as the ease with which rivals can copy new technology. Also we should say that from society's point of view, the fact that a certain combination of conditions leads to a greater incentive to innovate than another set does not necessarily mean the former is preferable.

Turning now to product innovations, let us consider the case where the new product is simply a more durable version of the old, for example a razor blade lasting twice as long. In section 6.1, we found that under certain cost conditions (represented in equation (6.3)), a monopoly industry and a competitive industry will make products of equal durability. As a corollary, there will be no incentive for a monopolist to delay innovation of such a more durable good beyond the time when a competitive industry would innovate, if the technology is freely known. Whether there will be *any* incentive for innovation or for inventive effort in this direction depends upon whether an equivalent amount of services can be produced more cheaply. If an innovation enables the marginal cost of services curve to be lowered and the inventor can capture rents, we are back in the Arrovian world; the inventor has more incentive to produce an innovation for a competitive industry.

More generally, the new product may be an imperfect substitute for an old one. For example, the invention might be an electric shaver, imperfectly substituting for the razor blade, with total demand for shaving equipment being increased.[7]

Consider the incentive to innovate, assuming knowledge sufficient to produce shavers is already available. It might be thought that a razor blade monopolist, with existing profits at stake, might be less likely to introduce shavers than a competitive razor blade industry. However Swan (1970) shows that if the cross-partial derivatives of the demand function are equal ($\partial p_i/\partial q_j = \partial p_j/\partial q_i$), if demand functions are homogeneous in outputs, and if constant returns to scale obtain in production of both goods – not unreasonably restrictive assumptions – the monopolist will be as ready to expand into the shaver market as the competitive industry. The reason, as White (1972) points out, is that monopoly restriction of output in the first market increases demand in the second beyond the level a competitive industry would experience, giving the monopolist a bigger incentive. However any production in the second market reduces profits in the first, thereby lowering the incentive. Because the cross-partials are equal, these effects happen to cancel each other out and monopolists will innovate into the same industries (though not produce the same output levels) as would existing competitive firms.

There is an interesting extension to this. While monopolists who stumble across possible substitute products may not find it profitable to innovate them, they will be very keen on patenting their discoveries in order to prevent others from innovating and so eroding existing monopoly profits. In other words, unused or 'sleeping' patents can be valuable in building up, or protecting, barriers to entry (see Gilbert and Newbery, 1982, for an analysis).

3. The impact of uncertainty

Uncertainty (or risk) can be introduced either as general market uncertainty (but as such it causes no problems peculiar to technical progress), specific uncertainty about the plans of rivals (which is discussed later in the chapter), or technical uncertainty. This last merits some consideration immediately.

Knowledge cannot be produced to order as easily as most things. If you employ someone to build you a garage, it is easy to specify fairly precisely what is required, to solicit estimates, to choose among them and to verify the final outcome. If, on the other hand, you employ someone to design you a fundamentally new product or process, there is much less to go on in comparing specifications. Even if the final outcome seems disappointing compared to the resources involved, it would be difficult to argue that the research team employed was lazy and worthless. Of course other aspects of business decision-making (e.g. choosing an advertising agency) involve this problem to a degree. However there are implications deriving from the fact that aspects of research necessarily involve a tenuous relationship between input and output.

One of the commonly-noted points is that small organisations may find research too risky an activity. The risk is that the project will go wrong and the firm will collapse. A firm with several projects is able to spread risk, but a small firm is unable to obtain fair insurance because of the 'moral hazard' problem that insurance may itself reduce effort. Also, internal sources of funds will normally be required, because the salvage value of an unsuccessful project will usually be too low to attract debt finance and the need for confidentiality will make equity finance difficult. This militates against those with slender resources (see, e.g. Galbraith, 1952). A rather different point is that since research can uncover unexpected outcomes, diversified firms (those with expertise in several fields) may be able most easily to make use of the results of their research.

These arguments generally suggest that larger organisations are more likely to engage in research programmes than small ones, and may well be more productive. Against this, large formal R&D divisions may be difficult to monitor for the same reason as identified earlier: have they worked hard and been relatively unlucky, or are they inefficient?

Exploring the influence of risk a bit more widely, we can enquire how much is socially acceptable. Suppose there are two research strategies on product innovation. Both would cost the same amount to pursue. One is known to reduce costs from c to c' per unit, the other has a fifty per cent chance of reducing costs by twice as much, from c to c'', with a fifty per cent chance of being useless. A risk neutral society would prefer the risky strategy, as can be seen by returning to figure 8.1. Assuming prices equal to marginal cost, society's expected benefit from the second option is (half area *efjk*) which is bigger than the certain benefit of *efgh* in the other case, simply because output expands as price falls.

It is also true that a firm seeking to maximise expected profits would prefer the riskier of the two projects. Increase in profit may be represented as increase in total revenue (increase in area under the marginal revenue curve) minus increase in cost, when unit cost falls from c to $\bar{c}$, say. Symbolically, writing profit-maximising output as a function of cost, $q^* = q^*(\bar{c})$, then:

$$\Delta\Pi \equiv \Delta R - \Delta C = \int_{q^*(c)}^{q^*(\bar{c})} (MR - c) \cdot dq$$

Translating this into areas in figure 8.1, the expected value (half) of area *elnk* is greater than the certain value *elmh*. However, the firm does not capture all the benefits of its actions; the expected value of the increase in consumer surplus is greater in the risky case (half $p_1 r t p_3$) than the risk-free ($p_1 r s p_2$).[8] Hence, a risk neutral firm will indulge in risky projects to an extent that is less than optimal for a risk neutral society. The point is made in more detail in Dasgupta and Stiglitz (1980*a*).

4. Diffusion processes

In this and the following sections, time is introduced into the analysis rather more explicitly, so relieving models of the false dichotomy between inventions which are instantaneously innovated and those which are not innovated at all. Innovations can, and generally do, diffuse gradually through the industry (or indeed the economy); innovations can be imitated or be subject to rivalry from similar innovations. In this section we cover the relatively straightforward approach of diffusion models and in the next we deal with the more heterogeneous analyses of rivalry. Both have limitations, which we mention in section 6.

It is generally held that innovations diffuse through industries roughly according to a sigmoid or s-shaped curve as exemplified in figure 8.5. This is

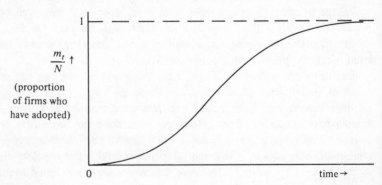

Figure 8.5

necessarily an over-simplification; some innovations (e.g. diesel traction on the railways) never diffuse completely. However it is, at the most basic level, what diffusion theory seeks to explain. At the second stage, one is interested in the determinants of the parameters describing the path. Partly because we are essentially talking here about an industry of similar firms adopting a similar (process) innovation produced exogenously to the industry, much of the focus has been on the structure of the demand (innovation-using) side. Let us look at some suggested processes.

Mansfield's work (at least on inter-industry diffusion) is based upon a model of epidemics. The central assumption is that, within a short time span, the proportion of non-adopters deciding to adopt a given process (the proportion of people catching the disease) is proportional to the proportion of firms already using it (proportion of people with the disease). Possible reasons for the hypothesis suggested by Mansfield (1968) for the diffusion context are, (i) that as more experience and information accumulate regarding the use of the new process, risk of adopting is reduced, competitive pressures mount, and so more adopt, (ii) that even if profitability is difficult to estimate, the observation that a large proportion have adopted will prompt favourable consideration.

If the total number of relevant firms is N, and the number who have adopted by time t is m_t, the proportion of those who have not so far adopted (called here non-adopters for brevity) adopting in the interval to $t + 1$ is $(m_{t+1} - m_t)/(N - m_t)$. Rewriting this in continuous time, the hypothesis may be expressed as:

$$\frac{\mathrm{d}m_t}{\mathrm{d}t} \cdot \frac{1}{N - m_t} = \frac{\beta m_t}{N} \tag{8.5}$$

with β being the constant of proportionality. Notice we can rearrange (8.5) to read[9]

$$\frac{\mathrm{d}\ln\left[m_t/(N - m_t)\right]}{\mathrm{d}t} \equiv \frac{N - m_t}{m_t} \cdot \mathrm{d}\,\frac{\left[m_t/(N - m_t)\right]}{\mathrm{d}t} = \beta \tag{8.6}$$

Hence, by integrating:

$$\ln\left(\frac{m_t}{N - m_t}\right) = \alpha + \beta t \tag{8.7}$$

where α is the constant of integration. Finally, taking the exponential of both sides of (8.7) and rearranging we have:

$$\frac{m_t}{N} = \left[1 + \exp\left(-\alpha - \beta t\right)\right]^{-1} \tag{8.8}$$

which is the equation of a *logistic curve*, an example of the s shape. The parameter β displaces the curve to make it more or less elongated and is known as the 'speed' of the diffusion process.

Mansfield suggests a second stage to the analysis. Once equation (8.8) has been estimated for a group of industries over time, the estimated values for β can be related across industries to such economic features characterising them as profitability, firm size, concentration and so on. However this is rather *ad hoc* and the basic mechanism lacks much in the way of economic content, so it is worthwhile looking at alternative routes to the same result.

Salter (1960) developed a model based upon cost minimisation and perfect knowledge. A diffusion path emerges because firms happen to have different vintages of capital equipment, later vintages being more efficient. The basic idea is that firms operating old plant have sunk resources in such plant which cannot be recovered.[10] If so, then it is only the operating, or variable, costs of such plant which are of importance. However, in deciding to introduce new plant, total costs become relevant.

Thus, when a process is innovated, only those plants for which the unit operating cost is greater than the unit total cost of the new technology will immediately be replaced; if a firm has a number of vintages of plant, some may be scrapped and some retained. Later on, as the new technology becomes cheaper, still further improved, or as factor prices move favourably, more plant will be replaced until eventually the innovation diffuses throughout the industry. The upshot is that there will be a diffusion path, or curve, the shape of which will depend upon factors such as the age distribution of equipment, the time paths of the price of the innovation and wages relative to the price of the product.

More recently, Reinganum (1981) has developed a model in which, in contradistinction to the above, the firms have identical capital. Early innovation carries penalties as well as benefits compared to procrastination: the benefit is that profit increases most for those who adopt earliest (and this is one feature which makes her model more sophisticated in one respect than those which follow) but the costs of adjustment involved in quick adoption are higher. After placing sensible restrictions upon the way these functions change over time, Reinganum finds that, despite the firms being identical, the Cournot–Nash solution involves the firms innovating in sequence such that a diffusion process occurs. The effect of market structure (firm numbers) on the timing of the diffusion process is shown to entail a complex amalgam of forces; it is not possible to say whether large number industries are speedier or slower at diffusion than small number ones. The only real problem with her model is whether the rather neoclassical assumptions involved may be too far from the truth to allow sensible predictions. For this reason it is useful to look at similar ideas placed within a more behavioural context.

One useful way of doing this is through what is called a *probit model*, as used by David (1969) and Davies (1979b). Here we assume an index, say z_i, can be devised for which, the higher the value, the more likely is an individual to adopt the innovation. In the probit model if the individual's index exceeds a critical value, say $\bar{z}_i$, the innovation will be adopted. To be operational, this index must be related to various characteristics of the adopter and/or the innovation.

More specifically, assume the index z_i is firm size, and that at a critical firm size the innovation is adopted. Possibly, the innovation allows lower variable costs (say, reduced labour costs) at the expense of a high sunk capital cost incurred on innovation. The larger the firm, the more likely is the excess of revenue over total variable cost to exceed fixed cost,[11] so making innovation profitable. Supposing, as time progresses, that real wages rise or that the real price of the equipment falls, then progressively smaller firms will become of critical size (assuming this is equivalent or, at least, related in some way, to the size at which innovation becomes profitable) and will adopt. In order to close the model it only remains to specify the way in which firms are distributed and the way in which prices change.

To take a specific example, based on Stoneman and Ireland (1983), assume the capital lasts for ever and that only one unit need be purchased to adopt the innovation. The initial demand curve relating the price of the capital good relative to variable costs, r/w, to the number of units, so to the number of firms in the industry, y, who will adopt at that price, will slope downwards. Its shape will depend upon the distribution of firm sizes, $f(s_i)$. In particular, only those firms at or above critical size will adopt, critical size changing as prices change. Thus what is relevant is the *cumulative* distribution of firms above size $\bar{s}$, or $F(\bar{s})$. Given their assumption that firm sizes are distributed according to the *log-logistic* (very generally, a skewed bell-shaped distribution), the cumulative distribution will imply a demand curve along the lines of that drawn in figure 8.6. As times goes on, and by assumption r/w

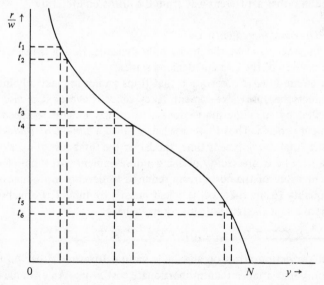

Figure 8.6

falls steadily, then at first relatively few firms adopt, then many, and finally few. This is exemplified by comparing the numbers adopting between time periods t_1 and t_2, t_3 and t_4, and t_5 and t_6, respectively, in the figure. Consequently, a sigmoid diffusion curve along the lines of fig. 8.5 results.

Actually, as Stoneman and Ireland (and others) have pointed out, such models treat the supply side of the market in a very cavalier way. Presumably the firms in the capital equipment business are doing it to make money. Suppose there is a monopoly seller. He will want to solve the intertemporal maximisation problem involved by an optimal pricing policy. Given that there may be intertemporal influences in the cost function (these are discussed in the next section) he is unlikely to set a constant or regularly falling price for the capital good. Moreover, oligopolistic interaction would make the problem more complex still. In the models we are about to discuss, these factors are treated in rather more detail, though the complications of having two vertically related markets are dropped.

5. Imitation and rivalry

Diffusion models analyse the spread amongst potential users of a specific innovation, often coming from an outside source. Another very common route to technical change is where firms in the user industry develop roughly similar projects, perhaps copying one another. This second route is more typical of product innovation than process innovation, and is often associated with rivalry amongst small numbers of firms. Timing can become of crucial importance in securing a market. For all these reasons, the literature has developed in rather a different way from the diffusion literature.

The basic ingredients

In order to make the model fully dynamic, timing is made to influence one or both of the cost and demand stages.

It is a commonsense observation that firms cannot immediately introduce new products because development takes time. However it is also widely believed that by spending more money, firms may be able to speed up the development process. Thus there is what is called a *time–cost trade-off*: the shorter the total development time, the larger the total cost of development. This idea may be expressed by defining a development cost function $C(T)$ as the present value of the cost stream required to develop a product of given *ex ante* quality (using the most efficient means) by time T. Formalising our assumptions about the trade-off function, we have:

$$C = C(T) > 0; \qquad C(0) \to \infty, \quad C' < 0, \quad C'' < 0. \qquad (8.9)$$

The final restriction arises because it is natural to assume that postponing innovation yields a more than proportionate cost saving. An example of such a function satisfying (8.9) is drawn in figure 8.7.

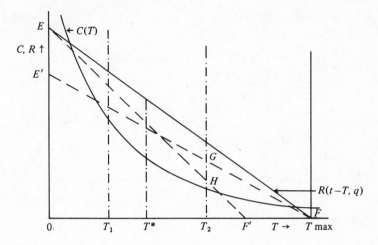

Figure 8.7

We have also plotted a net revenue function, R, as line EF, making the simplifying assumptions that the discount rate is zero, that however long or short the development time the eventual excess of current revenues over *production* costs is the same, and that the innovation immediately comes onstream once developed. (The last assumption is easily relaxed). Hence net revenues depend upon the output level q and the amount of time over which they are received $(t - T)$. We have taken it that once a certain period of time has elapsed, the project is eclipsed by others. The firm's problem is then simply to choose the development time T^* which maximises the difference between rewards and costs.

Of course, rivalry has not so far entered the picture. Nevertheless it is easy to show within this very simple construction that increased rivalry is likely to have conflicting influences on the firm's optimal development time (so, eventually, on the speed of technical change). One impact of increased rivalry will be to reduce the time interval before the product is eclipsed by a superior one, swinging the net revenue function round, say to EF'. More generally, increased rivalry is likely to increase uncertainty regarding future receipts, so reducing their expected values, with the same result. The other influence is that the firm's output share is likely to be lower in the presence of similar projects by rivals, causing a move to a line like $E'F$. Whilst this would tend to increase T^*, the other factor would likely reduce it.

In order to gain a greater appreciation of the possibilities involved, it is therefore necessary to specify the benefit function more fully. To see this, consider the decision tree for firm A, depicted in figure 8.8. Suppose both this firm (A) and its rival (B) are earning an amount of net revenue Π_e per period on existing goods. Then, if firm A innovates, so increasing (or at least not reducing) returns to Π_{11} say, one possibility is for these earnings

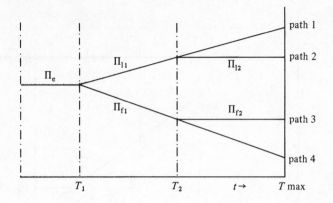

Figure 8.8

to persist to the end of our time horizon. Alternatively, the rival could imitate, from which time Π_{12} is earned. Another scenario is that B innovates first, whence A earns Π_{f1}, picking up to Π_{f2} (which may or may not be less than Π_{12}) if and when A imitates. Imitation may involve lower development costs than innovation though.

Now each branch of this decision tree (fig. 8.8) could be represented as a nonlinear revenue function on fig. 8.7. For example, path 2 might give $EGHF'$. However since it is not known *a priori* which path will eventuate, it is normal to apply probabilities to the various cases, specifically to assess the rival's behaviour by means of a conditional probability density function. *Expected* net revenues from innovation at various times (yielding a probabilistic version of R) may then be compared with costs to derive an optimal T, T^*.

This procedure has been adopted by Kamien and Schwartz in a series of papers (see their 1982 book for references; also see Fethke and Birch, 1982). Much of the interest in Kamien and Schwartz' models lies in how rivalry affects the optimal development period T^*. They find that the shortest development period may either occur when there is no rivalry at all, or (particularly when the project is an important one) when there is an inter-mediate intensity of rivalry.[12] The intuitive explanation they give for this is as follows: If, from a situation free of rivalry, the threat of rivalry increases, there is a probability of later profits being pre-empted. This will encourage the firm to go for a shorter development time. However as rivalry increases still further, pre-emption becomes very likely, the prospect of winning the race recedes, and the cost of shortening development time rises ever faster, so the firm may well come to the point of deciding to cut its losses and go for a longer development period. Thus, to the extent to which we can iden-tify rivalry with market structure, Kamien and Schwartz' results suggest that an intermediate structure between monopoly and competition may be most stimulating for innovative activity.

Actually in one respect, models of this type have taken a retrograde step from those discussed in section 3. Although uncertainty has been allowed in the revenue function, it has been dropped from the cost side. Indeed this can lead to peculiar conclusions for the reason which follows.

The obvious extension to Kamien and Schwartz' work is to allow for interactive effects between rivals. Their firm knows about its rivals in general terms, but does not believe it influences them. However, a recurrent theme of ours has been the recognition of interdependence between firms. Presumably this should hold also for R&D decisions, so that the firm should be viewed as one amongst a group of (say Cournot) firms in this respect. But in that case, in a symmetric model, each would behave in the same way; each would innovate at exactly the same time, so the rewards for innovating would be low, especially perhaps compared with the rewards for being first. Consequently, each firm could potentially increase profits by spending more to innovate earlier, assuming others act differently. If they all act like this though, each is likely to make losses, so none, realising the symmetry, would want to innovate. Essentially we are looking here at (what can be) a Bertrand-Nash situation, with no true equilibrium.[13]

For this reason, it is usual for modellers to reintroduce technical uncertainty into the development cost (time–cost trade-off) function at the same time as they allow game-theoretic types of interactions between firms, so increasing complexity greatly. Examples of models with this type of framework are Loury (1979) and Dasgupta and Stiglitz (1980b). We do not propose to discuss these models here.

6. Endogeneity of market structure

There is one criticism which may be applied to nearly all models of rivalrous product development such as those in the previous two sections. They feature processes which would result in early adopters doing better than others. Consequently, after the innovatory phase the model describes, industry structure would have changed. Thus, from a longer-term viewpoint, as with advertising, industry structure not only influences, but also is influenced by, the research process. The determinants of market structure are covered more fully in the chapter following this, but it is useful to consider briefly two links from research activity to market structure, albeit within the very simplest of frameworks.

Let us first follow Dasgupta and Stiglitz (1980a) in exploring the link between research activity and concentration. If we take a simple model of process innovation as discussed in section 1 (see equation 8.4) but embed the firm within an industry of like-minded firms, we have a typical profit function for firm i as:

$$\Pi_i = p(Q) \cdot q_i - q_i \cdot c(x_i) - x_i \qquad (8.10)$$

In order to simplify presentation here, we have assumed a separable cost function, so $c(x_i)$ is marginal (and average variable) cost of production, influenced negatively by increases in research spending. Assuming Cournot conjectures on output, the first-order condition for maximisation with respect to output[14] is:

$$\frac{\partial \Pi_i}{\partial q_i} = p + q_i \frac{dp}{dQ} - c(x_i) = 0$$

Rearranging in the manner familiar from chapter 2, we have:

$$[p - c(x_i)]/p = 1/N\eta \qquad (8.11)$$

Now, if we make the assumption of completely free entry usual in monopolistic competition models, we also have the zero profit condition:

$$[p - c(x_i)] \cdot q_i = x_i \qquad (8.12)$$

each firm's price-average variable cost margin is just sufficient to cover the costs of research. In a symmetric free-entry equilibrium, with (8.11) and (8.12) true for each firm (and firm sizes equal, so $Nq_i = Q$), we have by simple substitution:

$$\frac{Nx_i}{pQ} = \frac{1}{N\eta} \qquad (8.13)$$

This says that the industry research/sales ratio will be inversely proportional to the number of firms in the industry, that is directly proportional to industry concentration since all firms are of equal size. But it also says that there is a simultaneous relationship between research intensity and concentration, not a causal flow from one to the other.

Of course this model is extremely simple. The burden of models discussed in the previous section is that rivalry is unlikely to lead to equality in firm sizes, except perhaps over a very long period. Instead, uncertainty leads to some firms being 'lucky' and growing as a result, others being unlucky. This may be because particular firms establish particular policies or rules of thumb that happen to work in a given environment. For such reasons, Nelson and Winter have suggested in a series of papers (1977, 1978 and 1982) that the interaction between market structure and innovation should be studied as an evolutionary process, and that this is the true Schumpeterian message. Such processes as they adopt, being to some extent *ad hoc*, are most easily studied using simulation techniques. Hence, the conclusions can only be indicative, and we cannot do justice to their nuances here.

We turn now to a rather different influence on structure arising through rivalry with outsiders. Innovation can be the tool with which entry barriers are created, by putting potential entrants at a cost disadvantage. If so, the presence of potential entrants might itself distort the direction in which

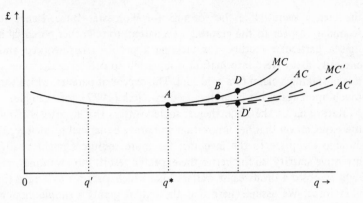

Figure 8.9

research efforts are oriented. Levin (1978) has made some explorations into this topic. His firms wish to allocate research effort as far as possible in the direction of maximising the rate of reduction of unit cost. His basic conclusion is that the higher are the quasi-rents earned by established firms, the more research effort will be biased towards *scale-augmenting* technical change. The intuitive reason for this is revealed by considering figure 8.9. If a typical firm in the industry is operating between q' and q^* on its cost curve earning zero quasi-rents, it will be interested only in innovations shifting the cost curves downwards. However, if operations are at a point such as B or D where quasi-rents are earned (due to entry barriers), the firm would be interested both in downward-shifting and scale-augmenting innovations, since both reduce production costs. If working at D, moving optimal scale out from A to D' will be particularly attractive to established firms.[15]

7. The economics of patents

It is not straightforward to calculate the economically optimal rate of technological change.[16] However, there is one rather narrower question where fairly straightforward trade-offs can in principle be identified, and that is the optimal life for patents. Here we shall look only at simple cases; others can be dealt with using the same basic framework, though more complex analytical tools.

The main reason why patents are offered is fairly obvious, and has to do with the basic features of knowledge we have already covered. It would almost certainly be cheaper to photocopy this book than to buy it, and it would similarly be cheaper to take a Xerox machine to pieces and copy its construction than to discover how to make it from scratch. The author and the inventor are offered the temporary monopoly protection of copyright and patent to assist them in the costly process of developing their basic ideas to fruition.

Actually, in the inventor's case, it might be possible and profitable to keep the idea a secret, like the formula for Worcester sauce. Hence there is a secondary aspect to the granting of a patent, to tell other potential inventors that a particular method for tackling a problem has worked and is now circumscribed. Here information is imparted to others in the same way that it is in staking a claim to a gold find. This aspect of patents, which we will not touch upon again, has been discussed by Kitch (1977), for example.

Returning to the main theme, society offers the inventor a monopoly in the expectation that her innovation will prove beneficial to society. The more durable the prize to the inventor, the more resources might be diverted to inventive activity, so the better the expected result. But awarding a monopoly right imposes a deadweight welfare loss, which lasts for as long as the patent is in force. We assume here that the patent grants a simple monopoly and has no further implications, and we abstract from questions of uncertainty.

To investigate the trade-off outlined above in a little more detail, let us consider first the case of a nondrastic invention, as depicted in figure 8.10. Expenditures on research (X) culminate over a period into a reduction in the firm's unit costs from c to c' so, we assume, producing benefits according to a function $B(X)$, with $B' > 0$, $B'' < 0$. The reduction in costs is insufficient for the monopoly price to be below c in this case, so the benefit is merely the shaded area of cost difference multiplied by existing output. (Therefore the restriction on $B(X)$, which merely imposes diminishing returns to inventive input, seems sensible). Consumers benefit after the patent expires to an extent $A(X)$, as illustrated.

Formalising the problem, the firm wishes to invest in research up to a point at which net benefits are maximised. Thus, the firm chooses X in:

$$\max_{X} V = \int_{0}^{T} B(X) \cdot e^{-\rho t} \cdot dt - X \qquad (8.14)$$

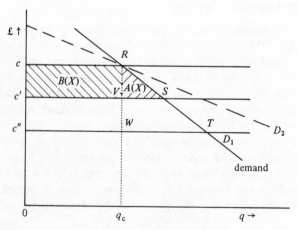

Figure 8.10

where T is the length of the patent and ρ the continuous rate of discount. The interpretation of X, more strictly, should be the present value of a series of research expenditures undertaken which will yield benefits $B(X)$ from the date the patent is filed ($t = 0$). It is not difficult to accept that increases in T will increase X and so $B(X)$.

As far as society is concerned, it wishes to maximise welfare:

$$W = \int_0^\infty B(X)\, e^{-\rho t} \cdot \mathrm{d}t - X$$

$$+ \int_T^\infty A(X)\, e^{-\rho t} \cdot \mathrm{d}t$$

(8.15)

which is the sum of the direct benefits (to consumers after T, to firms up until then) and the indirect benefits to consumers after T, minus the research costs. The firm's maximisation (8.14) defines a relationship between T and X, and society wants to find the optimal patent life T^* by maximising W with respect to T, subject to that.

In order to get much further, it is necessary to make some connection between $A(X)$ and $B(X)$. Nordhaus (1969), who first formalised this problem, assumed a linear demand curve with an arc elasticity of demand η over the range RS in fig. 8.10. The solution for optimal patent life may then be written, after some manipulation:

$$T^* = \frac{1}{\rho} \{\ln\, [1 + \eta B(1 + k)] - \ln\, (\eta B k)\}$$

(8.16)

where k relates to the curvature of the $B(X)$ function, specifically $k = -B'' \cdot B/2(B')^2 > 0$.

To summarise, it is possible to show that there is a general trade-off between promotion of progress and deferred societal benefits which justifies the award of monopoly rights for a specified period. At this stage, it is open to the investigator to select suitable values for the parameters and so to suggest a possible compromise patent length.

Notice also though, that the optimal length of patent varies from industry to industry, because the parameters will differ in the cross-section. Thus as demand becomes more elastic, it may be straightforwardly shown from (8.16) that T^* falls. This has a very sensible intuitive interpretation. In figure 8.10, with demand curve D_2 rather than D_1, the deadweight loss area is larger relative to the benefits. The larger proportionately the loss is, the quicker it should be eradicated *ceteris paribus*, so leading to a shorter optimal life. It can also be shown that the easier is the invention, measured in terms of benefit from given expenditure, the shorter is the optimal life. Consider expenditure X reducing costs from c to c'' rather than c to c'. Benefits double but deadweight loss more than doubles (to RTW from RSV) so we should not

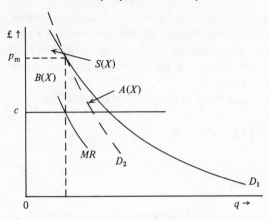

Figure 8.11

wait as long for it. Lastly and most importantly, if the benefits are fixed and do not depend upon the amount of research put in, optimal patent life is zero: if the inventor's input is not affected by length of patent then society should have the benefits immediately.

Of course we have so far been dealing only with a very simple and rather specialised case. Let us look briefly at two extensions. First, assume the invention is drastic and assume it is a product introduced onto the market for the first time. We now have to consider also the consumer surplus $S(X)$ which is gained immediately. Figure 8.11 shows the basic idea, with demand curve D_1 being the latent demand for the product, which becomes realised when costs fall from infinity to c. As we may recall from chapter 1, there is a bias against products with inelastic demands, in that setting a simple monopoly price only captures a relatively small proportion of the benefits. For this reason also we might wish goods in inelastic demand to be subsidised relative to others by having a longer optimal patent life.

As a second possible suggestion, we should note, with Berkowitz and Kotowitz (1982), that implicit in equation (8.14) is the notion that the inventor is a monopolist. An alternative view is of a group of inventors each trying for different outcomes and different patents. The returns to research will then become only normal, in the sense that discounted benefits will be equated with costs, so the maximum value of the functional V will be zero. The upshot is that an alternative constraint has to be fed into (8.15). On parameterising the solution, they find this alternative model calls for much shorter patent lives than were suggested by the analysis of Nordhaus.

Notes on the literature

An early paper which makes many thoughtful comments on the determination of optimal resource allocation for technical change is Arrow (1962). Two very useful recent works on the areas covered in this chapter are Dasgupta and Stiglitz (1980*a*) and Kamien and Schwartz (1982). The former is particularly useful on the impact of the nature of information as a good which makes technical change require special analysis. Kamien and Schwartz provide an excellent survey of almost all aspects of the innovatory process. So much so indeed, that in sections 5 and 6 we have deliberately curtailed analysis of some more complex studies since we have nothing to add. One area which they do strangely neglect is studies of the diffusion process. Luckily Davies (1979*b*, ch. 2) provides a very readable survey before proceeding in later chapters to develop his own model. On patents, Scherer (1972) develops a graphical analysis of Nordhaus' model whilst Usher (1964) comments on the various implications for product innovation.

9

The determinants of market structure

The paradigm with which we started this book focused upon elements of the structure of industries being comparatively stable and looked at the influences of these on performance. As we have proceeded though, we have had to modify this undirectional viewpoint. For example in chapter 5 we analysed motives for vertical integration, the extent of which might be thought to be a structural feature of an industry. In chapter 7, we looked at influences on, as well as of, advertising. Here, we examine two key and inter-linked structural features of industries, the determinants of industry concentration and the causes of changes in market structure.[1]

In the first section, we look at measures of concentration as indices of market power. We found in chapters 2 and 3 that, when all firms in an industry are the same, the number of firms is normally a key influence on the performance of that industry (e.g. as expressed in its price–cost margin). In addition, when, for some reason like differing cost levels, firms are unequally sized in a given way, the extent of that inequality will also affect performance. Thus it is useful to have a summary measure of the established industry structure; a measure of industry concentration.[2]

Once one has a measure of concentration and can compare levels across industries, it is interesting to analyse why it varies. One can either look at the determinants of concentration from the point of view of the fundamental forces involved – scale economies, stochastic influences and so on, as in section 2, or through the mechanisms by which such forces are resolved – entry, exit, internal growth and external growth (mergers). These latter factors are discussed in section 3 where we move to the dynamics of market structures.

Finally, the analysis of this chapter provides a perspective from which we can take another look at the implications of market structure for societal welfare, something which is done in the final section.

1. Measurement of industry concentration

The purpose of a measure of industrial concentration is to provide a summary statistic reflecting the distribution of firms in an industry, indexing one element of that industry's 'market power'. It is generally agreed this should

166

be a one-dimensional measure, incorporating the two relevant aspects of industry structure, namely firm numbers (N) and size inequalities (I). Thus, we can represent a candidate index of concentration, C, as:

$$C = f(N, I); \qquad f_N < 0, f_I > 0 \qquad (9.1)$$

for it is natural to assume, on the basis of almost any theory of oligopoly (see chapter 2) that the smaller the number of firms and the more unequally sized they are, the more market power they can exert as a group. This means that when one industry is talked about as more concentrated than another, there is some content to the statement.

On the basis of equation (9.1) then, for any particular index we could, in principle, construct a series of 'iso-concentration' curves, as Davies has called them, higher curves representing more concentrated industries. A representative family of curves is drawn in figure 9.1 (after Davies, 1979*a*).

Although the discussion has not proceeded very far, we have already glossed over several points, principally regarding inequality. The measurability of an index is not assured unless we have a measure of firm numbers (where there may be problems in defining the industry boundaries). In addition, and more importantly, there is no naturally appropriate way to measure size inequalities, nor a formula for combining these with firm numbers.

Given the need to measure inequality, we require a convention for measuring size. Candidate units are money sales, money assets, numbers in employment, and so on. None of them are ideal for every purpose: money values are obviously affected by price movements, input measures are affected by changing factor proportions and intensities of use of the stock. The choice is therefore governed by the purpose in hand (for example, whether we wish to compare indices cross-sectionally or over time) and by data availability.

Any measure of inequality will presumably be based upon the relative shares (given our chosen size measure), $s_i = q_i/Q$, of the firms.[3] Of course, if all the firms were the same size, $s_i = 1/N$ for all i. In general there will be an

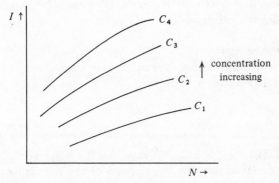

Figure 9.1

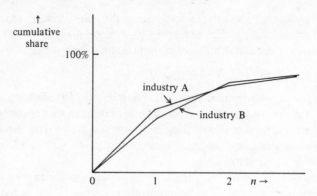

Figure 9.2

inverse relationship between numbers and shares. There is therefore an alternative, and also enlightening, way of thinking of concentration, namely as a weighted sum of firm shares:

$$C = \sum_{i=1}^{N} s_i \cdot g(s_i); \qquad 1 \geqslant g(s_i) \geqslant 0 \qquad (9.2)$$

where $g(s_i)$ is a weighting scheme.

Let us think of the firms in the industry being ranked largest to smallest, with the nth largest being indexed n. We could plot a cumulative share curve as in figure 9.2, in which the shares of successive firms are added vertically until the whole industry has been considered. Now, if the curves for comparisons in which we are interested (cross-sectional, or the same industry at different times) never crossed, the higher curve would represent a more concentrated situation than the lower. Thus any acceptable measure having the properties in (9.2) would provide as good a ranking of industries as any other. Our discussion could then focus on cardinal properties alone. Unfortunately, there is nothing to guarantee this, so the choice of an index ranges rather more widely. Before we turn to criteria for choice between indices, we discuss some candidate measures.

Concentration measures

We begin with the simplest type of measure, the *concentration ratio*. The n-firm concentration ratio is defined as:

$$CR_n = \sum_{i=1}^{n} s_i$$

In terms of (9.2) $g(s_i) = 1$, $i = 1, 2, \ldots, n$; $g(s_i) = 0$, $i = n + 1, \ldots, N$. It is therefore a *discrete* index referring to one point on the cumulative concentration curve, which means that for different values of n, a given industry can appear both more and less concentrated than another. However it is empirically popular, partly because of its easy interpretation, and government statistical sources provide values for 3-digit industries in many countries, (e.g. CR_5 for U.K. CR_3 for West Germany and a wide range including CR_4, CR_8 and CR_{20} for the U.S.).

Most other measures are not discrete but summary measures, that is they encapsulate the whole size distribution. One of the most straightforward of these is the *Hirschman–Herfindahl index*, which we encountered in discussions of oligopoly theory. Herfindahl's index is:

$$H = \sum_1^N s_i^2,$$

the sum of the squared shares. Thus the weight $g(s_i)$ is the share itself. Hirschman's measure was the positive square root of this, while a more complex measure of similar general type has been developed by Horvath (1970). It has been shown by Adelman (1969) that the Herfindahl index may be expressed as $H = (v^2 + 1)/N$, where v is the coefficient of variation (standard deviation/ mean). Since the coefficient of variation is a statistical measure of inequality, this expression shows clearly the two influences in equation (9.1) coming through in a measure encountered first in oligopoly theory (equation (2.6)). If all firms are the same size, $H = 1/N$. The Herfindahl varies between zero and one, and the more unequal are firm sizes (given N), the larger is the index.

One can also define a *numbers equivalent* to the Herfindahl H_{ne}, by taking its reciprocal. On the basis that H is a correct measure of market power, its numbers equivalent is an intuitively appealing way of expressing a given unequal market structure in terms of the number of firms of equal size to which it is equivalent.

A more complex weighting scheme is involved in Entropy indices. The basic or *first-order Entropy* is:

$$E = -\sum_1^N s_i \log s_i,$$

so the weight applied is minus the logarithm (traditionally to the base 2) of the market share;[4] a rationale will be provided below. It is designed as a measure of uncertainty or disorder. When all firms are of equal size, it is easily seen that $E = \log N$. In addition, when firms are very unequal in size, E tends to zero. Therefore it is important to note that E is an inverse measure of concentration. For this reason, a 'redundancy' measure R has been defined as $R = \log N - E$, and there is also a relative first order entropy measure $E/\log N$ and an associated redundancy measure $1 - (E/\log N)$. A numbers equivalent variant could be defined as antilog E.

Another general class of indices are those represented by the *Rosenbluth* or *Hall–Tideman* index (which we impartially label *RHT*):

$$RHT = 1 \Big/ \left[2 \sum_1^N is_i - 1 \right]$$

Here, the weight is provided by the rank (largest to smallest) of the firm. The idea is to emphasise the depressing effect of the number of firms, since small shares are multiplied by large rank numbers.

There are also indices which are more properly thought of as *inequality measures*. Obvious examples are the variance of the distribution of sizes and the coefficient of variation. Another is the variance of the logarithms, which has attractive properties if the underlying distribution is lognormal (see section 2). A much-used index, sometimes wrongly called a concentration index, is the *Gini coefficient*. This is best developed by reference to the *Lorenz curve*. If a cumulative concentration curve (figure 9.2) is scaled so that the *y*-axis measures the cumulative proportion of industry size accounted for and the *x*-axis the cumulative proportion of firms, the result will be a curve bowed above the diagonal running from the top right- to the bottom left-hand corner, as in figure 9.3. This curve is the Lorenz curve (except that the normal convention is to rank the firms smallest to largest so it appears as a mirror image to the curve we have described).

The Gini coefficient is double the area between the diagonal and the Lorenz curve and so measures the fractional extent of inequality since the area of the whole triangle above the diagonal is half a unit. It can be shown that the Gini coefficient may be written:

$$G = \left(N + 1 - 2 \sum_1^N is_i \right) \Big/ N$$

so it is apparent that $G = 1 - 1/(N \cdot RHT)$, a relationship with the *RHT* index which is broadly similar to the relationship between the coefficient of variation and the Herfindahl.

Firstly, we present examples of more complex combinations of the basic

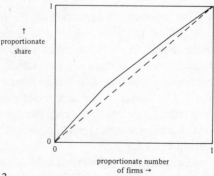

Figure 9.3

Table 9.1.

Distribution				Index				
	CR_4	CR_8	H	H_{NE}	E (Base 10)	RHT	L_2	L_3
A	0.8	1	0.2	5	0.699	0.2	0.5	0.33
B	0.7	0.9	0.28	3.57	0.771	0.179	2.5	2.11
C	0.6	0.8	0.13	7.69	0.939	0.139	0.5	0.556
D	0.4	0.8	0.1	10	1.0	0.1	0.5	0.33

A 0.2×5	(5 firms)	C $0.2 \times 2, 0.1 \times 4, 0.05 \times 4$ (10 firms)
B $0.5, 0.1, 0.05 \times 8$	(10 firms)	D 0.1×10 (10 firms)

index types we have described. One fairly promising one is *Hannah and Kay's numbers equivalent index*:

$$n(\alpha) = \left[\sum_1^N s_i^\alpha \right]^{1/(1-\alpha)} \qquad \alpha > 0$$

This is in fact the antilog. of the general entropy of order α. There are two special cases: when $\alpha = 2$, it becomes the Herfindahl numbers equivalent and as $\alpha \to 1$ its logarithm can be shown to tend to the first order entropy.

The Linda class of indices are based upon the concentration ratio (and like it, are discrete indices) but allow for inequalities between large firms. The *Linda index* for the n largest firms is:

$$L_n = \frac{1}{n(n-1)} \sum_{i=1}^{n-1} \frac{n-i}{i} \frac{CR_i}{CR_n - CR_i}$$

This is quite a popular index in European Community studies of industrial structure. It is easily verified that if all firms up to the nth largest are of the same size then $L_n = 1/n$. Furthermore, if the $(n + 1)$th firm is much smaller than its predecessors, the index L_{n+1} will be much larger than L_n. Hence it has been suggested that the 'oligopolistic arena' should be defined by the number of firms for which a minimum value of the L index is reached.

Examples of the concentration indices (except Hannah and Kay's) are given for four simple distributions of firm sizes in table 9.1. Notice that these agree *roughly* in ranking the four distributions *A–D* in descending order of concentration, though the Herfindahl judges *B* more concentrated than *A* and the Linda indexes calculated behave rather erratically.

Criteria for choice between measures

Having presented the reader with a bewildering array of indices, we should suggest some criteria for choice between them.

One important criterion is provided by *economic theory*. We have already seen in section 2.1 that if firms differ only in the level of their marginal costs and if they act non-cooperatively, the Herfindahl index is theoretically relevant for price cost margin studies. Schmalensee (1980) extends this result to some differentiated product models. It is also the most appropriate index if firms act as postulated by Stigler's theory of oligopoly. On the other hand, Saving's model (1970) provides some justification for using the concentration ratio, or possibly the Linda index. The entropy index has its basis in information theory and is a measure of the 'uncertainty' associated with a particular structure.

We can briefly illustrate the basic theory behind the entropy measure by means of an example. Suppose we hear Mr. Brown bought a particular make of cat food. If this make was the only one on the market, the informational content of that statement would be zero ($=\log 1$), whereas if he bought an unusual brand, the informational content would be high. It is therefore sensible to make informational content a decreasing function of the probability of purchase (which equals the share of the ith firm). The log of the reciprocal ($\log 1/s_i$) is chosen as the precise measure satisfying this since it is additive in the case of independent events; it is relevant if Mrs. Smith also buys cat food independently of Mr. Brown. Thus, the informational content of the statement regarding their purchases of brands one and two is:

$$e(s_1, s_2) = \log\left(\frac{1}{s_1 s_2}\right) = \log\left(\frac{1}{s_1}\right) + \log\left(\frac{1}{s_2}\right) = e(s_1) + e(s_2)$$

The expected information obtained given the sales distribution is:

$$E(s_1, s_2) = \sum_{1}^{2} s_i \log\left(1/s_i\right)$$

Hence the entropy measure. It must be admitted though that the present author finds it difficult to relate this more closely to industrial concentration.

A second, and perhaps more fundamental, basis for choice than economic theory is the *axiomatic*.[5] If we could agree on a set of criteria which should be satisfied by a reasonable concentration index, we could delimit the range of plausible concentration indices by reference to it. Now, we have already suggested some criteria, though not very formally — for example that numbers lower and size inequalities raise concentration and that if one concentration curve lies everywhere above another, the former is the more concentrated industry. The problem comes in devising additional criteria which are generally acceptable yet narrow the field sufficiently to be useful.

Two examples of sets of criteria are provided by Hannah and Kay (1977), and Hause (1977). They do have similarities — both make the assumption that mergers should increase concentration and that if a very small firm enters the effect on the index should be negligible, and they are both attracted to indices with numbers equivalent properties. Both therefore rule out some candidate measures (e.g. the concentration ratio and the Linda index). But there are also differences: Hannah and Kay focus on their index complying with the anti-Gibrat and Gibrat process (which we discuss in the next section) while Hause bases his model firmly on the Cournot–Nash equilibrium (see chapter 3) as a lower bound for a reasonable index, firms improving on non-cooperation if possible. As a consequence, the class of indexes Hannah and Kay are interested in do not always satisfy Hause's 'theoretically reasonable criteria', nor do Hause's indexes satisfy a cardinalisation criterion which Hanna and Kay class as 'appealing' and which their measure satisfies.

A third basis for choice is by means of statistical criteria. For example, the entropy index has the property of *decomposability*. Suppose the industry has two sub-industries (say, nationally advertised breakfast cereals and own-brands) then the overall entropy may be broken down into its constituent elements from the sub-industries.[6] Also, if a particular statistical distribution is valid for the industry in question, the choice of index is made easier; the relevant example here is the lognormal distribution of firm sizes. In that case, most indices are governed simply by N and σ^2, the variance of the logs. of size, as Hart (1975) explains. Therefore, once these values are known, the indices calculated from them contain no further information, they merely rearrange it, and σ^2, along with N, might as well be used directly.

We should warn the reader against a further possible basis for choice: the *a priori*. A particular economist may believe one measure superior to another because he feels, for example, that if an industry has one large firm it matters little whether there are also one hundred or one thousand small firms, so an index which gives this property would meet his approval. In other words, referring back to figure 9.1, one economist may believe a particular trade-off between numbers and inequality is most sensible. He is entitled to his opinion, but so is an opponent believing the opposite. We seek a more positive (non-normative) approach.

Lastly though, we must turn to more practical matters. If information on all sizes is not available, all measures will be approximations. Not unnaturally, firms may be reluctant to reveal their size, and in collecting statistics the (government) agency may be required to publish only aggregates. Thus it may group firms into size categories (firms with between 100 and 200 workers, etc.) giving the total employment/output accounted for by firms in that category. Such a table is known as the *first moment distribution* of firm sizes. It may additionally publish particular summary measures. The economist's task is then to derive his chosen summary statistic or indicator from the data at his disposal. This can either be done by assuming a particular statistical distribution like the lognormal, or by making some approximation, as discussed by Schmalensee (1977) for the Herfindahl index, and Horowitz (1970) for the entropy, for example. It is here, if anywhere, that the otherwise unfavoured concentration ratio scores, since it requires far less information, is often available directly from published sources, and does not suffer from problems of changing industry definitions and their effects on firm numbers to any great extent.

Thus, if all indices agree closely in ranking of concentration, and one needs only ordinal properties, it is sufficient to choose an index which is accurately measured with the information available. Hence the popularity of the concentration ratio in empirical work. And indeed, many researchers (e.g. Scherer, 1980, ch. 3; Sawyer, 1971) have found close rank correlations between various measures. However, Hause (1977) sounds the warning that there is no necessary reason for high rank correlation and that, particularly within highly concentrated industrial groups where the ranking is arguably most critical, the measures are not in fact highly correlated.

A final practical point: information regarding concentration is often available only for domestic firms, yet imports and exports must be expected to influence the true level of concentration existing. The difficulties in making the consequent adjustments are most easily illustrated using an example, and we take the case of the n-firm concentration ratio (CR_n); similar factors arise in other cases (see e.g. Lyons, 1981 on the Herfindahl). The most sensible approximation (see e.g. Green Paper, 1978) is:

$$CR_n \, \text{adj} = \frac{S_n - CR_n \cdot EX}{S + IM - EX} \tag{9.3}$$

where S is sales (so S_n is the sales of the top n) IM is imports and EX exports. The crucial assumptions necessary for this measure to be accurate are that large firms export in proportion to their size in the industry, that importers are not among the top n firms and that imports provide real competition (rather than being introduced by domestic firms). More generally, in choosing an index one has to assume the same economic theory holds good for both domestic producers and importers.

2. Determinants of the level of concentration

In any economy, concentration by any measure varies very widely, for example in the U.K. in 1978, the five-firm concentration ratio was 99% in tobacco and 12% in leather goods.

It also appears that, as a general rule, the industries which are highly concentrated tend to be the same ones from country to country[7] and similarly with the unconcentrated ones; examples of the former are motor vehicle assembly and cigarette manufacture, of the latter are various varieties of timber and clothing manufactures. One suggestion is therefore that deterministic factors are at work; that concentration is, at least ostensibly, determined by scale economies and the like. Other observers (e.g. Simon and Bonini, 1958) take an entirely different view, believing that probabilistic influences are paramount. In this section we cover both viewpoints and discuss a reconciliation.

Before we start, we should point out that any attempt to explain a level of concentration assumes that the chosen concentration measure is an interesting thing to explain. There is little point in developing a sophisticated model to explain a particular concentration index if that index is not believed to be itself a good measure of market power or anything else. Moreover, if one can 'explain' a particular measure well by reference, say, to firm numbers and a size inequality index, nothing may in fact have been explained except the mathematical relationship between firm numbers, size inequalities and that concentration index. These points recur and have bedevilled many empirical studies of the determinants of concentration.

An example may illustrate the factors involved. We know the Herfindahl index may be expressed as $H = (v^2 + 1)/N$, where v is the coefficient of variation of firm sizes. It would patently be silly to regress H on v^2 and N and pretend we had explained anything. But also, we must want to explain the Herfindahl because we believe in some theory which makes it relevant, for example that cost differences between firms explain their relative size. Assuming we believe the Cournot model to be a true representation of the industry, we can derive from equation (2.7), writing $C_i' = c_i$, that:

$$\frac{q_i}{Q} = \eta \left(1 - \frac{c_i}{p}\right) \tag{9.4}$$

which, summed over all firms, is:

$$1 = N\eta - \eta \frac{\Sigma c_i}{p} \tag{9.5}$$

From (9.5) we can derive p to substitute into (9.4) which is then squared and summed to yield:

$$H = \Sigma q_i^2/Q^2 = -N\eta^2 + 2\eta + [1 - N\eta]^2 \Sigma c_i^2/(\Sigma c_i)^2 \tag{9.6}$$

The second element of the last term of this is reminiscent of the Herfindahl itself, and may be broken down in the same way, viz: $\Sigma c_i^2/(\Sigma c_i)^2 = (1 + v_c^2)/N$, where v_c is the coefficient of variation of marginal costs. Substituting this into (9.6) and rearranging gives us, finally:

$$H = (1/N) + (1 - \eta N)^2 v_c^2/N \tag{9.7}$$

Clarke and Davies (1982), from which this derivation comes, also develop a more general case involving some measure of collusion, which gives rise to a slightly more complex formula incorporating the degree of collusion. Therefore from (9.7) it is no more an explanation of H to use, along with other variables, N and v_c^2; we must seek explanations for the number of firms and the distribution of costs in order to explain the fundamental determinants of concentration. We now turn to consider such things.

The role of 'technology'

Turning to the technological explanation, the prime consideration is economies of scale. To put things at their simplest, suppose the long-run average cost curve for firms in the industry is 'U' shaped. In that case, over a long period all firms can be expected to gravitate towards the lowest point on the average cost curve, the minimum efficient scale (MES), so the equilibrium number of firms in the industry is given by relative market size (RMS), that is: industry output/MES. This begs the question of how industry output is determined, since it will depend on the price the firms charge for their product, but it will do as a first approximation.[8] A complication arises when cost curves are 'L' rather than 'U' shaped, for firms might choose a size above MES, but most writers simply say that RMS gives the maximum number of firms in equilibrium. If a concentration measure with a numbers equivalent property is being used, then the equilibrium number of firms translates straightforwardly into a value for the concentration index. Therefore concentration can be regressed cross-sectionally on RMS to test this model.

The simple model outlined above assumes the firm operates one plant producing one product only, but most firms produce an array of products and may operate several plants, which is *prima facie* evidence that these things prove worthwhile. Economies of scale can arise generally (see Scherer *et al.*, 1975) as product-specific (involved with the volume of production of a single product, as is the case with learning effects), plant-specific (related to the volume of production in the possibly multiproduct plant), or multi-plant economies of scale (associated for example with economies of increased flexibility), economies of distribution or promotion, or, more vaguely, economies of scope (the modern term for what were known as economies of joint production; for a definition, see Willig, 1979). This complicates matters somewhat, and means that different methods for measuring scale economies will capture different aspects of a firm's overall scale structure. It is therefore sensible to look briefly at methods of estimating MES in order to progress.

Some methods of deriving MES are in fact designed to measure the shape of the whole scale curve. An example is the *technological or engineering cost study* (empirical cases include Haldi and Whitcomb, 1967, and Pratten, 1971). This obtains very much an *ex ante* measure of cost, computing costs for various plant sizes synthetically under various headings like equipment cost, investment cost and operating cost by questioning businessmen, or from trade journal sources. The usual result obtained is of plant scale economies up to very high levels in most industries, implying an MES often exceeding the level of total U.K. production. Critics point out that this type of study tends to ignore many important and complicating features of the real world such as diseconomies of transportation, administration and alienation and so presents a misleading picture of an ideal economy dominated by a few large single-plant firms.

An alternative source of information on the whole cost curve which can take some account of pecuniary effects is *statistical cost analysis*. The basic idea is very straightforward. Average cost is related to output for a cross-section of different-sized firms in the same industry using functional forms allowing for minima (e.g. the quadratic). An extensive analysis was performed by Johnston (1960), but such studies have attracted strong criticism from

Friedman (1955) who made two main points. First, accountants' treatment of capital costs poses difficulties since it will tend to make *ex post* and *ex ante* costs differ by ironing out mistakes and consolidating good fortune. This problem may be circumvented if it may be assumed that the production function is homothetic,[9] in which case factor proportions do not vary with the output level as long as input prices remain unchanged, so capital costs are simply taken as a constant fraction of total costs. This is the method of Fuss and Gupta (1981). The other, more telling, criticism is based upon the 'regression fallacy' or Galton effect; those firms who are observed to be producing low outputs are less likely than average to be operating above their normal output level, so that some of their costs will be appropriate to firms normally producing higher outputs. The argument works in reverse for firms producing the largest outputs. This tendency for the more extreme outputs to be associated with cost levels appropriate to less extreme outputs will flatten the estimated average cost curve.

A method which obtains information on the size–output relationship in a much more gross overall sense is the *Rate of Return* study (see e.g. Hall and Weiss, 1967, Samuels and Smyth, 1968). The idea here is to capture the overall suitability of various sizes to the market environment by relating profitability across firms to firm size, together with various control variables. The results for the U.S., but not the U.K., show benefits to size up to very large scale.

Another very gross measure of the size-scale economies relationship is the *Survivor Technique*. The method here is to find MES based upon a 'survival of the fittest' concept. If, on looking at the firm size distribution classed by size groups, we find firms moving away from smaller size classes into one particular size class over time, that indicates that, in a very overall sense, the size class which gains contains the MES. Examples of this approach are Saving (1961), Shepherd (1967) and Rees (1973). The difficulty is that technology may change, there may be no perceptible movement, or movement may be in contradictory directions, and hence results are commonly obtainable only for a small subset of industries.

A more recent method due to Lyons (1980) again makes use of inferences based upon observed data to obtain minimum efficient size, but this time in the much more limited context of minimum efficient plant size. Most small firms have only one plant, while large firms often have several plants, presumably because single plant scale economies have been exhausted, or because those which remain are more than outweighed by diseconomies of transportation or other multiplant effects. From the first moment distribution of plant sizes, the point in the size distribution where the average firm has $1\frac{1}{2}$ plants can be found; Lyons' measure of minimum efficient plant size is half this output level, since at that output level the average firm would just about find it worthwhile to operate two plants.

Lastly, because of the extensive amount of work needed to produce many of these indices, some researchers have fallen back on more *ad hoc* measures of minimum efficient plant size, for example the median of the first moment distribution of plant sizes.

Returning to our main thread, the explanation of concentration, we can observe that some measures of minimum efficient scale are rather unsuited to the task, on the grounds of tautology. The clearest examples are rate of return studies – where the measure will be bound up in the reasons for the distribution of profitability among firms, which may itself be partly explainable by concentration – and the survivor technique, where we would be using recent changes in the observed size distribution to explain that size distribution cross-sectionally. But other measures may be affected less directly, such as the *ad hoc* one described above, since the observed plant size distributions may relate closely to observed firm size distributions in the cross-section. This problem is discussed in detail in Davies (1980*b*).

It should also be clear that, in the case of a measure of minimum efficient *plant* size alone, additional variables are required to capture multiplant economies, promotional economies etc. The sort of variables which have been used tend to be *ad hoc* measures such as the plants/firm and advertising/sales ratios.[10]

If we suppose that a regression of concentration on a minimum efficient plant scale proxy, the plants/firm ratio and advertising/sales produces a good fit, can we conclude that the technological explanation for concentration is the truth? Unfortunately, we cannot. Apart from the difficulty regarding spurious correlation we have mentioned above, there is a more fundamental problem. It could be argued that concentration may be high because entry is difficult, that is because barriers to entry are high. And the sort of variables which have been used to explain concentration could with little imagination be thought of as proxies for barriers to entry.[11] Hence a quite different interpretation is possible: namely that concentration is actually determined by equilibration of the costs and benefits of a *desire to monopolise* and only seemingly by the logic of technology.

There is another general criticism of the 'technological' approach. It can explain why there might only be a certain number of firms at or above a given size in an industry, but it cannot really provide an explanation of the variance in their sizes. We return to this point in a slightly different guise at the end of the section.

The stochastic processes explanation

The polar alternative to the view that concentration is a mechanistic result of technology is the assertion that it is pure (statistical) chance. Suppose a hundred million people simultaneously throw dice and are awarded points corresponding to the number which comes up. At the end of the first throw some will have scored six and on average one in 36 will score a six on both first and second throws. Others will score one both times. Even after ten throws there may be a few who have always scored six, a few who have always had low numbers and a mass with a middling number of points. It is clear that we cannot applaud the high scorers for their skill, nor castigate them for cheating, yet the result is a distribution of people who started alike but ended up unequal.

What factors determine the extent of the inequality? Suppose that every time two dice are thrown rather than one; in that case the average (expected) score is 7 rather than $3\frac{1}{2}$ and after any given time has elapsed we would expect a more dispersed distribution because some people will have scored 12 every time and others 2 (so that after, say, six throws, the difference between maximum and minimum scores is 60, whereas with one die it would have been 30). Alternatively, moving back to one die, suppose we narrow the range of outcomes by knocking one spot off the side with six and adding it to the side with one. This will make the distribution less dispersed.

To modify this parable for the purpose in hand, we can think of a stochastic process of firm growth with the distribution of growth rates facing each firm at any point in time being fixed across all firms, that is independent of previous success or current size. This conforms to *Gibrat's law of proportionate growth* and the limiting distribution generated is in fact the *lognormal*, that distribution which is normal when its log values are plotted.[12] An example of the lognormal is drawn in figure 9.4. We have seen intuitively that the larger the mean growth rate and the larger its variance (the parameters of the lognormal), the more unequal will expected firm sizes be at any point in time.

This model can be adjusted to cater for entry, exit and non-random processes. If a constant rate of 'births' is allowed (new firms, or firms growing from below some minimum critical size) the distribution will be one known as the Yule (see Simon, 1955) which can be approximated in its upper tail by the Pareto distribution, which is in turn not markedly different from the lognormal, (though Quandt, 1966, has some success in discriminating between

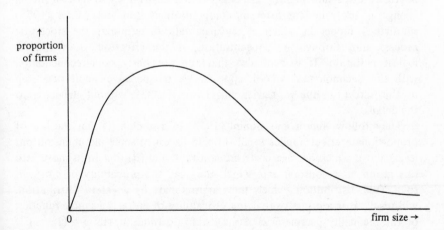

Figure 9.4

them). The complication of allowing firms below a certain size to become 'bankrupt' and leave the industry is also easily introduced. Even if there is serial correlation from one period to another in individual firms' growth rates, the distribution of firm sizes eventually generated can be close to the Yule (see Ijiri and Simon, 1964).

One criticism of the 'stochastic processes' viewpoint is that, if size distributions are purely due to chance, then why are similar industries highly concentrated across countries? A possible, but not entirely convincing, answer would be that those industries have reached a fairly mature and therefore concentrated structure in their life cycle, whereas others which are experiencing a high rate of births have not been subject to random processes long enough to have become concentrated, or whatever.

There is also a criticism of interpretation. It is unlikely that any of the chief executives of any of the biggest companies in any country would agree it was just by chance that their company was large (any more than it is unlikely that a winner at 'monopoly' would agree the losers were equally as skilful). It may have been subject to random shocks and it may have made some lucky choices, but some or even most of the small influences may have been purposive efforts by individuals or groups within the company, and we should not denigrate them by calling them chance. Gibrat's law simply says that these stochastic factors are unrelated to the size of the firm.

More fundamentally, even if we can explain the relative firm sizes in every industry by a statistical distribution which could be purely the outcome of chance, there is still room for other factors if the parameters of the distribution we have used vary across industries. We must then ask what factors differ from industry to industry to explain this variation in parameters. Weiss (1963) suggests and tests for the possibility that there is greater dispersion in firm size changes in industries where style or model change is the prevalent form of competition. Nelson and Winter (1978) simulate a model in which a key parameter determining the stochastic process and, through it, concentration, is the effectiveness of technological imitation. It is here also that the possibility of a reconciliation with the 'technological school' appears. We pursue an example of a step in this direction due to Davies and Lyons (1982), without delving into the details.

They follow Simon and Bonini (1958) in assuming (i) that the law of proportionate effect applies to all firms in excess of some minimum output level, above which average costs are constant, and (ii) that firms move into this group at a constant rate which they call the probability of entry, θ, so a Yule distribution, which they approximate by a Pareto distribution, will result. It is a property that the probability of entry is a simple function of the inequality parameter α of the Pareto distribution, viz: $\alpha = (1 - \theta)^{-1}$. It is also true for the Pareto distribution that:

$$\bar{s}_{mes} = (\alpha/\alpha - 1)\,MES \tag{9.8}$$

where $\bar{s}_{mes}$ is the average size of all firms in excess of MES. Then given that the suboptimal sector is a fraction y of total industry output, they show that the 5-firm concentration ratio (their chosen explanand) may be written as:

$$CR_5 = (1-y)^{1/\alpha}\left\{\frac{5\alpha}{\alpha-1}\frac{MES}{S}\right\}^{(\alpha-1/\alpha)} \tag{9.9}$$

Now, the parameter α may be obtained from (9.8), given $\bar{s}_{mes}$ and MES, and y is also available once MES is known. Thus, given an independent estimate of MES, a series for CR_5 may be calculated synthetically. Davies and Lyons' procedure is to obtain MES using the Lyons method described earlier in order to calculate (9.9), then to confront this series of values with the published statistics (see section 10.4). It therefore appears that technology can have an influence on the stochastic process via MES; further work in the direction of identifying the economic determinants of $\bar{s}_{mes}$ (or α) and y would complete the picture.

3. The dynamics of industry structure

In attempting to explain the dynamics of structure, we must not lose sight of one fundamental point. In theory, the equilibrium structure – to be specific, the level of a given concentration index – is to be explained by the levels of its various determinants (onto which stochastic factors impinge). Thus, *changes* in equilibrium concentration should be explainable by *changes* in the levels of the various determinants, so a proximate explanation of structural changes can be formulated using suggestions from the previous section: changes in technological factors and/or the desire and ability to monopolise. To say that the level of anything brings about changes in *equilibrium* concentration is, in the limit, nonsensical.

Nevertheless, it is perfectly permissible for levels of variables to influence the speed of movement between one equilibrium and another. Thus, in a differentiated product industry, for different reasons, a change in concentration of 5 percentage points between two periods might be partly explained by a change in consumer preferences and partly by the type of good sold in the industry (e.g. whether it is frequently purchased or not). In addition, we should not neglect the influence of other stochastic factors such as Galton's effect, which in this context means that if concentration is high this is likely to be partly due to chance, and *vice versa*, so that a change in concentration can be expected to be inversely linked with its previous level. This effect will interact with the Gibrat process, as explained in Hart and Prais (1956, p. 172).

Now, the *mechanism* by which concentration changes in an industry actually take place could be any of the following: entry into the industry, exit from the industry (including exit by merger or takeover) or a change in relative sizes of firms within the industry. In addition, shifts among firms' relative sizes could occur without concentration changing. These things can be responses both to equilibrium and disequilibrium phenomena. Thus, for example, increased economies of scale are often cited as the reason for a merger. Since we have already discussed many of the fundamental forces involved, we concentrate for the rest of this section on the mechanisms by which they are resolved.[13]

Determinants of entry

Entry into an industry occurs because it presents profitable opportunities. This does not necessarily mean the firms already in the industry are showing high profits; they might be inefficient or be disguising profits in various ways. Rather, the firm seeking to enter is interested in its potential profits, which will depend upon the characteristics of the industry after entry has occurred.

However, if we treat the situation analogously with our discussion in chapter 4 of the problem facing the established firm(s), we must assume that pre-entry values for industry magnitudes have some relevance to the decision to enter. There we took it that price was the main signal to a potential entrant. From the entrant's point of view, of course, price on its own is no guide; it must be compared to costs. Perhaps more relevant still would be profitability – the entrant is essentially making an investment and wants a return on this, so the existing ratio of profit to capital may be more important than the profit–revenue ratio. In addition, the expected profitability of the investment will have to be traded off against its risk, i.e. variability in industry profitability. Another key feature influencing the entry decision will be factors affecting the prospects and attractiveness of making the investment, such as industry growth rates and established firm reactions.

Profitability, risk and growth are all things suggested by standard microeconomic theory as likely to influence entry. In addition, given our discussion in chapter 4, those things known as barriers to entry should make it less likely. In fact, inclusion of measures for scale economies, product differentiation advantages and other barriers in models explaining entry, can be seen as an alternative test of the limit pricing thesis. However, we must reiterate that things which are deterrents to one firm are not necessarily so to another – a particular firm contemplating entry may have an established brand name in a related field together with an extensive distribution network, or may be an importer who has reached minimum efficient scale in production through sales elsewhere. We also leave open the question of whether entry is better measured by numbers or market share of entrants.

Determinants of exit

It is tempting to assume that exit can simply be treated as negative entry and in fact (probably for reasons of data availability) many empirical workers use figures for net entry when analysing the determinants of entry.

Unfortunately, things are not quite that simple. In order to treat exit as negative entry it would be necessary for things which made entry less likely to make exit more likely. Some factors would fit this pattern: low or non-existent average profitability and slow growth or decline would make exit (by one of the least efficient) more likely, as well as discouraging entry. Consistency would require in addition that high barriers to entry made exit *easier* — to take a concrete example, if the relevant part of an estimating equation is:

$$\text{net entry} = a - b \cdot \text{barrier} \qquad (a, b > 0)$$

then high barriers could make net entry negative while low barriers could mean it was positive, *ceteris paribus*.

Now, factors which encourage firms to remain or retain capacity in an industry despite low profits have been called (e.g. Caves and Porter, 1976) *barriers to exit*. In general if barriers to entry and barriers to exit are both high, then in times of booming demand, profits would be abnormally high, while in periods of slump they will be unusually low. Conversely, if both barriers are low, the situation is near to competitive. If entry barriers are high and exit barriers low (a case we described above), profitability will be permanently high, and *vice versa*.

In several cases, high barriers to entry will make for high barriers to exit also, in contrast with the 'net entry' treatment. To take some examples, if the capital costs of a plant are high and its value in any alternative use is comparatively low, this may mean a firm is more likely to mothball the plant in the hope of future upturn than to sell out completely. If scale economies are extensive, a firm may be more unwilling to cut back output somewhat than if they were trivial. If firms are vertically highly integrated (and entry into one sphere alone is consequently difficult) they may rely largely on internal transactions and so be inclined to disregard what market signals they receive regarding the profitability of operating a particular division. On the other hand, some barriers to entry may not be applicable as barriers to exit; an example is patent protection. Finally, some possible barriers to entry may indeed make exit easier: if an industry is populated by diversified firms this may make single product entry harder but it may also make it easier for a firm to contemplate exit.

We must not forget, of course, that the size of the barrier (to entry or exit) will depend upon the characteristics of the likely entrant or leaver, and these characteristics may differ between them. But the general point is that there is no overall reason for believing that the higher are barriers to entry the lower are barriers to exit (nor, indeed, *vice versa*). An analysis of the determinants of exit should be separate from one determining entry and should feature variables measuring poor prospects (low profits, low growth) and barriers to exit.

Mergers

It is usual to make three classifications of mergers: horizontal, vertical and conglomerate. Vertical merger has been covered in chapter 5, and conglomerate merger is essentially influenced by the desire to pool risk and by capital market factors, which are really outside our scope. Nevertheless, mergers between firms in the same industry contribute to the dynamics of industry structure and so should at least be mentioned. Here, we are really concerned only with two types of merger.

The first is where two firms in the same industry join together. The alternative would have been either for both to remain or for one to leave the industry. Presumably these did not occur because they were less (privately) advantageous; in the latter case the benefits were seen as sufficient to avert closure of the weaker. If the merged firm is to continue to operate as two entirely separate divisions, the reason for the merger must have been to gain horizontal market power or possibly, in a differentiated product industry, to pool risk. If the merged firm is to become unified in a more than trivial sense then there may be some real industrial logic involved. For example, the plants might be altered in size, say one expanding and another contracting or closing, with the reason being to gain economies of scale. Alternatively, the merged firm may aim only to exploit goodwill or distribution networks. However even if the existing plants are retained, product-specific economies might be realised as production schedules are re-jigged between plants to provide longer runs. Additional benefits envisaged as a result of the merger may be improvements in vertical relationships (tailoring of specifications etc.), advantages in marketing, broader-based R and D programmes, or economies of administration.

The second type of merger with which we are concerned here is entry by merger. The alternative would have been exit of the resident firm and entry by the other. Again there must have been seen to be advantages in the arrangement entered into; either technical or pecuniary economies on the production side, or factors on the demand side such as goodwill and demand complementarities.

Thus, horizontal mergers can be seen as beneficial if they allow lower costs, but not necessarily so if there are concomitant increases in market power; we are then firmly into the world of the 'Williamson trade-off' (see section 1.3). There will virtually always be a *private* incentive for horizontal merger and, in an attempt to screen out socially undesirable ones, horizontal mergers are usually subject to some governmental control. Thus, the extent of merger activity is largely inversely proportional to the perceived severity of the control.

Determinants of intra-industry stability

Entry, exit and merger will influence other firms in the industry as well. But even without these influences, substantial changes can take place in an industry in the sizes of individual firms. As we saw in the previous section, a larger average growth rate and a larger variance in that rate will tend to make firm sizes in the industry more disparate, *ceteris paribus*. But as well as natural or stochastic variation, there will be a plethora of other influences at work, both stabilising and destabilising.

Those influences we have already mentioned – entry, exit and merger – can be included among destabilising influences since they upset the established order. Also, the pace of discovery of new cheaper processes for making established products and the frequency of introduction of new products will affect the balance among firms, as we said in chapter 8. If established firms' marginal cost curves are sharply rising at current outputs then output increases are expensive, so that imbalances resulting from various causes will tend to be corrected mainly by price, whereas flatter marginal cost curves will result in destabilisingly large movements in outputs.

The sort of factors implicit in our discussion in chapter 3: the characteristics of the players of the game (including purchasers) or what have been called *behavioural understandings* (Caves and Porter, 1980) will also be of importance here. Tacit understandings regarding the extent of competition on various fronts are an obvious example. As we saw in chapter 3, the relative speed of reaction to various instruments – price, advertising, new product developments, etc. can also have a substantial influence upon equilibria and, plausibly, on movements around equilibria. Also of importance will be the ease of movement between separate segments of the industry (see Porter, 1976).

This area of intra-industrial dynamics is one economists are only beginning to explore systematically, though case studies undoubtedly provide extensive evidence of the phenomena at work.

4. Concentration and welfare

The conclusion of the welfare analysis of chapter 2 is that concentration is undesirable since it implies oligopolistic interaction leading (to a greater or lesser extent) to prices above costs. That point remains true, but the analysis of this chapter has indicated that the problem of finding an ideal structure is not straightforward: pure competition is not attainable in all cases. Partly as a consequence, the level of concentration does not provide a proper welfare criterion.

Also, we may reflect, the work of this chapter has brought us a long way from the view that the structure of industry directly determines performance. Though structure may be slow to change, it is basic technological factors and stochastic features, together with firm conducts, which ultimately determine both structure and performance.

A very simple model will illustrate some aspects of this. Suppose a number of firms operate as Cournot firms towards each other, producing a homogeneous good. Then, from equation (2.7a) (again writing $C_i' = c_i$), the price–cost margin varies directly with the Herfindahl index of concentration:

$$\frac{\Pi + F}{R} = \frac{pQ - \Sigma c_i q_i}{pQ} = \frac{H}{\eta} \qquad (9.10)$$

However, this is not a causal relationship, since both concentration and price–cost margin are essentially determined by cost and demand conditions. Moreover, consumer surplus CS will be (in this case) a direct function of price so that, using (9.10):

$$CS = g(p) = g\left(\frac{\Sigma c_i q_i / Q}{1 - H/\eta}\right) \qquad g' < 0$$

A fall in firm numbers, keeping average cost levels ($\Sigma c_i q_i / Q$) unchanged, which raises H will raise the price–cost margin and will lower consumer surplus. Society as a whole will be worse off as deadweight loss will increase. However, a fall in average cost levels, keeping the Herfindahl constant, will leave the price–cost margin unchanged but will increase consumer surplus – a welfare improvement which the concentration index has not picked up. Other manipulations are possible, like the case where a Cournot duopoly turns into a Stackleberg leader–follower situation: here, concentration (H) rises, but the price–cost margin falls, as does price.

To take another series of examples, if we suppose an industry is a natural monopoly then the first-best solution (assuming away other imperfections elsewhere in the economy) is for one firm to produce all the output, for it to charge marginal cost and for the losses engendered to be borne by means of a lump sum subsidy. Assuming subsidy solutions are ruled out, there may still be profitable alternatives involving various numbers of firms. As the number of firms grew, price would certainly be expected to move into line with costs, but these costs would be above the cost levels obtainable by the monopolist. Yet we should not forget the importance of potential entry. As we saw in chapter 4, even in the natural monopoly case, *if* the market is perfectly contestable then it automatically exhibits desirable welfare properties.

Relating this to our earlier discussion, if cost levels are determined solely by technological or efficiency considerations, then high concentration provides no proof of any intent to monopolise. We also know that any breakup of large established firms would raise those firms' cost levels, and so average industry cost levels, at the same time as aiding a reduction in price *unless* entry is easy. Alternatively, if concentration levels are seemingly the result of technological logic, but instead have been maintained by entry barriers, there is evidence of intent and hence breakup of large firms, prohibition of mergers and so on, are more likely to improve societal welfare. Yet another possibility is that the firm size distribution in an industry is largely the result of chance. Here there is no evidence of intent to monopolise; any monopoly policy should not be seen as a punishment for intent, nor as a penalty for

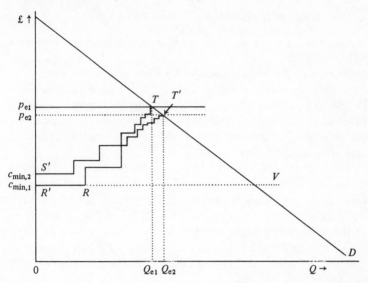

Figure 9.5

success. Thus an established industry structure may be determined by cost conditions, chance, or strategic action. As we have seen though, it may be difficult to decide which story to believe. Therefore we would be into the area of the 'Williamson trade-off'.

To illustrate the trade-off, let us consider the model of equation (9.10). Here, the largest firms in the industry will be those with the lowest cost levels, since from equation (2.7) we have:

$$(p - C_i')/p = s_i/\eta \qquad (s_i \equiv q_i/Q) \qquad (9.11)$$

Thus, at the initial equilibrium output price combination (Q_{e1}, p_{e1}), we have a welfare loss compared with pricing at the marginal cost of the lowest cost firm $(c_{min,1})$ shaped something like the step-sided area RTV in figure 9.5 (adapted from Dixit and Stern, 1982). Supposing that breaking up the largest firm results in higher costs for the largest firm, but lower prices, p_{e2}, and correspondingly higher output, Q_{e2}, then that area has to be compared with $R'S'T'V$; not an easy matter. Mergers may, in principle, be analysed by the reverse process. Entry conditions complicate things further.

The important point is that, even if a concentration measure perfectly encapsulates market power, it is not only the level of concentration that matters, nor even necessarily (as Blackorby, Donaldson and Weymark, 1982, have recently suggested) some combination of that with industry output, though that is undoubtedly better,[14] but also the reason why that level prevails. In section 10.6, we shall look at some studies which have made first steps towards disentangling empirically the components of higher profitability in concentrated industries.

Notes on the literature

Much of the material covered in the present chapter has been developed in articles primarily of an empirical nature which we have referenced as they occur, so not all aspects of the literature are covered below.

A good discussion of the problem of measuring concentration is provided by Hannah and Kay (1977), particularly chs. 2 and 4. Also of relevance is Encaoua and Jacquemin (1980). The links between the various indices under the assumption of lognormality are easily accessible in Davies (1979a); a more extensive discussion is Hart (1975).

Gold (1981) provides an exhaustive discussion of the concept of scale economies relevant to the technological explanation of concentration. In general, we have tried to avoid becoming immersed in the mathematical statistics which are necessary for a full understanding of the lognormal and of the stochastic processes explanation. For those who wish to pursue this, a text such as Freund (1971) should provide the basics while Simon (1955) develops the various distributions used. Simon and Bonini (1958) is a classic paper espousing the stochastic viewpoint, but also covering the competing explanations of concentration.

The determinants of entry and exit are covered in Orr (1974) and Caves and Porter (1976) respectively. The latter authors (1980) have also looked at dynamics. An important recent piece of work on mergers is Mueller (1980).

The recent survey by Curry and George (1983) is useful on many areas covered in this chapter and, in particular, will provide a starting point for reading the relevant aspects of the vast literature on merger activity. On welfare aspects, and indeed on the subject area of this chapter more generally, there is an important new book by Baumol, Panzar and Willig (1982).

10

A guide to the empirical work

Evidence enabling the industrial economist to test his or her theories is available from several sources. There are individual firms which can be studied in the way a business historian might look at them – analysing production arrangements, pricing and investment policies, boardroom decisions and so on. Alternatively, a questionnaire approach could be adopted – asking firms how they set their prices, how they decide advertising allocations etc. Yet again, reports by antitrust enforcement agencies, price commissions, regulatory agencies and governmental committees could be gleaned for insights, as indeed could consultants' and receivers' reports. A further, popular, source of information is cross-sectional (normally cross-industry) statistical analysis, usually based upon published data from governmental or other central agencies.

In this chapter, we review evidence preponderantly from this last source. First because the sum total of all types of evidence is too large to cover within a primary theoretical book. Second, because such statistical analyses are relatively popular and also provide a relatively homogeneous source of information. There are drawbacks though; the limitations in the range of questions which can be answered will become apparent in what follows.

Even given this limited compass, the material below cannot be said to constitute a detailed review: a great many studies are omitted. In fact, we provide something more nearly in line with the title of the chapter – a guide. It is also a guide to the pitfalls. Hence our tone in discussion may often seem critical, but many of the papers mentioned were, at the time, pathbreaking. It is always easier to be critical given the benefit of hindsight.

The empirical tradition in industrial organisation is longstanding and is fairly firmly embedded within the structure–conduct–performance paradigm, more particularly the view that structure determines performance, usually as represented by some profitability measure. Consequently, much of the literature is aimed at pragmatic tests of this link, and the purpose of our first and second sections it to outline what we see as the main thrust of this considerable body of material. We then move onto more subsidiary hypotheses involving advertising (section 3) and the determinants of research intensity and concentration (section 4). As we have pointed out, the initial paradigm has (justifiably) dropped somewhat from favour and with this has come

189

the rise in simultaneous equation analyses (section 5). The final section is essentially on the welfare or policy implications. The ordering of material in this chapter then, follows roughly the order of theoretical chapters in the book.

1. The central hypothesis: structure influencing profitability

The message of the straightforward oligopoly models of chapter 2, as embodied for example in equation (2.6), is that there are a small number of important influences on the profit–revenue ratio. These include the level of industry concentration, the elasticity of demand for the industry's product, and the beliefs of the firms about how other firms in the industry react. Later work in chapter 2 suggests that another important influence is the extent of product differentiation in the industry, whilst the work of chapter 3 indicates that concentration can itself influence the way firms believe others may react; high concentration may make collusion easier. As a rather rough rule then, the hypothesis is:

$$\frac{\Pi + F}{R} = f(\text{'concentration'}, \eta)$$

Chapter 4 adds the important proviso that, whereas the industry might wish to perform in the way specified above, it may be constrained in doing this by the threat of competition from outside. Thus, the extent to which it is able to operate as above depends upon the height of entry barriers. The modified hypothesis (given, e.g. equation 4.3) reads:

$$\frac{\Pi + F}{R} = g(\text{'concentration'}, \text{'barriers'}, \eta) \tag{10.1}$$

This is what we take to be the central structure performance hypothesis. Presumably we could hope to estimate an average relationship across industry. However, Sawyer (1982) claims that such an estimating equation is methodologically suspect because it relies on two different views: that firms are short run profit maximisers yet that they price with regard to entry. Essentially, the point must be that the two theories have not been properly integrated.

There are two further methodological points. First, and connected with the above, theory is not explicit as to the functional form of g. This is usual in economic theory (consider for example, the demand curve). But theory does not even suggest conclusively whether the function should be additive in 'concentration' and 'barriers'. On an eclectic view of the theory, both can be seen as necessary but not sufficient for profitability. Additivity implies that an increase in concentration has the same impact on profitability whether barriers are high or low (which is unlikely but not inconceivable) whereas the eclectic view suggests some multiplicative form might be appropriate. The empiricist is therefore left to experiment on this point.

Second, estimates of elasticities of demand for industrial goods are difficult to obtain. For this reason it is common to leave this variable out of estimating equations on the lines of (10.1). Thereby, economists assume implicitly that elasticity is random across industry. An alternative approach, adopted for example in Cowling and Waterson (1976), is to take the ratio of (10.1) for each industry at two points in time, and to assume η varies in the same way across industries over this time period. Having put this variable aside, we proceed by discussing the rest of formulation (10.1).

On a rather different matter, the suggestion in section 2.4 is that if indeed 'concentration' does have a positive influence on profitability, then welfare losses may be generated. Much the same might be said about 'barriers'. These beliefs lie at the back of the minds of many empirical workers and often influence their concluding discussions. We shall examine this view later in the chapter.

The dependent variable

Our development in chapter 2 started with the price–cost margin. Then, by assuming marginal cost could be approximated by average variable cost, we moved to the profit–revenue ratio.[1] However, although this measure is widely used as the dependent variable in structure–profit studies (particularly in the U.K.), other studies (particularly for the U.S.) have employed an alternative denominator, mostly equity capital or total assets. Here we denote the ratio of profit to 'capital', somehow measured, Π/K.

Bain (1951), in his pathbreaking empirical work, made it clear that he was using Π/K rather than Π/R for empirical convenience. However Benishay (1967), for example, has argued that profitability is what would be equalised by competitive forces, so that the argument for using Π/K is to be found in the null hypothesis: what would happen with perfectly free entry. In fact, the main problem is one of measurement, for in pure economic terms profit on anything would tend to zero as entry became free and established industry numbers became large.

Essentially, the difficulty lies in measuring capital. Assuming for simplicity all costs can be designated as either due to labour or capital used up (worn out) in the productive process,[2] profit may be defined as: $\Pi = R - wL - rK$. Here R is revenue, w is the unit cost of labour (L) while r is the return on capital stock (K) to cover its depreciation, interest payments etc. If our data source gives a measure of profit before subtracting variable capital costs, measured profits are $\Pi_M = R - wL$. Then assuming our economic hypothesis, specifically in terms of the true profit–revenue ratio, is $\Pi/R = f(C, B)$, where C and B are an index of concentration and an index of 'barriers' respectively, our relationship as measured is:

$$\frac{\Pi_M}{R} = f(C, B) + \frac{rK}{R} \tag{10.2}$$

The null hypothesis, when $f(C_0, B_0) = 0$, is then seen to relate the profit–revenue ratio to the capital revenue ratio, which potentially varies widely across industries. On the other hand, if we have available a measure of capital stock, K, the same economic hypothesis leads to:

$$\frac{\Pi_M}{K} = \frac{R}{K} \cdot f(C, B) + r \tag{10.3}$$

Albeit yielding a slightly more complex alternative hypothesis, this formulation provides us with a much more attractive null hypothesis than (10.2), since r can plausibly be assumed roughly constant across industries and thus may be estimated as a constant. Hence the argument for using Π/K.

Now, we have been assuming that the 'cost of capital' variable is unknown but that capital stock is known. However there is still a question of how to measure this in an economically meaningful way, that is how to measure its opportunity cost. One approach uses the historical cost type of measure such as obtained from a balance sheet. A superficially more attractive measure is shareholder's equity, though this has the grave disadvantage that, if the capital market were working perfectly (and abstracting from considerations of risk), profit on equity would be equalised across all firms since the capital market would include discounted value of monopoly profits in determining the valuation of shares. Thus there would be a mixing of two different hypotheses (and see also Fisher and McGowan 1983).

To summarise: both alternative types of dependent variable measure have disadvantages caused by the problem of subtracting from the dependent variable the cost of capital used up. The form of (10.2) indicates that those who choose to use profit on revenue should include an additional dependent variable (as, in fact, most do) to proxy the capital revenue ratio,[3] while (10.3) indicates that a slightly more complex functional form should probably be used by devotees of the profitability measure.

A final alternative, available only in certain cases, is to use price directly rather than one of the proxies. The difficulty is obvious: prices cannot be compared across industries without some common measuring rod. However, if industries or sectors of an industry face similar demand and cost conditions but different competitive conditions, this approach may be tenable. For example, bank interest rates might be compared between cities where banking is concentrated in the hands of a few, and cities with less concentrated banking facilities. A recent example of this type of analysis can be found in Geithman, Marvel and Weiss (1981); in their samples more concentrated areas face higher prices. An ingenious alternative approach along these lines is Nickell and Metcalf (1978). They related concentration and barrier measures to arguably more accurate estimates of monopoly profit based upon associating supermarket own brand prices with economic production costs, and they concluded that prices are substantially raised above costs by such structural variables.

Adjustments regarding concentration

We discussed concentration measures in the previous chapter, so we have little to add here. Empirically, by far the most popular measure is the concentration ratio, (most commonly CR_4 or CR_8 for the U.S., CR_5 for the U.K., CR_3 for West Germany, because these are what happen to be published). However although the concentration ratio itself has a rather doubtful pedigree, it is quite usual either to adjust it for various factors or to include additional variables in the regression to take account of these factors.

Thus for example, given a particular theory about how importers behave, a particular adjustment to domestic firms' concentration is required to obtain concentration faced by final consumers. A theoretical example was suggested in equation (2.11) and a pragmatic version appears as equation (9.3). A very popular alternative is to include the ratio of imports/sales and the ratio of exports/sales as determinants of profitability additional to concentration.

For some industries the market cannot be said to be national; an example might be bread. In such cases it is common to include a regional *dummy variable*, that is an explanatory variable taking on the value unity when the industry is regionalised (say) and zero otherwise. This variable will then hopefully pick up the differential effect and so cater for concentration being measured on a national basis. Other common examples of the use of dummy variables are where a durable goods dummy is employed, also where a consumer (rather than producer) goods dummy is used. These are perhaps best seen as crude attempts to allow for different general classes of demand elasticities. (As we have said already, demand elasticity is not usually available.) They might also be used to allow for bilateral power, of which more later.

Measures of entry barriers

There are basically two general methods of measuring entry barriers. The earlier, now much less popular but not necessarily inferior, method is due to Bain (1962). The other appears first to have been used by Comanor and Wilson (1967). Neither, it must be said, really attempts to measure the expectational elements which have been stressed in recent theoretical work (see chapter 4).

Both methods attempt to capture several possible dimensions of entry barriers, principally those in Bain's three categories mentioned in section 4.1: absolute cost advantages, product differentiation advantages and economies of scale. We should add here that, as well as real economies of scale, pecuniary economies of scale can have a very similar effect.

Product differentiation *advantages*[4] were considered by Bain to arise for three reasons: patent control over superior products, control of superior distributive outlets and accumulated preferences of buyers for particular products. The last of these received extensive discussion in section 7.3 and in fact it is often assumed, following Bain's empirical work, that the prime potentially empirically measurable creator of such a barrier is advertising.

An absolute cost advantage might arise for several reasons. Among these are control over the optimal production techniques, imperfections in the markets for factors of production favouring established firms, (for example control over the best sources of a mineral input), rising supply prices for factors of production forcing large-scale entrants to envisage higher costs (possibly for established firms as well as themselves) if they enter, and money market conditions (possibly imperfections) imposing higher interest rates or capital rationing on new entrants. At least the last two of these may be linked in with scale conditions operating in the industry, and this is often done in empirical work. Let us turn to the methods of measuring such multifarious effects.

In his work, Bain assesses the height of barriers to entry under four headings: scale economies, product differentiation, absolute cost and capital requirements. The fourth of these is essentially the capital rationing case we noted under absolute cost advantages, while the category 'absolute cost' caters for the rest, principally control over raw materials. For each industry, under each of these four heads, Bain assesses the height of the barrier on the basis of knowledge of his own and primary and secondary industry sources. Thus one of three categories is chosen: unimportant, moderately important or very important. An overall barrier into each industry is then derived as either very high, substantial or moderate-to-low, not by averaging but rather by an intuitive weighting scheme which means the weights ascribed to each type of barrier vary from industry to industry. Overall then, there is a large element of subjectivity involved in assessing the ease of entry into each of his industries; the reader must place a very high level of trust in the worker's judgment. The methodological view that there are a small number of distinct categories rather than a smooth continuum of barriers to entry must also be accepted.

To give the flavour of this approach within the modern context of regression analysis, we quote an example from Mann (1971), a disciple of Bain. Here, the dependent variable (Π/K) is average profit on net worth earned by the leading firms over the period 1950–1958, with concentration, CR_4, utilised as a continuous rather than discrete explanatory variable. The final variable is a dummy (d_H) taking on the value unity if the industry (according to Mann's revision of Bain's estimates) has high barriers to entry:[5]

$$\frac{\hat{\Pi}}{K} = 7.28 - 15.86\, d_H + (0.06 + 0.23\, d_H) \cdot CR_4$$

$$\quad (1.36) \quad (6.85) \qquad (0.02) \quad (0.09)$$

$(R^2$ not reported).

Based upon this, Mann concludes that 'the effect of concentration on profitability is greater in the presence of high barriers to a statistically significant degree' (p. 292), though note also the significantly negative coefficient on d_H by itself.

Comanor and Wilson's approach, while again utilising concentration, economies of scale, absolute capital requirements and the effects of advertising as independent variables, could hardly be more different. Their basic ethos is that (widely available) statistical measures proxying each of the effects of entry barriers should be used rather than personal assessment of their importance. Further they assume that the weights on each of the variables should be those average values ascribed by cross-industry regression analysis rather than a varying subjective weighting scheme. (There are parallels here with hedonic pricing models met in chapter 6). With this approach, the reader must put his faith in the efficacy of the various proxies in capturing the various effects (and in these proxies being of roughly equal importance across the industries chosen) rather than in the authors' knowledge of individual industries. The proxies Comanor and Wilson choose for the barriers are as follows: for economies of scale the measure is 'average plant size among the largest plants accounting for 50 per cent of industry output . . . divided by total output in the relevant market' (p. 428). Thus the plant size first moment distribution table is split by interpolation at the output size level representing 50 per cent of industry output and the average size of plant in terms of output in the group containing the larger plants is obtained. In order to derive the absolute capital requirement measure, they simply multiply this average output level by the ratio of total assets to gross sales in the industry. Two alternative advertising measures were employed: advertising outlays per dollar of sales and 'average advertising expenditures per firm among firms which account for 50 per cent of industry output' (p. 428).

To give one example from among the great number of equations Comanor and Wilson estimate in order to explain profit on equity averaged over the period 1954–1957 for 41 U.S. consumer goods industries, consider the following (weighted to correct for heteroskedasticity):

$$\frac{\hat{\Pi}}{K} = 0.040 + 0.29\frac{A}{S} + 0.013\ KR + 0.0084\ G$$
$$\phantom{\frac{\hat{\Pi}}{K} = 0.040 + }(0.15)\quad (0.0027)\quad (0.0084)$$
$$\phantom{\frac{\hat{\Pi}}{K} = }+ 0.028\ RID \qquad R^2 = 0.76$$
$$\phantom{\frac{\hat{\Pi}}{K} = }(0.0015)$$

Here, A/S is the advertising/sales ratio, KR is the log of the capital requirements variable we discussed, G is the log of the growth in demand over the period and RID is a regional industry dummy variable to account for the fact that three industries sell primarily in local markets. All these except demand growth (which we discuss shortly) are significantly different from zero with the expected positive sign and the overall fit (admittedly boosted by correction for heteroskedasticity) is good.

One point which may puzzle the reader, is why neither scale economies nor a concentration index is represented in their equation. The reason is a high level of multicollinearity between these two and the capital requirements barrier which means that separate effects are difficult to disentangle. Comanor and Wilson thus drop one or more of these three variables from the most of their equations without significantly worsening the overall fit.[6] Statistical reasons for this multicollinearity are not hard to find. Recalling the definition of the capital requirements barrier, we see that if the assets/ sales ratio were constant across the industries, this barrier would be a constant proportion of their scale economies measure and the multicollinearity would be 'perfect'. Thus, if the ratio is approximately constant, so the measures are very similar, it becomes difficult to know, when only one of the variables is included, which effect is being picked up. The capital requirements barrier is in fact rather naive, for it assumes a potential entrant, whatever its identity, will face problems in funding its investment in the new industry. This may be the case when a completely new firm considers entry but is fairly unlikely if the potential entrant is, for example, the Ford Motor Company.

The scale economies measure also can be criticised. There are two separate points here. Firstly, as Comanor and Wilson admit, their proxy is likely to be strongly related statistically to concentration measures, whether or not there is a technical relationship linking them (see section 9.2), for it is related to plant concentration, which is likely to be correlated with firm concentration. Thus it becomes difficult to say whether one or both affect profitability; again the problem of multicollinearity appears. Secondly, it is unlikely that such a simple summary measure captures at all adequately the three separate dimensions of a scale curve we noted in section 4.2. One measure which goes part way towards meeting this criticism is employed in Caves *et al.* (1975). They multiply a Comanor and Wilson-type measure (MEPS) by a dummy variable taking the value one when the cost disadvantage of operating plants below MEPS is, say, 10 per cent of operating those above MEPS, and zero otherwise. Luckily also, this measure is less highly correlated with concentration than is MEPS. Interestingly, the statistical significance of concentration improves when their variable is used rather than MEPS.

For reasons we will come on to in section 3, researchers have been critical of Comanor and Wilson's results on advertising. The basic point here is that advertising intensity is not necessarily a very good measure of barriers; advertising per firm might be a better one, given the sort of mechanisms discussed in section 7.3.

More generally, although the method of capturing entry barriers via statistical proxies employed by Comanor and Wilson and their followers is superficially attractive, it has to be very carefully executed in order to avoid critical comment on the details of the actual proxies.

Demand growth

Rather surprisingly, Comanor and Wilson make no real economic arguments for their use of the demand proxies measure. Other studies make rather dubious arguments. For example in Holterman (1973) we read that 'In a growing market . . . it takes time for supply to increase through entry of new firms or the expansion of capacity of existing firms, and during this time higher profits are made by existing firms in the industry' (p. 121). Our problem with this argument is that, if demand is growing at a known constant rate, there seems no particular reason to expect lags before output expands. Unplanned growth or decline would perhaps be more germane.

However there are more specific economic arguments which may be adduced in favour of including a growth term. Caves (1972), for example, argues that behaviour by established firms in a fast growing industry is likely to be different from that in a static industry, since in the latter the firms are merely taking buyers from each other and vigorous competition may well lower profits for all. In a growth industry, the future returns from capturing a set of loyal customers by vigorous competition now may well be large. This indicates a negative relationship between demand growth and profit margin would be expected. Another hypothesis suggesting a negative relationship is that if a potential entrant envisages the industry growing, a scale economy barrier is likely to be less of a threat, as she can expand with the market to optimal size (unless of course scale economies increase at a similar or greater rate due to scale augmenting technical progress).[7] It is therefore perhaps surprising that growth usually attracts a positive coefficient. On the other hand, as Baron (1973) points out, expected future growth may either make it more or less worthwhile for the established industry to retard entry in pursuit of an optimal long run strategy. For still further arguments relevant to the inclusion of a growth term, see Johns (1962) for example.

2. Further considerations and results

Most studies of the Comanor and Wilson type relating profitability to concentration and entry barriers assume the relationship with concentration changes smoothly. An important sub-branch of the literature takes a different view. Also, most studies, while including concentration in one form or other, take no account of possible influences of market power in related sectors, as discussed in chapter 5, but some do. We discuss both these points below, then provide a very brief summary of results more generally.

A critical concentration ratio?

Some economists believe concentration only has an impact on performance once it rises above a certain level. A plausible theoretical reason is that an industry may be able to switch from non-cooperative to cooperative behaviour once the dominance of a few large firms becomes significant.[8] Empirically the problem is to identify this point, assuming it is roughly constant across industries.

White (1976) analyses two models designed to do this. One involves a dummy variable for concentration (D), along with various barrier variables (B_j) along the following lines:

$$\frac{\Pi}{K}i = \alpha + \beta D_i + \sum_j \gamma_j B_{ji} + u_i$$

Here the barrier variables accord roughly with those used by Comanor and Wilson, but concentration has an influence only by giving a discrete jump in the intercept. The value for concentration which does this is not fixed *ex ante*, but is derived as the optimal split value within the regression process itself; that is the equation is estimated for a number of values and the best explanation chosen. White finds that both this and his other model yield an optimal split at a four-firm concentration value of about 57 per cent, in a study on U.S. data.

Geroski (1981*b*) has performed some more complex experiments on U.K. data. His model is of the form:

$$\frac{\Pi}{R}i = \alpha + \beta C_i + \sum_b \phi_b D_b CR_i + \sum_j \gamma_j B_{ji} + u_i$$

Thus concentration has a normal linear effect plus an effect which varies from class to class, the slope coefficient being ($\beta + \phi_b$) when concentration is in the *b*th size class. He defined 16 size classes but then grouped these somewhat. The final empirical relationship between margin and concentration is not continuous nor does it show a single clean break; it is not even monotonically increasing.

Recent work by Bradburd and Over (1982) suggests that the critical concentration ratio may differ depending on whether concentration is rising or falling. They believe this may be because collusion is easier to sustain than initiate.

Taken together, these studies put the idea that there is a smooth relationship between profitability and concentration into some doubt. However the theoretical justification for a constant critical value across industries is very weak, and some more detailed tests (e.g. Geithman, Marvel and Weiss, 1981) cast doubt upon it empirically also.

The impact of bilateral market power

Few empirical studies have troubled to pay serious attention to bilateral power, though sometimes people include *ad hoc* variables like the extent to which purchases are made by governmental agencies, with the hope of dealing with the main problems.

Early examples of studies including more specifically formulated variables are those by Brooks (1973) and Lustgarten (1975) on U.S. data. Both employ the *buyer concentration ratio* $BCR_i = \Sigma_j\, a_{ij} \cdot CR_{4j}$. Here then, buyer concentration in industry i is the weighted average of four-firm seller concentration ratios in the j purchasing industries, where the weights (a_{ij}) are the proportions of i's output which are sold to the various purchasers, derived from the input–output matrix.[9] Lustgarten finds this index to be a significant negative determinant of price–cost margins when used alongside seller concentration and the capital–output ratio, and Brooks finds it influences profitability negatively in a simple model of the Comanor and Wilson type: the more concentrated are buyers, the lower is sellers' profitability. However Guth, Schwartz and Whitcomb (1977), making adjustments which reduce sample size appreciably, find Lustgarten's variable no longer significant.

A Herfindahl-type variant of *BCR* was used alongside a measure of *successive* market power, as well as the ordinary Herfindahl index, in some work by Waterson (1980) on U.K. data. The successive power measure, based upon a Cournot-type model (see section 5.1), may be written as:

$$H_{pi} = \sum_j a_{ij} \bigg/ \left(1 - \frac{H_j}{\eta_j}\right),$$

where H_j is the Herfindahl index of concentration for the jth industry and η_j (the modulus of) that industry's demand elasticity, which was assumed constant across industries in the empirics; a_{ij} is as defined above. The format of the estimating equation derived from the work of Cowling and Waterson (1976) mentioned earlier. Estimation for 1968/1963 produced the result that the *BCR*-type measure was a significantly negative, and H_p a significantly positive, determinant of price–cost margins. The first result ties in with what Lustgarten and Brooks found for the U.S., whilst the implication of the second (given the formula for H_p above) is that a rise in selling power of a purchasing industry *raises* the margin in the selling industry. Perhaps these two measures can be thought of as picking up different aspects of the two effects noted in section 5.4, a rise in concentration in a purchasing industry raising the total margin achievable, but lowering the *share* of this for the selling industry.

The studies listed above all concentrate on the influence of downstream market power, but upstream market power is also a potential influence on performance. The effect of unions' bargaining over wage rates is likely to be predominant amongst such factors, but although several studies (e.g. Weiss, 1966*b*, Geroski, Hamblin and Knight, 1982) have related earnings to concentration and unionisation, to employ unionisation as an explanatory variable in a structure–profitability study is less common. One paper which does this is Hollander (1981). Using Canadian data, he relates various profitability measures to seller concentration, and percentage unionisation, along with some other variables. Increases in buyer concentration (at lower levels),[10] or in unionisation, appear to have some dampening effect on profitability, but they are not both significant at the same time.

A brief summary of empirical results

There have been a very considerable number of studies relating various profit measures to concentration, entry barrier proxies and so on; in 1974 Weiss surveyed 81 such studies, Böbel (1978) covered nearly 100 and there have been many more since then. They differ in being estimated for different countries (apart from the U.S. there have been several for Canada, over 10 for the U.K., at least one for most West European countries), for different samples, for different time periods, and they differ in the variables they include, the way they measure them, and the functional form. It would not be sensible to attempt another survey of results, but we can try to draw a few strands together.

The overwhelming majority of these studies have some measure of statistical success in relating the basic structural variables to profitability. Concentration, in one form or another, very commonly features as a significant positive influence. At least some of the variables used as proxies for entry barriers (particularly advertising intensity) usually prove significant in any particular study. Industry growth measures and dummy variables to account for foreign trade influences and different general types of markets are also quite successful. It is perhaps true that the measure of success achieved in relatively open economies (e.g. the U.K.) is less than that in relatively closed economies like the U.S., but that might be as expected.

Given this preponderant weight of evidence, there are really three questions of importance. First, is there a serious minority of dissenters on the results as they stand? Second, are the statistical techniques used likely to lead to misleading results? Third, how are we to interpret the results; is the only interpretation the standard one emanating from oligopoly theory?

As far as the first question is concerned there are obviously some studies which find opposing results. For example, possibly a majority of U.K. studies find concentration not to be a significant determinant of profitability. It is also true, perhaps, that people tend not to get negative results published as often as positive ones, though in this area they might have some novelty. One forceful critic was Brozen (e.g. 1970, 1974) who claimed that high profitability did not persist in concentrated industries in the U.S., but his work generated its own counterblast (e.g. Qualls, 1974, who demonstrated that it did persist where entry barriers were high).

On the second question, we have already pointed out the statistical problems which can arise in interpreting the relative impact of measures of concentration and measures of scale economy entry barriers, but these problems are likely to understate rather than overstate the true importance of those variables. There are also problems with advertising intensity as a measure of product differentiation advantages; we turn to this in the next section. Another potentially important problem is whether single equation estimation is a valid technique, or whether some of the explanatory variables are in fact jointly determined along with profitability. We come to that in section 5. The last question is discussed at some length in section 6; in fact this is the area where most of the controversy resides at present.

3. Relationships involving advertising

As we saw in chapter 7, one of the most basic direct questions regarding advertising is: what is the effect on the price elasticity of demand? More indirectly, does advertising raise profit margins for established firms? Another important question is whether concentration influences advertising. We consider all these below. A further hypothesis, that advertising influences concentration directly,[11] perhaps by increasing scale economies, is discussed in the next section.

Unfortunately, it would be hazardous to come to any firm conclusion as to the influence of advertising on the price elasticity of demand. Though a large number of studies have looked at the effect of advertising on the demand for products or brands, most suffer from problems of simultaneous equations bias. If the demand for the products of an industry depends upon advertising and various other variables, but advertising expenditures in turn depend upon sales (and other factors), yet only the demand function is estimated, there will be a bias imparted to the coefficients of this relation akin to that derived in econometric textbook examples of demand and supply systems where only one of the equations is estimated. Schmalensee (1972) shows this bias is likely to be in the direction of exaggerating the effects of advertising on industry demand. Even more importantly for our present purpose, the overwhelming majority of such studies estimate functions which do not allow advertising effectively to influence the price elasticity of demand. Many use the double-log (log–linear) form in which price and advertising elasticities are constant parameters to be estimated, so that by definition advertising cannot affect the price elasticity.[12] However Lambin (1976), in a wide-ranging study of the impact of advertising upon various branded goods in Western Europe, finds *some* support for the idea that those brands which are more intensively advertised are also those with relatively low price elasticities, implying higher prices, *ceteris paribus*.

Having said this, we should mention an often-quoted study of Benham (1972) on the price of eyeglasses (spectacles). If advertising does indeed raise industry demand (questionable in general) and at the same time lower unit costs (perhaps due to production scale economies) or lower unit profits (because demand becomes more elastic) then it can lower price. Benham in fact found prices to be lower in states of the U.S. where advertising was allowed than where it was prohibited. It would be unwise to generalise from this instance though. In any case it is often more relevant to enquire into the effects of a bit more or less advertising rather than a total ban. As Butters (1976) points out, there is no necessary conflict between believing advertising *per se* is important in allowing entry and believing its large-scale use may make entry more difficult (and see also section 7.4).

Advertising intensity as a barrier?

Since direct estimates of the effects on price elasticities of demand has proved difficult, let us turn to indirect methods. Superficially this appears straightforward; as we have said, Comanor and Wilson (among others) obtained a significant coefficient on advertising intensity in multiple regression analysis of profit on capital against various market structural variables, and other studies have found a positive coefficient on advertising intensity when explaining profit–revenue ratios. There are, however, two problems in relating the empirics back to the theory; we treat the least serious first.

If we assume advertising has a dynamic effect, then established firms hold advertising capital which does not appear on balance sheets as such. Will this raise the measured rate of profit on capital by understating capital stock? To investigate this, we use a little algebra based upon Telser (1969). Let Π be profit before deduction of anything to do with advertising, K be physical capital and A_K advertising capital, while A is current advertising outlay and A_d is the depreciation of advertising capital. The true rate of return on capital may then be written as:

$$r^* = \frac{\Pi - A_d}{K + A_K}$$

while the measured rate of return, r, is $(\Pi - A)/K$. The difference between these may be written:

$$r^* - r = \frac{\Pi - A_d - (\Pi - A)[(K + A_K)/K]}{K + A_K}$$

Simplifying this gives:

$$r^* - r = \left[\left(\frac{A - A_d}{A_K} \right) - r \right] \frac{A_K}{K + A_K}$$

The first expression in square brackets is the proportionate rate of growth of advertising capital. If this is markedly smaller than the measured rate of return on capital, the true rate of return on capital will be somewhat smaller than the measured rate. An attempted correction of Comanor and Wilson's results by Weiss (1969) found this effect weakened but did not destroy the relationship between profitability and advertising intensity.

Having found the result largely immune from the first attack, consider the second. Define firm i's profit revenue ratio as the difference between the price-average *production* cost margin and the advertising–sales ratio[13] i.e.:

$$\frac{\Pi}{R}i = \left(\frac{q}{q}\right)i\left(\frac{p-AVC}{p}\right)i - \frac{A}{R}i \tag{10.4}$$

Referring back to the Dorfman–Steiner condition, we find from (7.5) and (7.7) we may write for firm i:

$$\frac{A}{R}i = \left(\frac{p-\mathrm{d}C/\mathrm{d}q}{p}\right)i \cdot \eta_{Ai} \tag{10.5}$$

Now, supposing average variable costs to be (approximately) equal to marginal costs, we may substitute (10.5) into (10.4) and rearrange to obtain:

$$\frac{\Pi}{R}i = \frac{A}{R}i\left(\frac{1}{\eta_{Ai}} - 1\right) \tag{10.6}$$

Assuming for simplicity η_{Ai} is constant across all firms in the industry, we may aggregate (10.6) to yield the industry relation:

$$\frac{\Pi}{R} = \frac{A}{R}\left(\frac{1}{\eta_{Ai}} - 1\right) \tag{10.7}$$

Thus, if η_{Ai} does not vary too much across industries, a very strong correlation between the profit–revenue ratio and the advertising–sales ratio will result. This can carry over to the use of a profit on capital measure since multiplying (10.7) by R/K gives:

$$\frac{\Pi}{K} = \frac{R}{K} \cdot \frac{A}{R}\left(\frac{1}{\eta_{Ai}} - 1\right)$$

More fundamentally, what factors may be identified as causes of the correlation? One possibility, given (10.4) and (10.5), is the effectiveness of the industry's pricing discipline. Supposing a number of industries to be alike except in the extent to which price collusion obtains, then those pricing nearest to joint-profit maximising levels would have the highest values for Π/R and A/R. The more orthodox alternative suggestion is that heavy advertising makes demand curves less price elastic, so increasing the price–production cost margin and, incidentally, the profit–revenue ratio. There are many other possible mechanisms; Needham (1976) presents a fairly comprehensive analysis of these. The main point is already clear, however. The observed results of the Comanor and Wilson type allow us to say that increases in price relative to production costs, increases in the advertising–sales ratio and increases in the profit measure are associated, but do not allow us to conclude that any particular causal mechanism had produced this. Work with simultaneous equation systems can potentially help here.

The influence of concentration on advertising
      Theoretically, a link from concentration to advertising can come about through Dorfman–Steiner mechanisms. As we saw in chapter 7, it is

possible that the relationship may turn out to be non-linear, and most recent studies allow this to be so. In estimating such a relationship cross-sectionally, it is important to allow for the differing extents to which goods are advertisable (producer versus consumer goods, durable versus non-durable etc.) as these will affect the productivity of advertising. Additionally, inter-temporal effects such as introductory campaigns for new goods may be relevant.

As an example of a fairly straightforward analysis along these lines, we list an equation estimated by Cable (1972) for a fairly homogeneous sample of 26 U.K. consumer good industries, mainly food products:

$$\frac{\hat{A}}{R} = -0.0789 + 0.722\,H - 0.957\,H^2 + 0.126\,D + 0.0013\,N$$

$$(0.273) \quad (0.402) \quad\;\; (0.0308) \quad (0.00058)$$

$$-0.448\ \text{new}\ B - 0.0023\ G \qquad R^2 = 0.3932$$

$$(0.676) \qquad\quad (0.0025)$$

Notice that advertising is linked to the Herfindahl index of concentration through a quadratic function, with both terms achieving significance. The results suggest maximum advertising intensity occurs at an H value of about 0.4 ($2\frac{1}{2}$ firm equivalents). The other variables are a dummy picking up durability (D) and the number of brands (N), both of which are positive and significant, also the ratio of new brands introduced over a specified period (new B) and industry sales growth, which were insignificant. A similar relationship was obtained by Sutton (1974) on another sample of U.K. consumer goods.

Ornstein (1976) has claimed such findings may merely be statistical artefacts. He suggests that larger firms may in general have larger price-cost margins because of greater efficiency.[14] If so, the Dorfman–Steiner condition (e.g. equation 7.10) implies we would expect greater advertising intensity for them. But larger firms are relatively more important in concentrated industries. Hence there is an alternative explanation flowing not from concentration to advertising (with *possible* anticompetitive implications), but simply a simultaneous relationship, with advertising perhaps acting as a vehicle for achieving production scale economies. His empirical results, suggesting that the concentration advertising relationship holds equally for consumer and producer goods, provide confirmation for this view, in his opinion.

On the other hand, Bradburd (1980) claims that Ornstein's empirical work is at fault in adopting too loose a definition of producer goods. When Bradburd omits from the sample industries for which sales to producers and consumers are almost evenly matched, the results for producer goods become insignificant. This indicates Ornstein's hypothesis is suspect.

4. Other common hypotheses

In this section we cover the most important of the empirical hypotheses coming from the work discussed in chapters 8 and 9.

The determinants of technical change

Most aspects of technical change are difficult to measure. Obviously, it is most important to know the key factors influencing the swiftness of diffusion or imitation. However, innovations are heterogeneous in nature with some being much more important than others, so it is difficult to identify factors varying in the cross-section which contribute to speedy change. Nevertheless there has been some work done on diffusion, notably by Mansfield (1968), Romeo (1977) and Davies (1979*b*). All find variables corresponding to profitability of investment to be relevant in explaining the 'speed' of diffusion (see section 8.4). Mansfield and Romeo both suggest that concentration has a negative influence on diffusion speed, but Davies (1980*a*) points out, and his results suggest, that it has conflicting influences. If critical size for adoption is falling over time, then diffusion is swifter in small number industries, but slower as firm sizes become more unequal, *ceteris paribus*.

In fact, much more work has been done to discover determinants of inputs into the innovative process such as R and D expenditure or number of patents issued, with the former index in particular attracting a lot of attention. The usual hypothesis here comes from the Galbraithian and Schumpeterian views that large firm size[15] and a concentrated market structure increase R and D intensity.

Now obviously there are many other factors of importance besides size and concentration, most notably the likely productivity of that research expenditure. This in turn will depend upon the type of industry ('naturally progressive' or not, producer/consumer good, durable/non-durable good etc.), also on the likely extent of appropriability (whether the technology can be utilised overseas, or in other divisions, whether technology normally comes from another branch of the firm etc.). Thus it is usual to include a number of dummy variables to account for such things. Herein, often, lies a problem. Just why are some industries naturally more progressive? If they also tend to be those industries which are populated by a few large firms, obvious empirical difficulties can result.

To take an example, Scherer (1967*a*) estimated the determinants of a measure of R and D inputs: the *proportion* of engineers and scientists in the workforce (e_i), across 56 U.S. industry groups for 1960, identifying four general industry types. He obtained the result:

$$\hat{e}_i = 16.4 + 0.155\, CR_{4i} + 38.4\, \text{Elec}_i + 35.7\, \text{Chem}_i - 14.3\, \text{Trad}_i$$

$$(0.109) \qquad (9.0) \qquad\quad (6.6) \qquad\quad (4.1)$$

$$R^2 = 0.728 \ \text{(three other, insignificant, dummies omitted)}$$

where Elec, Chem, and Trad are dummy variables representing industries classified to the electrical, chemical and traditional groups, their coefficients illustrating (sensible looking) differential effects compared with the base case, General and Mechanical Industries. Concentration, CR_4, is insignificant. However in another version of the model, concentration exhibited a significant positive influence. Since the electrical and chemical areas also tend to be the most concentrated, multicollinearity is likely to make interpretation difficult.

More recently, studies in this area have employed more sophisticated methods. A good example is Shrieves (1978). He started with a large number of product market and technological characteristics, the former representing such things as proportion of sales of consumption goods, proportion of sales of investment goods, etc., the latter being a breakdown of the areas of discipline of the scientists employed. These characteristics were then distilled (by a statistical technique called factor analysis) into a smaller group comprising those indicated by sample observations to be the most important. His results show a positive link existing between R and D and concentration for those industries producing material inputs and consumer goods, but not for other classes such as specialised durable equipment. He explains this in terms of varying ease of appropriability (as determined by ease of imitation) of research in the various areas. R and D expenditure rises less than proportionately with firm size in his sample, against the 'Schumpeterian' view. In fact this is a common result.

Another recent example in this area is Farber (1981), who includes buyer concentration as well as the usual structural and opportunity variables. He estimates a simultaneous system of equations involving R and D intensity, advertising intensity and concentration. As we saw, recent theoretical work (Dasgupta and Stiglitz, 1980*a*) suggests a simultaneous approach is appropriate. We discuss simultaneous equation systems in the next section.

The determinants of concentration

In the previous chapter we identified two basic determinants of concentration, technological considerations and stochastic processes. People have attempted estimates of the effects of these factors on concentration, but the work is not without its problems. Most people in this area, for example, choose to explain the concentration ratio, though the reason for employing that as a summary *explanatory* measure is normally only a pragmatic one. Also, there is the problem of tautology we discussed at the beginning of section 9.2, which afflicts many studies.

One paper which recognises some of the problems is Ornstein *et al.* (1973). They suggest a logarithmic estimating function of the form:

$$\ln CR_4 = \alpha + \beta_1 \ln N + \beta_2 \ln (VA/P) + \beta_3 \ln (K/L) + \beta_4 PD$$
$$+ \beta_5 (\text{Gov}/R) + \beta_6 G + \beta_7 V_g + u.$$

where CR_4 is the 4-firm concentration ratio, N, R, K and L have their usual meanings (number of firms, sales revenue, capital and labour), VA/P is value added per plant, PD is a product differentiation proxy (sometimes based upon advertising intensity), Gov/R is the ratio of government purchases to total, G is industry growth rate and V_g its variance (rather than the theoretically appropriate intra-industry variance). Here N is meant to be a proxy for relative market size (which would be measured by *optimal N*). But of course its influence as measured is essentially tautological, and the same can be said for R/N, which sometimes appears. Perhaps therefore, those equations from which these variables are dropped are the most sensible.

Of the variables remaining, value added per plant, the capital labour ratio and the product differentiation proxy may be said to measure technological forces, while G and V_g represent the stochastic processes explanation and (Gov/R) is meant to be a rough proxy for countervailing power effects. In a typical example of their estimations, coefficients β_2, β_3, β_4, β_7 all are positive and significant, so there is evidence for both schools of thought.

Davies and Lyons (1982), whose approach we covered in chapter 9, tested their model by regressing actual concentration on concentration calculated according to (9.9). In a sample of 100 U.K. industries, they obtained an R^2 of 0.9, and the coefficient on concentration was very nearly one, providing strong confirmation that both technology and stochastic processes are important.

However, there is a further view which cannot be discounted on the basis of the evidence. Some, at least, of the measures for technological influences could equally be proxies for entry barriers, which arguably affect concentration. The precise interpretation can be of some importance too: entry barriers might be created deliberately to concentrate the industry, whilst if the underlying technology determines concentration, the implications are essentially benign. It is difficult to surmount this problem.

As we have said, changes in the various factors may be expected to induce changes in concentration. Hart and Clarke (1980) perform regressions on U.K. concentration *changes* between 1958 and 1968 on this basis, finding that increases in a scale economies proxy (the proxy we criticised earlier) increase concentration significantly, as do increases in a proxy for multiplant economies. The previous level of concentration exerts a dampening influence, in line with Galton's effect, discussed in sections 9.2 and 9.3. Hart and Clarke's other variables perhaps are more dubious.

5. Simultaneous equation systems

As we have said many times, the causal link between variables is not necessarily uni-directional. Cross-sectional empirical studies increasingly have taken this into account. Most of the equations discussed above have been estimated as part of a simultaneous system. These systems, like macroeconomic models, show a tendency to grow increasingly large.[16]

One of the earliest attempts was due to Strickland and Weiss (1976). They suggested a three equation model where advertising intensity is determined by concentration, the price–cost margin and various exogenous variables, where the level of concentration is determined by technological factors and advertising intensity, and where the margin is determined by concentration, advertising intensity and the usual types of barrier to entry proxies. Specifically, their model is as follows:

$$\frac{A}{R} = \alpha_1 + \beta_{13}\frac{\Pi}{R} + \beta_{12}CR_4 + \beta_{14}CR_4^2 + \gamma_{11}\frac{CD}{R} + \gamma_{12}\,\text{Dur} + \gamma_{13}G + u_1 \,(10.8)$$

$$CR_4 = \alpha_2 + \beta_{21}\frac{A}{R} + \gamma_{21}\text{MES} + u_2 \tag{10.9}$$

$$\frac{\Pi}{R} = \alpha_3 + \beta_{31}\frac{A}{R} + \beta_{32}CR_4 + \gamma_{31}\text{MES} + \gamma_{32}\frac{K}{R} + \gamma_{33}G + \gamma_{34}\text{Dis} + u_3 \,(10.10)$$

where Π/R, A, R, MES and K and G take on their usual meanings of price–cost margin (profit–revenue ratio), advertising, sales, minimum efficient scale, capital and growth rate, CR_4 is the 4-firm concentration ratio, CD is sales to final consumers, Dur is a durable good dummy and Dis is a measure of geographical dispersion.

There is an important statistical problem with this model, a problem of identification. Roughly, equation (10.10) cannot be distinguished empirically from a linear combination of it and equation (10.9), since it excludes no variable included in the latter. More formally, equation (10.10) fails the rank (sufficiency) condition for statistical identification. Hence the results they obtain are misleading.

Martin (1979) modifies their model to solve the identification problem by introducing additional variables into equation (10.9).[17] He assumes an adjustment mechanism whereby concentration adjusts gradually towards its long run value. Consequently, past values for concentration and profitability matter in determining current concentration. He estimates his model separately for producer and consumer good groups and finds substantial differences between the two samples. Concentration and the price cost margin are the most important determinants of advertising intensity, at least for consumer goods. Concentration, as might be expected, is heavily influenced by its past level. The most important influences on the price cost margin are positive effects due to advertising intensity and the growth rate, together with a negative effect of import intensity, whilst concentration, incidentally, is insignificant.

A variant of this model has also been estimated by Pagoulatos and Sorenson (1981). Their innovations are to include estimates for price elasticity of demand (which is helped by their restricting the sample to food industries) and to incorporate foreign trade variables in the price–cost margin equation.

They find that price elasticity and advertising intensity are the most important determinants of the margin. Advertising has important interactive effects elsewhere also.

Examples of two rather larger models are the work of Caves *et al.* (1980) for Canada, and Neumann, Böbel and Haid (1979, 1981, 1982) for West Germany. Caves' study involves the estimation of a 15 equation model jointly explaining seller concentration, cost disadvantage of small plants, minimum efficient scale, imports as a percentage of Canadian purchases, proportion of output exported, market share of foreign subsidiaries, advertising intensity, R and D intensity, diversification into and diversification out of an industry, profitability, proportion of employees covered by collective agreements, average wages of production workers, technical efficiency, and proportion of capacity in plants larger than MES. There are obviously a great number of explanatory variables, including several obtained from matched U.S. industries. The model has very much an open economy character to it, with domestic industries being influenced, and their performance tempered, by tariffs, relative efficiencies, extent of foreign ownership, etc.

The Neumann, Böbel and Haid study (1982) has nine endogenous variables, some of which are matched in Caves' work, some different, reflecting the differing traditions and industrial policies. For example, one equation is designed to explain the extent of cartelisation, a longstanding feature of German industry.

It would obviously be difficult to summarise the results from either of these models.

6. Profitability and public policy

As we said, the basic hypothesis behind the empirical studies covered in the first two sections is that oligopolies, protected by barriers to entry, are able to price substantially above costs and so earn high profits compared to atomistic industries. The 'critical concentration' school is perhaps the most explicit on this. The logical implication of the generally confirmatory findings is that oligopolistic industries impose deadweight welfare losses on the community.[18] Then, if technological change is not unnecessarily retarded and if intervention is cheap, the suggestion is that society would benefit from dominant firms being broken up, horizontal mergers prohibited, and barriers to entry demolished. Or would it? There are other views on this question we should discuss.

Demsetz (1973) put forward a completely contrary view. Firms in an industry are not all the same size and presumably those which dominate do so for some reason. In his view, it is because they are more efficient. To translate this into concrete terms, a higher industry price–cost margin can come about either because prices are higher (the view espoused above) or because costs are lower, so the standard empirical finding does not necessarily lead to the conclusion commonly drawn.

Demsetz finds profitability (Π/K) is positively and significantly associated with concentration only for the largest firms in his sample of industries. Carter (1978) regresses the price–cost margin for the largest four firms on industry concentration, advertising intensity and capital intensity, and finds all variables significant. When he regresses the price–cost margin for the fifth to eighth firms on the same *industry* magnitudes, concentration is no longer significant.[19] These results are consistent with the efficiency interpretation.

Nevertheless, such findings also are consistent with the view that large firms are able to earn supernormal profits because they happen to be the ones which achieve production scale economies or promotional economies (the 'technological' view of concentration), and/or because they succeed in colluding together. In this case, they would no longer necessarily receive either acclaim or blame. Demsetz-type tests are rather too blunt-edged a tool to allocate acclaim or blame. To exemplify the point, consider the simple homogeneous product model represented by (2.5). Substituting into it the definition of α on p. 23 yields:

$$\frac{p - C_i'}{p} = \frac{\alpha}{\eta} + \frac{(1 - \alpha)}{\eta} s_i$$

Hence, larger firms would have larger price–cost margins even if α, the collusion parameter, were almost unity. The point is explained in more detail in Clarke, Davies and Waterson (1983). Moreover, the averaging of results conceals the fact that in some U.S. industries profitability actually falls with firm size (Marcus, 1969).

Peltzman (1977) developed a more fully structured model which simultaneously explains the development of concentration and profitability. The mechanism is that some firms (presumably the more efficient) adopt cost-reducing innovations more swiftly, then find greater outputs optimal as a result of their lower costs. Thus in industries susceptible to such changes, concentration increases, with the largest firms being the most profitable. He formulated a very complex model along these lines and obtained seeming empirical verification. However the model is so complex it is difficult to separate out the various effects, and Scherer (1979) noted that, as a matter of fact, most recent concentration increases in the U.S. had not come about by the mechanism Peltzman suggested.

Porter (1979) has developed the concept of *barriers to mobility* (mentioned in chapter 4) to suggest a general alternative to the Demsetz view. This is that individual industries, while selling the same product, are nevertheless made up of groups of firms with group characteristics. For example a manufacturer of unbranded detergents, whilst obviously in the same industry as branded detergent manufacturers, nevertheless faces a very different market position. Entry into the branded group might be very difficult for an outsider and moderately difficult even for the unbranded firm. This is because of barriers to mobility within the industry. Hence there will generally be industry-wide traits of market structure which determine average profitability. But there will also be differential traits within the industry, with the extent of competition/collusion between groups, differences in the scale of firms between and within groups and costs of mobility between groups, as well as the differential abilities of managements, creating efficiency differences. Because small firms may be able to develop specialised niches of the market, Porter's view allows for the small firms to be more profitable in some industries.

In a pragmatically-structured cross-sectional test of his hypothesis on U.S. data, Porter divided industries into the larger and smaller firms based upon the size distribution tables. He found very considerable differences between firms in the leader and follower groups in the explanation of profitability (the former being more profitable on average, though not significantly so). In the follower group industry growth and capital requirements had a significantly positive effect on profitability, though advertising intensity and a scale economies barrier variable had an insignificant effect, whilst in the leader group these results were reversed.

Porter's empirical work is thus broadly consistent with the idea that different barriers impact differently on profitability within different strategic groups for the reasons discussed above (see also Newman's work, 1978). It is also broadly consistent with Nickell and Metcalf's (1978) finding of prices substantially higher for branded than unbranded supermarket products in concentrated industries in the U.K., whilst on average concentration is often found to exert an insignificant influence on profitability in the U.K. It is definitely against the pure efficiency view that inter- and intra-industry structural elements are unimportant in determining intra-industry profitability differences. The difficulty is to decide quite what compromise view is appropriate.

In this connection, one area which is becoming increasingly important is analysis using detailed data sets at the level of the firm or product line. This enables a more detailed investigation of intra-industry behaviour, such as the relationship between profitability and firm size (Shepherd, 1972) or even, by inference, conjectural variations (Geroski, 1982a). Newly available data sets in the U.S. such as PIMS (see e.g. Gale and Branch, 1982) and the F.T.C.'s Line of Business data set (see e.g. Ravenscraft, 1983) will greatly assist in this work.

One important task for the future is to quantify the extents to which efficiency, scale economy and other structural effects, and collusion, contribute to inter- and intra-industry profitability. In the course of this analysis, such studies are likely to cast light also on the determinants of industry structure.

Notes on the literature

The methodology underlying the basic structure–profitability relationship is critically discussed in Phillips (1976), Cowling (1976) and Sawyer (1982). As far as the existing empirical literature is concerned, the surveys by Weiss (1971, 1974) cover a great deal of ground, particularly regarding the structure–profitability hypothesis. Comanor and Wilson (1979 and subsequent discussion, 1980) survey much of the material on advertising, and Kamien and Schwartz (1982, chapter 3) provide an excellent survey on R & D. Curry and George (1983) cover the determinants of concentration.

Of course the literature is continually growing. As well as those journals with Industrial Economics/Industrial Organisation in their title, other common sources of empirical work are the *Review of Economics and Statistics*, the *Southern Economic Journal* and the *Journal of Law and Economics*.

Notes

1. Introduction: the analytical framework

1. The analysis of this problem is discussed, in much greater detail, in chapter 6.
2. We do not therefore agree with Triffin (1949) that in the limit it is impossible to analyse the equilibrium of a group of firms without looking at the general equilibrium.
3. An example of a justification along these lines is Stigler's theory of oligopoly (1964) discussed in chapter 3.
4. Some valiant attempts have been made to assess the general equilibrium impact of price changes both empirically (see, e.g. Bergson, 1973) and theoretically (see e.g. Ireland, 1978).
5. Thus, it is no justification to say that, since some people still buy the product, its price cannot be excessive.
6. Suppose the demand curve is $p = a - bQ$. Then total revenue is $pQ = aQ - bQ^2$, so marginal revenue $(\mathrm{d}pQ/\mathrm{d}Q)$ is $a - 2bQ$.
7. There were later comments by Ross (1968) and De Prano and Nugent (1969).
8. There are of course other reasons for nationalisation, many of them political; we mean legitimate in the sense of economically defensible.
9. There are specific theories of the firm which suggest alternative maximands to profit. They have not been developed to any real extent to consider the firm's reaction to *industry* constraints and we will not discuss them here.
10. However, we should warn the reader against some such trade-off analysis. If some X-inefficiency arises because employees are improving their own positions then part of the increase in costs is not a loss to society but merely a transfer. Unfortunately, the X theory is silent on what portion of costs might be considered to be pure transfer, and on how this relates to product market conditions.
11. This *might* provide an explanation why mergers often turn out worse than expected, as is found by Meeks (1977) for example.
12. Of course, price can always be defined as average cost plus a markup. Thus in order for a cost-plus theory to have content, there must be some things which do *not* influence the markup.
13. The administered pricing hypothesis is tested in a rather different manner. See, for example Weiss (1966*a*) and Phlips (1971), but also (1980).

214 *Economic theory of the industry*

2. Classical theories of oligopoly

1. If it is not, there is little that can be done to find industry magnitudes.
2. Strictly here fixed costs are a problem, which we ignore.
3. To take an algebraic example, if $p = 300 - (q_1 + q_2)$ and $C_i = 20q_i$, $(i = 1, 2)$ the reaction functions are easy to find from (2.2) as $q_i = 140 - q_j/2$ $(i \neq j)$. Also, substituting back into (2.1), the isoprofit contours for firm 1, for example, are of the form $280q_1 - q_1^2 - q_1q_2 = \overline{\Pi}_1$.
4. By this we mean the ψ_j already take into account reactions to firms apart from m.
5. Hence the *analytical* irrelevance of firm numbers argued for by Archibald (1959); beliefs matter as well.
6. See also Aaronovitch and Sawyer (1981, p. 137) for an example of a similar model and Cubbin (1983).
7. The interested reader should consult Efroymson (1943) who develops an alternative assumption for the boom.
8. The dynamics here are therefore only necessary in order that we can examine stability; we are not interested in any properties of the equilibrium path (which would constitute true dynamic analysis) apart from its direction. This point, and the general methodology behind it involving the Correspondence Principle, is discussed in general terms in Samuelson (1947, chs 9–11).
9. A simple example along these lines is given in Henderson and Quandt (1971) pp. 226–7.
10. There are other measuring rods, and hence other versions of the formulae that follow. Here we are talking about fixed number industries; welfare under monopolistic competition is considered in chapter 6.

3. Oligopoly: the game-theoretic approach

1. Telser (1972, p. 133) shows that the Nash point is in fact a generalisation of the minimax solution to cover both constant and non-constant sum games.
2. If, however, price was the decision variable in a homogeneous product oligopoly, the non-cooperative solution would be for price to equal marginal cost: this is the Bertrand–Nash equilibrium.
3. Notice though that this does rule out a constant elasticity demand function for example.
4. This does not mean the Stackleberg model is of no interest, as we see in chapter 4, since the rules of the game need not be the same for both players.
5. Friedman (1977), Telser (1972) and Nicholson (1972) all provide analyses which run to some extent parallel with our exposition. We mention individual contributions where relevant.
6. The payoff under joint profit maximisation is often spoken of in the game-theoretic literature as *Pareto-optimal*. It is so only from the point of view of the firms in the industry and this terminology should be distinguished clearly from that used in welfare economics where consumers are brought into account.
7. We are talking here of non-collusive oligopolists. Part of the feasibility of a collusion may be bound up in identifying or labelling particular consumers.

8. The question of quality as it relates to product differentiation is considered in chapter 6.
9. See d'Aspremont *et al.* (1981), also Shubik, ch. 11.
10. Alternatively, the industry products need not be homogeneous if the firms can agree amongst themselves about the objective differences between them.
11. The question of why imperfect cartels should exist, is probably very much connected with the fact that in most cases cartels are illegal, so that the less formal gathering is involved, the better.
12. Since a binomial model is appropriate here (as those who know some statistics will appreciate), this is $(1 - \rho) \cdot \rho \cdot n_0/n_s$.
13. We are continually looking at the situation from the position of the firms rather than taking a societal viewpoint in this chapter.
14. Notice that in the earlier theoretical discussion we always assumed complete information, in that the players' actions were mutually recognised as giving rise to particular payoffs to both parties. Games with incomplete information have been discussed by Harsanyi (1967).
15. Lest the reader becomes confused here, we should mention that Friedman's second article contains a remarkably impersonal critique of his 1963 paper.

4. A consideration of the effects of potential entry

1. This is not precisely Modigliani's definition.
2. In fact, Schmalensee (1981*a*) analyses Modigliani's case using the basic framework of Dixit's model, which we are about to develop.
3. Matters become more difficult if there is a sequence of potential entrants, as we see in the next section.
4. We should mention at this juncture that Wenders (1967) has shown that, given the sorts of values Bain calculates as reasonable for the level of price above marginal cost attainable without inducing entry into various industries, blockaded entry (i.e. monopoly price below limit price) would require *extremely* elastic demand curves.
5. Dixit develops a simple algebraic model where he demonstrates these results for particular cost and demand curves.
6. The approach can in fact run into difficulties even when only the established firms are being taken into account, specifically where one is considering exit from the industry.
7. On this point, see also von Weizsäcker (1980*b*) p. 46.
8. Another example, 'rational conjectures', is discussed in Geroski (1981*a*).
9. Schmalensee's (1981*a*) variant is also relevant here.
10. Our definitions here follow Baumol and Willig (1981), though others (e.g. Grossman, 1981), make similar distinctions.
11. The existence of rental markets makes the distinction we are drawing fuzzier, though it does not eliminate it.
12. In addition, see again Grossman (1981), also Waterson (1981), and the debate in *A.E.R.*, June 1983.
13. Pyatt's model sometimes has market share being eroded, as in many cases the established firm maximises short run profits.
14. In the case of an increase in industry growth rate they seem rather dubious given the limited nature of the model (Kamien and Schwartz) or the unusual way in which growth is introduced (see Ireland on Gaskins).

216 Economic theory of the industry

15. The figure also illustrates the gist of Baron's point, though in a deterministic model.
16. Benefits and costs are not, of course, measured on the same scales in figure 4.10, which contains insufficient information to enable us to perform measurement.
17. In fact, some of the more recent papers examine established industry structures other than monopoly; see e.g. Kamien and Schwartz (1975), Lippman (1980) but also Reynolds (1982). Reynolds finds that industry price increases as the industry becomes more collusive. Also the earlier predictions on whether a dominant firm declines are of potential importance in time-series work.
18. Though Demsetz (1982) demurs from this consensus.

5. Monopoly power in vertically related markets

1. One aspect of these inter-relationships we will not cover here is co-ordination between powerful firms producing substitute products selling to the same industry, for example a merger between manufacturers of electrical and belt-driven fans for cars. In essence, this is an oligopoly problem.
2. In this chapter we assume that the relevant second-order maximisation conditions are always satisfied.
3. The joint profit maximising price/single stage monopoly price and the costs B faces in the two-stage parametric (or myopic) pricing model are identical for many demand functions — see Greenhut and Ohta's (1976) analysis, discussed in the next section.
4. One slight difficulty is whether the price–quantity negotiations envisaged above between A and B could take place if B were not also the sole (or possibly, an important) purchaser of factor A. A sole purchaser possesses potential monopsony power. In our example this cannot be exercised in the normal manner since B does not face upward sloping supply curves. On the other hand, being an important purchaser means B is less likely to accept A's price as given, and thus more likely to enter into price–quantity negotiations.
5. If the reader is unwilling to accept this, he should work through the exercise of verifying that these costs can easily be added onto the basic costs of battery and tyres or subtracted from the (joint) derived demand curve without substantive changes, as in our analysis of the previous subsection.
6. Until comparatively recently, an independent firm manufactured steel body panels for major British motor manufacturers to their specifications.
7. Adelman (1955) and Laffer (1969) both attempt to measure this as a structural feature.
8. The ideas here flow from Coase's (1937) fundamental insight that the formation of the firm itself is a suppression of the market mechanism, arising out of contractual difficulties.
9. McGee and Bassett (1976) provide a mathematical treatment along the same lines.
10. Though it could alternatively be more profitable to increase output, since the cost of producing any given output has fallen.
11. A more detailed analysis of *upstream* integration by a monopsonist into a perfectly competitive supply industry is provided by Perry (1978).

12. Point G is NOT given by the intersection of a marginal revenue and a marginal cost function shown in this figure, since we represent marginal revenue for the final product, not the derived curve for input A.

13. Another alternative, which would make the analysis of the next couple of paragraphs rather fatuous, would be for the firm to integrate to gain the scale economies but then sell the excess to unintegrated firms. In practice this may be ruled out by industry custom or because of specialised inputs, as in Porter and Spence (1977) below. However, the problem recurs in the next section.

14. Changes in other firms' output levels will shift this firm's derived demand curve, which complicates the analysis.

15. Another possible (though slightly artificial) example of something making vertical integration the resolution of two forces is Green's assumption of decreased technical efficiency in integrated concerns. See Kaserman (1978, pp. 490–2) for a discussion.

16. From *society's* point of view, integration is wasteful since, given a large number of integrated downstream firms, more input has to be held in total to satisfy the same fraction of the population, each of whom arrives at a particular firm in a random way. Holdings would be least with only one downstream firm. See also Perry (1982*b*).

17. It is clear that, depending upon the slopes of $MVP(D)$ and $MC(S)$, q_B could be greater or less than q_A.

18. This point is made very clearly in Morgan (1949), which the reader should consult if he finds our abridged explanation unconvincing.

19. A pure profit maximising firm, for example, would be indifferent between £E from source e plus £F from source f, as compared with £$(E + F)$ from source g.

20. While discussing joint profit maximisation bilateral power models, we should also mention that in Stigler's (1964) theory of oligopoly, buyers enter the picture explicitly. However, Stigler specifically does not wish to discuss situations where the number of buyers are few, so that we shall not consider his paper further in the present context.

21. This combination of opposing effects arises also in Waterson (1980).

22. More general statistical tests have been attempted; see, for example, Guth *et al.* (1977).

23. See also Blois (1978) on a similar topic.

6. Models of product differentiation

1. Though in fact, as explained in Prais (1974) who considers a specific problem of the type we have in mind here, length of life is related also to brightness.

2. These essentially place restrictions on the curvature of $\gamma(s)$.

3. Other aspects of the literature we have not touched upon include (i) the importance of monopolistic price discrimination for the debate (on this see Coase, 1972) (ii) the use of regulatory devices to achieve an efficient result and (iii) the influence of second-hand markets (see e.g. Swan, 1972).

4. We discussed Chamberlin's (1962) model in chapter 2. On the relationship between a Chamberlinian and a Lancastrian group, see Archibald and Rosenbluth (1975). Essentially, we are coming up against the problem of industry definition here again.

5. Archibald and Rosenbluth (1975) make a minor distinction between these.
6. Actually, if both were sufficiently highly priced, neither might be bought. We shall have more to say on this in section 5.
7. Whether they actually do or not is essentially an empirical matter, and it is difficult to give any intuition on this.
8. The problem does not arise if the market is assumed to be circular rather than linear, as we say later on in discussing Salop (1979*a*), because it is not possible to foreclose an area of the market. However the circle may not be an appropriate analogy for some cases of product differentiation.
9. Notice from (6.11) that the first-order condition for maximising profit is:

$$\frac{\partial \Pi(p, N)}{\partial p} = \frac{d[(p - c)f(p)]}{dp} \cdot g(N) = 0, \text{ i.e. } \frac{d[(p - c)f(p)]}{dp} = 0,$$

a condition independent of N.
10. Hay (1976, appendix 2) has a numerical example which convincingly shows this.
11. Entry may nevertheless take place if potential entrants seek to serve previously unnoticed segments of the market.
12. This competition is an aspect of the rent transfer problem mentioned in chapter 1.
13. Some years ago there was a recurrent rumour that the major tobacco companies had registered plausible trade names for cigarettes containing cannabis on the assumption that its use would become legal.
14. However, Dixit and Stiglitz' model is like Chamberlin's and is rather different from spatial competition analyses. In it each product is an equally good substitute for any other product, rather than being a direct substitute only for two neighbours. The example of different coloured toothbrushes comes to mind.
15. See Lancaster (1975) and White (1977) for arguments on this, and Stewart (1979) for a special case.
16. Interestingly, an *unconstrained* optimum would in this case involve identical outputs from the producing firms, though more products would be produced (and prices would naturally equal marginal costs).

7. Advertising

1. If we wished to bring price into the analysis, we might specify the demand function as $q_i = q_i(p_i, p_r, A_i, A_r)$, where p_r is an index of rivals' prices. Notice incidentally that the model is incompatible with perfect competition since price is a decision variable — Telser (1964) builds a variant which is compatible.
2. Scherer (1980, pp. 387–9) argues that Cournot-type behaviour is much more likely on advertising than price, principally because of the time lags and uncertainty involved. On the effect of relative time lags, see our discussion of Nicholson's two-strategy model in chapter 3.
3. This is a simplified version of an example in Schmalensee (1977). A wide range of alternative general possibilities is catalogued in Lambin (1976), p. 26.
4. Note that $\partial Q/\partial A_i = \partial Q/\partial A$ when each firm's advertising is equally effective and there is no retaliation.

5. This is somewhat unrealistic given that price is the natural decision variable here, but we are merely deriving a simple example.

6. Second-order conditions require $\eta_{AQ} < 1$, see Schmalensee (1972, p. 377).

7. It is not clear in this particular example that advertising *intensity* is the correct explanatory variable though.

8. This is a very common terminology but is obviously slightly inaccurate; what we really mean is a range of output over which there are increasing returns to advertising expenditures; see also our comments regarding Spence (1980) below.

9. Ferguson (1974) makes the point that multimarket conglomerates benefit from quantity discounts just as much as large firms in a particular industry but that the implications are rather different. Notice incidentally that if diminishing returns do not eventually set in, the established industry faces a difficult co-ordination problem: it will be in each firm's individual interest to expand advertising to take advantage of increasing returns, yet such nonprice competition can compete away all monopoly profits, even assuming price collusion obtains. The point is made more formally in Stigler (1968, ch. 3).

10. Here the idea is that increased advertising increases the price at which a physical unit of output can be sold.

11. Notice we have not needed to make recourse to arguments on capital requirements barriers to entry here.

12. Notice this is rather different from the Dorfman–Steiner model: Williamson makes price a function of output and advertising.

13. The inverse demand function $p_i = p(q_i, q_j, A_i, A_j)$ is simply an alternative to the direct version $q_i = q(p_i, p_j, A_i, A_j)$ suggested in note 1 above.

14. This assumes the test standards referred to above are at socially optimal levels (which might not be the case for bureaucratic reasons).

15. See also Stigler (1961) on the implications of viewing advertising as a means of receiving information on prices.

16. The change in profit, and so in welfare, should include the resource cost of advertising.

17. Kotowitz and Mathewson (1979a) have extended this model by allowing for learning effects, among other things.

18. We are grateful to Avinash Dixit for a private communication which suggested the following analysis and the nature of the contrast with Dixit and Norman.

19. Without changing the nature of the problem, we abstract from Kotowitz and Mathewson's assumption that a certain proportion of consumers 'forget' about the product in each period.

20. In this problem, we are unconcerned about the triangular area of monopoly welfare loss *alongside* the monopoly profit rectangle.

21. On this, see also the interchange between Shapiro (1980) and Dixit and Norman (1980).

8. Technical change and market structure

1. Some people consider that a movement around a production isoquant is sufficient to qualify for the name innovation, but we do not take that view here.

220   *Economic theory of the industry*

2. We prefer the term 'technical change' to 'technical progress', because the latter carries with it the implication that all technically superior processes/products are socially superior as well.
3. This may strike the reader as a non-rigorous argument, but the point is made more formally (in a different context) in section 3.
4. Another way of saying this is that the monopolist and inventor are the same person, whilst the inventor in the competitive case is one of the firms which then licenses to others at a per unit royalty $(p' - c')$.
5. Note, though, that in both Arrow and Demsetz, the incentive/post innovation sales ratio is larger in competitive industries.
6. These include Kamien and Schwartz (1970) who take the case where both pre-innovation output and elasticity of demand are the same, also Ng (1971) who considers a second drastic invention.
7. Presumably some people who disliked shaving now decide against retaining their facial hair.
8. This generalises the argument of the previous paragraph to cover situations where price is not equal to marginal cost.
9. This is most easily verified by working from (8.6) back to (8.5).
10. Therefore, implicitly, the new technology cannot be embodied into the old plant.
11. We are obviously making numerous abstractions here, for example that there are no scale economies in the downstream sector, that the price of the capital good embodying the innovation is expected to change in a regular manner and so on. Many of these are discussed later.
12. Though Arrow's (1962) conclusion that preexisting profits retard innovation extends to Kamien and Schwartz' model also; new firms are likely to innovate fastest.
13. An early Cournot–Nash analysis of this situation is provided by Scherer (1967b).
14. There will be a first-order condition $\partial\Pi_i/\partial x_i$, but this is not required for our present purpose.
15. Scale-augmenting technical progress might also be attractive to firms in concentrated industries wishing to justify the industry structure to antitrust authorities (see section 9.4 on this).
16. It is not even clear that a free market would produce too little research. The argument extends from section 6.6. A firm introducing a new product does not take consumer benefit into account, but does not take the costs to other firms' products into account either.

9. The determinants of market structure

1. This implicitly subsumes also some aspects of the determinants of diversification, but it is usual and more direct to analyse diversification from the point of view of the firm, a task which is beyond the scope of the book.
2. Another facet of concentration is overall concentration, e.g. the share of the top 100 firms in the U.K. That is not our concern here.
3. Output is an ambiguous measure of size if the products of the industry are differentiated from each other, but it is still a natural index in symmetric oligopoly models.
4. Since $s_i < 1$, $\log s_i < 0$, hence the negative sign gives a positive E.

5. As in consumer theory, we can say 'Economic theory says demand curves slope downwards', and choose a functional form to satisfy that or we can proceed from more fundamental axioms regarding preferences.
6. See Theil (1967 chapter 8) for an application to car sales in the U.S.
7. See e.g. Horowitz (1970) for some empirical work on the E.E.C.
8. That question, together with the extension of the basic idea of multi-product space, is dealt with in Baumol and Fischer (1978).
9. See, e.g. Baumol (1977) for a definition and some discussion.
10. We discussed relationships between concentration and advertising in chapter 7 also.
11. See also Ornstein *et al.* (1973) on this point.
12. Just as the distribution of the *sum* of a large number of independent random influences tends towards the normal (by the Central Limit theorem), the distribution of the *product* of such influences tends towards the lognormal. See Aitchison and Brown (1957) for further discussion of the lognormal.
13. We should warn the reader that there is substantial disagreement on the relative impact of various factors; see the interchanges between Hart, Prais, Hannah, Kay and Sawyer in the *Oxford Bulletin* (1980) and the *Journal of Industrial Economics* (1981), for example.
14. The main problem here is in choosing the reference level of output. See also Donsimoni, Geroski and Jacquemin (1982).

10. A guide to the empirical work

1. In this chapter we essentially treat 'price–cost margin' and 'profit–revenue ratio' as synonymous. Every paper we know of assumes, explicitly or implicitly, that marginal costs may be equated with average variable costs.
2. For simplicity we neglect fixed costs in this discussion.
3. Or, as Qualls (1974) attempts, to subtract a proxy for this (in his case 6 per cent of equity capital) from the dependent variable. Such a procedure is potentially preferable econometrically.
4. It is quite clear that Bain was talking about product differentiation advantages, but other people are not always as explicit when discussing their proxies, though this is normally what they mean.
5. Standard errors are reported in brackets below the coefficients to which they apply; in all our reported equations we have given standard errors, even if *t* values were originally given. Roughly speaking, a coefficient may be said at a high level of confidence to be significantly different from zero if the absolute value of its coefficient is more than twice the standard error.
6. We do not mean to condone this as a procedure for dealing with multicollinearity problems; the problem essentially lies with the proxies themselves.
7. See section 8.6 on this point.
8. This reasoning does not, however, accord well with the tests actually performed, since inserting the hypothesis as stated into an equation like (2.9) would suggest profitability rising with concentration up to a certain level, then jumping to a plateau.

9. Thus it is implicitly assumed that in buying industries seller concentration approximates to concentration of buyers.

10. There is a non-linearity in the equation structure which means the effect can change sign.

11. If advertising increases concentration but also increases market share instability then it could be beneficial. There is also some literature on this latter point, see e.g. Reekie (1974).

12. See also Telser (1964 appendix I) for some useful points.

13. Data problems sometimes result in observers being unable to subtract advertising costs from the numerator of the profit–revenue ratio, which immediately puts the relationship between it and advertising intensity under suspicion. This is independent of the problem we are about to discuss.

14. We return to this point in section 6; it has considerable ramifications.

15. There is some doubt here as to what should be tested and what is actually being tested. See Fisher and Temin (1973), but also Rodriguez (1979) and Lunn (1982).

16. None of the models discussed below actually *tests* for simultaneity, nor for the appropriate dimensions of the simultaneous system. As such, they might either be too small or wastefully large for the information desired. A testing procedure is described in Geroski (1982b).

17. If these variables proved not to help the explanation, then the identification problem would not have been solved, but in fact some of them do help.

18. Though if, in an open economy say, domestic industrial structure appears not to influence profitability, then no such conclusion is warranted. Nevertheless, the subsequent material is of some interest even then.

19. For definitional reasons one would expect advertising intensity and the capital/sales ratio to be significantly positive here still.

References

In order to avoid unnecessary duplication, the following abbreviations have been used in the bibliography:

A.E.R. = *American Economic Review*
Bell J. = *Bell Journal*
Eca = *Economica*
E.E.R. = *European Economic Review*
E.J. = *Economic Journal* (also used as a combination, e.g. *Southern E.J.* = *Southern Economic Journal*)
Etrica = *Econometrica*
I.E.R. = *International Economic Review*
J.E.L. = *Journal of Economic Literature*
J.E.T. = *Journal of Economic Theory*
J.I.E. = *Journal of Industrial Economics*
J.L.E. = *Journal of Law and Economics*
J.P.E. = *Journal of Political Economy*
J.R.S.S. = *Journal of the Royal Statistical Society Series A*
O.E.P. = *Oxford Economic Papers*
Q.J.E. = *Quarterly Journal of Economics*
R.E. Stats. = *Review of Economics and Statistics*
R.E. Studs. = *Review of Economic Studies*
U.P. = University Press (e.g. Cambridge U.P. = Cambridge University Press)

Aaronovitch, A. and Sawyer, M.C. (1981), Price change and oligopoly, *J.I.E.*, **30**, 137–47.

Adelman, M.A. (1955), *Concept and statistical measurement of vertical integration*, National Bureau of Economic Research, Princeton N.J.: Princeton U.P.

(1969), Comment on the *H* concentration measure as a numbers equivalent, *R.E. Stats.*, **51**, 99–101.

Aitchison, J. and Brown, J.A.C. (1957), *The lognormal distribution*, Cambridge: Cambridge U.P.

Akerlof, G.A. (1970), The market for lemons . . . , *Q.J.E.*, **84**, 488–500.

Allen, R.D.G. (1938), *Mathematical analysis for economists*, London: Macmillan.

Andrews, P.W.S. (1949), *Manufacturing Business*, London: Macmillan.

Archibald, G.C. (1959), 'Large' and 'small' numbers in the theory of the firm, *Manchester School*, **27**, 104–9.

Archibald, G.C. and Rosenbluth, G. (1975), The 'new' theory of consumer demand and monopolistic competition, *Q.J.E.*, **89**, 569–90.

Arrow, K.J. (1962), Economic welfare and the allocation of resources for invention, *in* National Bureau of Economic Research *The rate and direction of inventive activity*, Princeton N.J.: Princeton U.P.

Arrow, K.J. (1975), Vertical integration and communication, *Bell J.*, **6**, 173–83.

d'Aspremont, C. *et al.* (1981), On the stability of collusive price leadership, Louvain, working paper 8101.

Bacharach, M. (1976), *Economics and the theory of games*, London: Macmillan.

Bain, J.S. (1951), Relation of profit rate to industry concentration in American manufacturing 1936–1940, *Q.J.E.*, **65**, 293–324.

(1954), Conditions of entry and the emergence of monopoly, *in* E.H. Chamberlin (ed.) *Monopoly and competition and their regulation*, I.E.A., London: Macmillan.

(1962), *Barriers to new competition*, Cambridge Mass.: Harvard U.P.

Baran, P.A. and Sweezy, P.M. (1968), *Monopoly capital*, Harmondsworth, Penguin.

Baron, D.P. (1973), Limit pricing, potential entry and barriers to entry, *A.E.R.*, **64**, 666–74.

Bator, F. (1957), The simple analytics of welfare maximisation, *A.E.R.*, **47**, 22–59.

Baumol, W.J. (1959), *Business behaviour, value and growth*, Macmillan, New York.

(1977), *Economic theory and operations analysis*, 4th ed., Englewood Cliffs N.J.: Prentice Hall.

(1982), Contestable markets: an uprising in the theory of industry structure, *A.E.R.*, **72**, 1–15.

and Fischer, D. (1978). Cost minimising number of firms and determination of industry structure, *Q.J.E.*, **92**, 439–67.

, Panzar, J.C. and Willig, R.D. (1982), *Contestable markets and the theory of industry structure*, New York: Harcourt, Brace, Jovanovich.

and Willig, R.D. (1981), Fixed costs, sunk costs, entry barriers and sustainability of monopoly, *Q.J.E.*, **96**, 405–31.

Benham, L. (1972), The effect of advertising on the price of eyeglasses, *J.L.E.*, **15**, 337–52.

Benishay, H. (1967), Concentration and price-cost margins: a comment, *J.I.E.*, **16**, 73–4.

Bergson, A. (1973), On monopoly welfare losses, *A.E.R.*, **63**, 853–70.

Berkowitz, M.K. and Kotowitz, Y. (1982), Patent policy in an open economy, *Canadian Journal of Economics*, **15**, 1–17.

Bernhardt, I. (1977), Vertical integration and demand variability, *J.I.E.*, **25**, 213–29.

Bertrand, J. (1883), Review of Cournot (1927) *in Journal des Savants*, 499–508.

Bhagwati, J.N. (1970), Oligopoly theory, entry prevention and growth, *O.E.P.*, **22**, 297–310.

Bishop, R. L. (1952), Elasticities, cross elasticities and market relationships, *A.E.R.*, **42**, 779–803.

(1963), Game theoretic analyses of bargaining, *Q.J.E.*, **77**, 559–602.

Blackorby, C., Donaldson, D. and Weymark, J.A. (1982), A normative approach to industrial performance evaluation and concentration indices, *E.E.R.*, **19**, 89–121.

Blois, K.J. (1978), A pricing model of vertical quasi-integration, *E.E.R.*, **11**,

291–303.
Böbel, I. (1978), *Industrial organisation*, Tübingen: Demokrit Verlag.
Bradburd, R.M. (1980), Advertising and market concentration: a re-examination of Ornstein's spurious correlation hypothesis, *Southern E.J.*, **46**, 531–9.
and Over, A.M. (1982), Organisational costs, sticky equilibria and critical levels of concentration, *R.E. Stats.*, **54**, 50–8.
Bresnahan, T.F. (1981), Duopoly models with consistent conjectures, *A.E.R.*, **71**, 934–45.
Brooks, D.G. (1973), Buyer concentration: a forgotten element in market structure models, *Industrial Organisation Review*, **1**, 151–63.
Brozen, Y. (1969), Competition, efficiency and antitrust, reprinted in Brozen (ed.) (1975).
 (1970), The antitrust task force deconcentration recommendation, *J.L.E.*, **13**, 279–92.
 (1971), Bain's concentration and rates of return revisited, *J.L.E.*, **14**, 351–69.
 (1974), Concentration and profits: does concentration matter?, reprinted in Brozen (ed.) (1975).
 (1975), *The competitive economy: selected readings*, Morristown, N.J.: General Learning Press.
Brunner, E. (1961), A note on potential competition, *J.I.E.*, **9**, 248–50.
Brush, B.C. (1976), The influence of market structure on industry advertising intensity, *J.I.E.*, **25**, 55–67.
Butters, G.R. (1976), A survey of advertising and market structure, *A.E.R.*, **66**, 392–7.
Cable, J. (1972), Market structure, advertising policy and intermarket differences in advertising intensity, *in* K. Cowling (ed.) (1972).
Capozza, D.R. and van Order, R. (1978), A generalised model of spatial competition, *A.E.R.*, **68**, 896–908.
Carlton, D.W. (1979), Vertical integration in competitive markets under uncertainty, *J.I.E.*, **27**, 189–209.
Carter, J.R. (1978), Collusion, efficiency and antitrust, *J.L.E.*, **21**, 435–44.
Cathcart, G. (1979), Cartel problems: detection and deterrence, Unpublished M.A. dissertation University of Newcastle.
Caves, R.E. (1972), *American industry: structure, conduct, performance*, (3rd. ed.) Englewood Cliffs, N.J.: Prentice Hall.
, Khalilzadeh-Shirazi, J. and Porter, M.E. (1975), Scale economies in statistical analyses of market power, *R.E. Stats.*, **57**, 133–40.
and Porter, M.E. (1976), Barriers to exit *in* R.T. Masson *et al.*, *Essays in honour of Joe S. Bain*, Cambridge, Mass.: Ballinger.
 (1977), From entry barriers to mobility barriers . . . , *Q.J.E.*, **91**, 241–61.
 (1978), Market structure, oligopoly and stability of market shares, *J.I.E.*, **26**, 289–312.
 (1980), The dynamics of changing seller concentration, *J.I.E.*, **29**, 1–15.
, Porter, M.E. and Spence, A.M. (1980), *Competition in the open economy: a model applied to Canada*, Cambridge, Mass.: Harvard U.P.
Chamberlin, E.H. (1962), *The theory of monopolistic competition*, (8th ed.) Cambridge, Mass.: Harvard U.P.
Clarke, P. and Davies, S.W. (1982), Market structure and price cost margins, *Eca.*, **49**, 277–87.
, Davies, S.W. and Waterson, M. (1983), The profitability-concentration

relation: market power or efficiency?. Mimeo, University of East Anglia.
Coase, R.H. (1937), The nature of the firm, *Eca.*, 4, 386–405.
  (1972), Durability and Monopoly, *J.L.E.*, 15, 143–9.
Cohen, K.J. and Cyert, R.M. (1975), *Theory of the firm*, (2nd. ed.) Englewood Cliffs, N.J.: Prentice Hall.
Comanor, W.S. and Wilson, T.A. (1967), Advertising, market structure and
  performance, *R.E. Stats.*, 49, 423–40.
  (1979), The effects of advertising on competition: a survey, *J.E.L.*, 17,
  453–76. Plus discussion (1980) *J.E.L.*, 18, 1066–78.
Cournot, A.A. (1927), *Researches into the mathematical principles of the
  theory of wealth*, New York: Macmillan. (Reprint).
Cowling, K.G. (ed.) (1972), *Market structure and corporate behaviour*,
  London: Gray Mills.
Cowling, K.G. (1976), On the theoretical specification of industrial structure-
  performance relationships, *E.E.R.*, 8, 1–14.
  (1982), *Monopoly capitalism*, London: Macmillan.
  and Cubbin, J. (1971). Price, quality and advertising competition . . . the
  U.K. car market, *Eca.*, 38, 378–94.
  and Waterson, M. (1976), Price-cost margins and market structure, *Eca.*,
  43, 267–74.
Cubbin, J. (1974). A measure of apparent collusion in oligopoly, Warwick
  Economic Research Paper no. 49.
  (1981), Advertising and the theory of entry barriers, *Eca.*, 48, 489–98.
  (1983), Apparent collusion and conjectural variations in differentiated
  oligopoly, *International Journal of Industrial Organisation*, 1, 155–63.
Curry, B. and George, K.D. (1983), Industrial concentration: a survey, *J.I.E.*,
  31, 203–55.
Cyert, R.M. and DeGroot, M.H. (1973), An analysis of cooperation and
  learning in a duopoly context, *A.E.R.*, 63, 24–37.
  and March, J.G. (1963), *A behavioural theory of the firm*, Englewood
  Cliffs, N.J.: Prentice Hall.
Dansby, R.E. and Willig, R.D. (1979), Industry performance gradient indexes,
  A.E.R., 69, 249–60.
Dasgupta, P. and Stiglitz, J. (1980a), Industrial structure and the nature of
  innovative activity, *E.J.*, 90, 266–93.
  (1980b), Uncertainty, industrial structure and the speed of R & D, *Bell J.*,
  11, 1–28.
David, P.A. (1969), A contribution to the theory of diffusion, Stanford Centre
  for research in economic growth, memo no. 71.
Davies, S. (1979a), Choosing between concentration indices: the iso-concentration curve, *Eca.*, 46, 67–75.
  (1979b), *The diffusion of process innovations*, Cambridge: Cambridge U.P.
  (1980a), Innovation, diffusion and market structure, *in* D. Sahal (ed.)
  Research, development and technical innovation, Lexington, Mass.:
  Lexington.
  (1980b), Minimum efficient size and seller concentration: an empirical
  problem, *J.I.E.*, 28, 287–301.
  and Lyons, B.R. (1982), Seller concentration: the technological explanation and demand uncertainty, *E.J.*, 92, 903–19.
De Bondt, R.R. (1978), Short run industry performance and potential
  competition, *J.I.E.*, 26, 267–72.
De Prano, M.E. and Nugent, J.B. (1969), Economies as an antitrust defense:
  Comment, *A.E.R.*, 59, 947–53.

Demsetz, H. (1969), Information and efficiency: another viewpoint, *J.L.E.*, **12**, 1–22.

(1973), Industry structure, market rivalry and public policy, *J.L.E.*, **16**, 1–9.

(1982), Barriers to entry, *A.E.R.*, **72**, 47–57.

Dickson, V.A. (1981), Conjectural variation elasticities and concentration, *Economics Letters*, **7**, 281–5.

Dixit, A.K. (1979), A model of duopoly suggesting a theory of entry barriers, *Bell J.*, **10**, 20–32.

(1980), The role of investment in entry deterrence, *E.J.*, **9**, 95–106.

(1982), Recent developments in oligopoly theory, *A.E.R.* (p&p), **72**, 12–17.

(1983), Vertical integration in a monopolistically competitive industry, *International Journal of Industrial Organisation*, **1**, 63–78.

and Norman, V. (1978), Advertising and welfare, *Bell J.*, **9**, 1–17. And reply, (1980), **10**, 728–9; another reply, (1980), **11**, 753–4.

and Stern, N. (1982), Oligopoly and welfare, *E.E.R.*, **19**, 123–43.

and Stiglitz, J.E. (1977), Monopolistic competition and optimum product diversity, *A.E.R.*, **67**, 297–308.

Dolbear, F.T. *et al.* (1968), Collusion in oligopoly: an experiment ... , *Q.J.E.*, **82**, 240–59.

Donsimoni, M-P., Geroski, P.A. and Jacquemin, A. (1982), Implicit beliefs and normative judgements in the use of concentration ratios, Louvain, working paper 8214.

Dorfman, R. and Steiner, P.O. (1954), Optimal advertising and optimal quality, *A.E.R.*, **44**, 826–36.

Eaton, B.C. and Lipsey, R.G. (1976), The introduction of space into the neoclassical model ... , in M.J. Artis and A.R. Nobay (eds) *Studies in modern economics*, Oxford: Basil Blackwell.

(1978), Freedom of entry and the existence of pure profit, *E.J.*, **88**, 455–69.

(1979), The theory of market preemption ... , *Eca.*, **46**, 149–58.

(1980), Exit barriers are entry barriers ... , *Bell J.*, **10**, 721–9.

(1981), Capital, commitment and entry equilibrium, *Bell J.*, **12**, 593–604.

Edgeworth, F.Y. (1925), *The pure theory of monopoly*, London: Macmillan.

Efroymson, C.W. (1943), A note on kinked demand curves, *A.E.R.*, **33**, 98–109.

Encaoua, D. and Jacquemin, A. (1980), Degree of monopoly, indices of concentration and threat of entry, *I.E.R.*, **21**, 87–105.

, Geroski, P. and Jacquemin, A. (1982), Strategic competition and the persistence of dominant firms: a survey, Louvain, working paper 8206.

, Jacquemin, A. and Michel, P. (1979), Price leadership versus monopolistic competition ... , Louvain, working paper 7905.

Fama, E.F. and Laffer, A.B. (1972), The number of firms and competition, *A.E.R.*, **62**, 670–4.

Farber, S. (1981), Buyer market structure and R&D effort: a simultaneous equations model, *R.E. Stats.*, **63**, 336–45.

Fellner, W. (1949), *Competition among the few*, New York: A.A. Knopf.

Ferguson, J.M. (1974), *Advertising and competition: theory, measurement, fact*, Cambridge, Mass: Ballinger.

Fethke, G.C. and Birch, J.J. (1982), Rivalry and the timing of innovation, *Bell J.*, **13**, 272–9.

Fisher, F.M. (1959), New developments on the oligopoly front ... , *J.P.E.*,

228   *Economic theory of the industry*

67, 410–13.
(1961), The stability of the Cournot oligopoly solution, *R.E. Stats.*, **28**, 125–35.
and McGowan, J. (1979), Advertising and welfare: comment, *Bell. J.*, **10**, 726–7.
(1983), On the misuse of accounting rates of return to infer monopoly profits, *A.E.R.*, **73**, 82–92.
and Temin, P. (1973), Returns to scale in research and development: what does the Schumpeterian hypothesis imply? *J.P.E.*, **81**, 56–70.
Foldes, L. (1964), A determinate model of bilateral monopoly, *Eca.*, **31**, 117–31.
Fouraker, L.E. and Siegel, S. (1963), *Bargaining behaviour*, New York: McGraw Hill.
Freund, J.E. (1971), *Mathematical Statistics*, 2nd. ed., Englewood Cliffs, N.J.: Prentice Hall.
Friedman, J.W. (1963), Individual behaviour in oligopolistic markets: an experimental study, *Yale Economic essays*, **3**, 359–417.
(1969), On experimental research in oligopoly, *R.E. Studs.*, **36**, 1969, 399–415.
(1977), *Oligopoly and the theory of games*, North Holland, Amsterdam.
and A.C. Hoggatt (1980), *An experiment in non cooperative oligopoly*, Greenwich, Conn.: J.A.I. Press.
Friedman, M. (1955), Comment, on a paper by C.A. Smith in National Bureau of Economic Research *Business concentration and price policy*, Princeton: Princeton U.P.
(1962), *Price theory: a provisional text*, Chicago, Aldine.
Fuss, M.A. and Gupta, V.K. (1981), A cost functions approach to the estimation of minimum efficient scale . . . , *E.E.R.*, **15**, 125–35.
Gabszewicz, J.J. and Thisse, J.-F. (1980), Entry (and exit) in a differentiated industry, *J.E.T.*, **22**, 327–38.
Galbraith, J.K. (1952), *American capitalism: the concept of countervailing power*, London: Hamish Hamilton.
(1954), Countervailing power, *A.E.R.*, **44**, 1–6.
(1969), *The new industrial state*, London: Penguin.
Gale, B.T. and Branch, B.S. (1982), Concentration and market share: which determines performance and why does it matter? *Antitrust Bulletin*, **27**, 83–106.
Gaskins, D.W., Jr. (1971), Dynamic limit pricing: optimal pricing under threat of entry, *J.E.T.*, **3**, 306–22.
Gehrig, W. (1981), On the complete solution of the linear Cournot oligopoly model, *R.E. Studs.*, **48**, 667–70.
Geithman, F.E., Marvel, H.P. and Weiss, L.W. (1981), Concentration, price and critical concentration ratios, *R.E. Stats.*, **63**, 346–53.
Geroski, P.A. (1981*a*), Rational conjectures and entry, Mimeo, University of Southampton.
(1981*b*), Specification and testing the profits concentration relationship . . . , *Eca.*, **48**, 279–88.
(1982*a*), The empirical analysis of conjectural variations in oligopoly, Mimeo, Louvain, May.
(1982*b*), Simultaneous equations models of the structure-performance paradigm, *E.E.R.*, **19**, 145–58.
, Hamblin, A. and Knight, K. (1982), Wages, strikes and market structure, *O.E.P.*, **34**, 276–91.

Gilbert, R.J. and Newbery, D.M.G. (1982), Preemptive patents and the persistence of monopoly, *A.E.R.*, **72**, 514–26.
Godley, R.J. and Nordhaus, W.D. (1972), Pricing in the trade cycle, *E.J.*, **82**, 853–82.
Gold, B. (1981), Changing perspectives in size, scale and returns: an interpretative survey, *J.E.L.*, **19**, 5–33.
Goldschmid, H.J., Mann, H.M. and Weston, J.F. (eds) (1974), *Industrial concentration: the new learning*, Boston: Little, Brown.
Green, H.A.J. (1976), *Consumer theory*, (revised ed.), London: Macmillan.
Green Paper (1978), *A review of monopolies and merger policy*, (Secretary of state for prices and consumer protection), London: H.M.S.O., Cmnd 7198.
Greenhut, M.L. and Ohta, H. (1975), *Theory of spatial pricing and market areas*, Durham, N.C.: Duke U.P.
    (1976), Related market conditions and interindustrial mergers, *A.E.R.*, **66**, 267–77.
    (1978), Reply, *A.E.R.*, **68**, 228–30.
    (1979), Vertical integration of successive oligopolists, *A.E.R.*, **69**, 137–41.
Greer, D.D. (1971), Product differentiation and concentration in the brewing industry, *J.I.E.*, **19**, 201–19.
Grossman, S.J. (1981), Nash equilibrium and the industrial organisation of markets with large fixed costs, *Etrica*, **49**, 1149–72.
Guth, L.A., Schwartz, R.A. and Whitcomb, D.K. (1977), Buyer concentration ratios, *J.I.E.*, **25**, 241–51.
Hadar, J. (1966), Stability of oligopoly with product differentiation, *R.E. Studs.*, **33**, 57–60.
Hahn, F.H. (1962), The stability of the Cournot oligopoly solution, *R.E. Studs.*, **29**, 329–31.
Haldi, J. and Whitcomb, D. (1967), Economies of scale in industrial plants, *J.P.E.*, **75**, 373–85.
Hall, M. and Weiss, L. (1967), Firm size and profitability, *R.E. Stats.*, **49**, 319–31.
Hannah, L. and Kay, J.A. (1977), *Concentration in modern industry*, London: Macmillan.
Harsanyi, J.C. (1963), A simplified bargaining model for *n* person co-operative games, *I.E.R.*, **4**, 194–220.
    (1967), Games with incomplete information played by Bayesian players, Part 1, *Management Science*, **14**, 159–82.
Hart, P.E. (1971), Entropy and other measures of concentration, *J.R.S.S.*, **134**, 73–85.
    (1975), Moment distributions in economics: an exposition, *J.R.S.S.*, **138**, 423–34.
    and Clarke, R. (1980), *Concentration in British Industry 1935–1975*, Cambridge: Cambridge U.P.
    and Prais, S.J. (1956), The analysis of business concentration: a statistical approach, *J.R.S.S.*, **119**, 150–81.
    Prais, S.J. and Sawyer, M.C. (1980), Industrial concentration: an interchange, *Oxford Bulletin*, **42**, 263–80.
    Prais, S.J., Hannah, L. and Kay, J.A., Symposium on bias and concentration, *J.I.E.*, **29**, 305–32.
Hause, J.C. (1977), The measurement of concentrated industrial structure and the size distribution of firms, *Annals of Economic and Social Measurement*, **6**, 73–107.

Hay, D.A. (1976), Sequential entry and entry-deterring strategies in spatial competition, *O.E.P.*, **28**, 240–57.
Hay, G.A. (1973), An economic analysis of vertical integration, *Industrial Organisation Review*, **1**, 188–98.
Henderson, J.M. and Quandt, R.E. (1971), *Microeconomic theory: a mathematical approach*, Tokyo: McGraw-Hill.
Hicks, J.R. (1935), Annual survey of economic theory: the theory of monopoly, *Etrica*, **3**, 1–20.
(1954), The process of imperfect competition, *O.E.P.*, **6**, 41–54.
Hoggatt, A.C. (1967), Measuring behaviour in quantity variation duopoly games, *Behavioural Science*, **12**, 109–21.
Hollander, A. (1981), Buyer concentration and profitability in Canadian industries, Proceedings of 8th annual conference of E.A.R.I.E.
Holohan, W.L. (1978), Cartel problems: comment, *A.E.R.*, **68**, 942–6.
Holterman, S.E. (1973), Market structure and economic performance in UK manufacturing industry, *J.I.E.*, **22**, 119–40.
Horowitz, I. (1970), Employment concentration in the common market: an entropy approach, *J.R.S.S.*, **133**, 463–79.
Horvath, J. (1970), A suggestion for a comprehensive measure of concentration, *Southern E.J.*, **36**, 446–52.
Hotelling, H. (1929), Stability in competition, *E.J.*, **39**, 41–57.
Ijiri, Y. and Simon, H.A. (1964), Business firm growth and size, *A.E.R.*, **54**, 77–89.
Ireland, N.J. (1972*a*), Concentration and the growth of market demand: a comment on the Gaskins limit pricing model, *J.E.T.*, **5**, 303–5.
(1972*b*), Harrod, profit maximisation and new entry, Warwick Economic research paper no. 23.
(1980), Roy's identity and monopoly welfare loss, *in* D.A. Currie and W. Peters (eds) *Contemporary economic analysis vol. 2*, London: Croom Helm.
Jacquemin, A.P. and Thisse, J. (1972), Strategy of the firm and market structure . . . , *in* K.G. Cowling (ed.), 1972.
Johns, B.L. (1962), Barriers to entry in a dynamic setting, *J.I.E.*, **11**, 48–61.
Johnston, J. (1960), *Statistical cost analysis*, New York: McGraw Hill.
Kalish, L., Hartzog, J. and Cassidy, H. (1978), The threat of entry with mutually aware potential entrants, *J.P.E.*, **86**, 147–55.
Kamien, M.I. and Schwartz, N.L. (1970), Market structure, elasticity of demand and the incentive to invent, *J.L.E.*, **13**, 241–52.
(1971), Limit pricing and uncertain entry, *Etrica.*, **39**, 441–54.
(1975), Cournot oligopoly with uncertain entry, *R.E. Stats.*, **42**, 125–31.
(1982), *Market structure and innovation*, Cambridge: Cambridge U.P.
Kaserman, D.L. (1978), Theories of vertical integration: implications for antitrust policy, *Antitrust Bulletin*, **23**, 483–510.
Kihlstrom, R.E. and Levhari, D. (1977), Quality, regulation and efficiency, *Kyklos*, **30**, 214–34.
Kitch, E.M. (1977), The nature of the patents system, *J.L.E.*, **20**, 265–90.
Kotowitz, Y. and Mathewson, F. (1979*a*), Advertising, information and product quality, *Bell J.*, **10**, 566–88.
(1979*b*), Informative advertising and welfare, *A.E.R.*, **69**, 284–94.
Koutsoyiannis, A. (1979), *Modern microeconomics*, (2nd. ed.), London: Macmillan.
(1982), *Non-price decisions: the firm in a modern context*, London: Macmillan.

Laffer, A.B. (1969), Vertical integration by corporations, *R.E. Stats.*, **51**, 91–3.

Lambin, J-J. (1976), *Advertising, competition and market conduct in oligopoly over time*, Amsterdam: North Holland.

Lancaster, K. (1966), A new approach to consumer theory, *J.P.E.*, **74**, 132–57.

(1971), *Consumer demand: a new approach*, New York: Columbia U.P.

(1975), Socially optimal product differentiation, *A.E.R.*, **65**, 567–85.

(1979), *Variety, equity and efficiency*, New York: Columbia U.P.

Lave, L.B. (1962), An empirical approach to the prisoners dilemma game, *Q.J.E.*, **75**, 424–36.

Leibenstein, H. (1966), Allocative efficiency versus X-efficiency, *A.E.R.*, **56**, 392–415.

Leland, H.E. (1977), Quality choices and competition, *A.E.R.*, **67**, 127–37.

Levhari, D. and Peles, Y. (1973), Market structure and durability, *Bell J.*, **4**, 244–8.

Levin, R.C. (1978), Technical change, barriers to entry and market structure, *Eca.*, **45**, 347–61.

Lippman, S.A. (1980), Optimal pricing to retard entry, *R.E. Studs.*, **47**, 721–31.

Loury, G.C. (1979), Market structure and innovation, *Q.J.E.*, **93**, 395–410.

Lowes, B. and Pass, C.L. (1970), Price behaviour in asymmetrical duopoly: some experimental observations, *Manchester School*, **38**, 29–43.

Luce, R.D. and Raiffa, H. (1957), *Games and decisions*, New York: Wiley.

Lunn, J. (1982), Research and development and the Schumpeterian hypothesis: alternate approach, *Southern E.J.*, **49**, 209–17.

Lustgarten, S.H. (1975), The impact of buyer concentration in manufacturing industries, *R.E. Stats.*, **47**, 125–32.

Lyons, B. (1980), A new measure of minimum efficient plant size in UK manufacturing industry, *Eca.*, **47**, 19–34.

(1981), Price-cost margins, market structure and international trade, *in* D. Currie, D. Peel and W. Peters (eds) *Microeconomic analysis*, London: Croom Helm.

Machlup, F. and Taber, M. (1960), Bilateral monopoly, successive monopoly and vertical integration, *Eca.*, **27**, 101–19.

Mann, H.M. (1971), The interaction of barriers and concentration: a reply, *J.I.E.*, **19**, 291–3.

(1974), discussion, p. 156 in Goldschmid *et al.* (eds).

Mansfield, E. (1968), *Industrial research and technological innovation*, London: Norton.

Marcus, M. (1969), Profitability and size of firm, *R.E. Stats.*, **51**, 104–7.

Marris, R. (1964), *The economic theory of 'managerial' capitalism*, London: Macmillan.

Marshall, A. (1920), *Principles of economics*, (8th. ed.), London: Macmillan.

Martin, S. (1979), Advertising, concentration and profitability: the simultaneity problem, *Bell J.*, **10**, 639–47.

McGee, J.S. and Bassett, L.R. (1976), Vertical integration revisited, *J.L.E.*, **19**, 17–38.

McKinnon, R.I. (1966), Stigler's theory of oligopoly: a comment, *J.P.E.*, **74**, 281–5.

Means, G. (1962), *The corporate revolution in America*, New York: Crowell-Collier.

Meeks, G. (1977), *Disappointing marriage: a study of the gains from merger*, Cambridge: Cambridge U.P.

Miller, J.P. (1954), Competition and countervailing power: their roles in the American economy, *A.E.R.* (*p&p*), **44**, 15–25.

Mills, D.E. and Elzinga, K.G. (1978), Cartel problems: comment, *A.E.R.*, **68**, 938–41.

Modigliani, F. (1958), New developments on the oligopoly front, *J.P.E.*, **66**, 215–32.

Morgan, J.N. (1949), Bilateral monopoly and competitive output, *Q.J.E.*, **63**, 371–91.

Mueller, D.C. (ed.) (1980), *The determinants and effects of mergers*, Cambridge, Mass.: Oelschlager, Gunn and Hain.

Murphy, J.L. (1966), Effects of the threat of losses on duopoly bargaining, *Q.J.E.*, **80**, 296–313.

Nash, J. (1950), The bargaining problem, *Etrica.*, **18**, 155–62.

Needham, D. (1976), Entry barriers and non-price aspects of firms' behaviour, *J.I.E.*, **25**, 29–43.

Nelson, P. (1970), Information and consumer behaviour, *J.P.E.*, **78**, 311–29.

Nelson, R.R. and Winter, S.G. (1977), Dynamic competition and technical progress, *in* B. Balassa and R. Nelson (eds) *Economic progress, . . . in honour of William Fellner*, Amsterdam: North Holland.

(1978), Forces generating and limiting competition under Schumpeterian competition, *Bell J.*, **9**, 524–48.

(1982), The Schumpeterian tradeoff revisited, *A.E.R.*, **72**, 114–32.

Nerlove, M. and Arrow, K.J. (1962), Optimal advertising policy under dynamic conditions, *Eca.*, **29**, 129–42.

Neumann, M., Böbel, I. and Haid, A. (1979), Profitability, risk and market structure in West Germany, *J.I.E.*, **27**, 227–42.

(1981), Market structure and the labour market in West German industries . . . , *Zeitschrift für Nationalökonomie*, **41**, 97–109.

(1982), Innovations and market structure in West German industries, *Managerial and Decision Economics*, **3**, 131–9.

Newman, H.H. (1978), Strategic groups and the structure-performance relationship, *R.E. Stats.*, **60**, 417–27.

Ng, Y.K. (1971), Competition, monopoly and the incentive to invent, *Australian Economic Papers*, **10**, 45–9.

Nicholson, M. (1972), *Oligopoly and conflict*, Liverpool: Liverpool U.P.

Nickell, S. and Metcalf, D. (1978), Monopolistic industries and monopoly profits or, are Kellogg's cornflakes overpriced?, *E.J.*, **88**, 254–68.

Nordhaus, W.D. (1969), *Invention, growth and welfare*, Cambridge, Mass.: M.I.T. Press.

Ogukuchi, K. (1964), The stability of the Cournot oligopoly situation: a further generalisation, *R.E. Studs.*, **31**, 143–5.

Omori, T. and Yarrow, G. (1982), Product diversification, entry prevention and limit pricing, *Bell J.*, **13**, 242–8.

Ono, Y. (1982), Price leadership: a theoretical analysis, *Eca.*, **49**, 11–20.

Ornstein, S.I. (1976), The advertising-concentration controversy, *Southern E.J.*, **42**, 892–902.

, Weston, J.F., Intriligator, M.D. and Shrieves, R.E. (1973), Determinants of market structure, *Southern E.J.*, **39**, 612–25.

Orr, D. (1974), An index of entry barriers and its application to the structure performance relationship, *J.I.E.*, **23**, 39–49.

and MacAvoy, P. (1965), Price strategies to promote cartel stability, *Eca.*, **32**, 186–97.

Osborne, D.K. (1964), The role of entry in oligopoly theory, *J.P.E.*, **72**, 396–402.

(1973), On the rationality of limit pricing, *J.I.E.*, **22**, 71–80.

(1976), Cartel problems, *A.E.R.*, **66**, 835–44.

Pagoulatos, E. and Sorenson, R. (1981), A simultaneous equation analysis of advertising, concentration and profitability, *Southern E.J.*, **47**, 728–41.

Pashigian, B.P. (1968), Market concentration in the US and Great Britain, *J.L.E.*, **11**, 299–319.

Peltzman, S. (1977), The gains and losses from industrial concentration, *J.L.E.*, **20**, 229–63.

Perry, M.K. (1978), Vertical integration: the monopsony case, *A.E.R.*, **68**, 561–70.

(1982*a*), Oligopoly and consistent conjectural variations, *Bell J.*, **13**, 197–205.

(1982*b*), Vertical integration by competitive firms: uncertainty and diversification, *Southern E.J.*, **49**, 201–8.

Phillips, A. (1976), A critique of empirical studies of relations between market structure and profitability, *J.I.E.*, **24**, 241–9.

Phlips, L. (1971), *Effects of industrial concentration: a cross sectional analysis for the Common Market*, Amsterdam: North Holland.

(1980), Intertemporal price discrimination and sticky prices, *Q.J.E.*, **94**, 525–42.

Porter, M.E. (1976), *Interbrand choice, strategy and bilateral market power*, Cambridge, Mass.: Harvard U.P.

(1979), The structure within industries and companies' performance, *R.E. Stats.*, **61**, 214–27.

and Spence, A.M. (1977), Vertical integration and different inputs, Warwick Economic Research Paper no. 120.

Posner, R.A. (1975), The social costs of monopoly and regulation, *J.P.E.*, **83**, 807–27.

Prais, S.J. (1974), The electric lamp monopoly and the life of electric lamps, *J.I.E.*, **23**, 153–8.

Pratten, C.F. (1971), *Economies of scale in manufacturing industry*, Cambridge: Cambridge U.P.

Prescott, E.C. and Visscher, M. (1977), Sequential location among firms with foresight, *Bell J.*, **8**, 378–93.

Pyatt, G. (1971), Profit maximisation and new entry, *E.J.*, **81**, 246–55.

Qualls, D. (1974), Stability and persistence of economic profit margins in highly concentrated industries, *Southern E.J.*, **40**, 604–12.

Quandt, R.E. (1966). On the size distribution of firms, *A.E.R.*, **56**, 416–32.

(1967), On the stability of price adjusting oligopoly, *Southern E.J.*, **33**, 332–6.

and McManus, M. (1961), Comments on the stability of the Cournot oligopoly model, *R.E. Studs.*, **28**, 136–9.

Raiffa, H. (1957), *in* R.D. Luce and H. Raiffa, *Games and decisions*, New York: Wiley.

Ravenscraft, D.J. (1983), Structure-profit relationships at the line of business and industry level, *R.E. Stats.*, **65**, 22–31.

Reekie, W.D. (1974), Advertising and market share mobility, *Scottish J.P.E.*, **21**, 143–58.

(1979), *Industry, prices and markets*, Oxford: Philip Allen.

Rees, R.D. (1973), Optimum plant size in UK industries: some survivor estimates, *Eca.*, **40**, 394–401.

234   *Economic theory of the industry*

Reinganum, J.F. (1981), Market structure and the diffusion of new technology, *Bell J.*, **12**, 618–24.
Reisman, D. (1980), *Galbraith and market capitalism*, London: Macmillan.
Reynolds, S. (1982), Limit pricing, conjectural variation and entry, *Economics Letters*, **9**, 195–9.
Rodriguez, C.A. (1979), A comment on Fisher and Temin on the Schumpeterian hypothesis, *J.P.E.*, **87**, 383–5.
Romeo, A.A. (1977), The rate of imitation of a capital embodied process innovation, *Eca.*, **44**, 63–9.
Rosen, S. (1963), Hedonic prices and implicit markets: product differentiation in pure competition, *J.P.E.*, **71**, 34–55.
Ross, P. (1968), Economies as an antitrust defense: comment, *A.E.R.*, **58**, 1367–72.
Rothschild, R. (1981), Cartel problems: note, *A.E.R.*, **71**, 179–81.
Rowley, C.K. (1973), *Antitrust and economic efficiency*, London: Macmillan.
Salop, S.C. (1979a), Monopolistic competition with outside goods, *Bell J.*, **10**, 141–56.
(1979b), Strategic entry deterrence, *A.E.R.* (*p&p*), **69**, 335–8.
Salter, W.E.G. (1960), *Productivity and technical change*, Cambridge: Cambridge U.P.
Samuels, J.M. and Smyth, D.J. (1968), Profits, variability of profits and firm size, *Eca.*, **35**, 127–39.
Samuelson, P.A. (1947), *Foundations of economic analysis*, Cambridge, Mass.: Harvard U.P.
Saving, T.R. (1961), Estimation of optimum size of plant by the survivor technique, *Q.J.E.*, **75**, 569–607.
(1970), Concentration ratios and the degree of monopoly, *I.E.R.*, **11**, 139–46.
(1982), Market organisation and product quality, *Southern E.J.*, **48**, 855–67.
Sawyer, M.C. (1971), Concentration in British manufacturing, *O.E.P.*, **23**, 352–83.
(1982), On the specification of structure-performance relationships, *E.E.R.*, **17**, 295–306.
Scherer, F.M. (1967a), Market structure and the employment of scientists and engineers, *A.E.R.*, **57**, 524–31.
(1967b), Research and development allocation under rivalry, *Q.J.E.*, **71**, 359–94.
(1972), Nordhaus' theory of optimal patent life: a geometric reinterpretation, *A.E.R.*, **62**, 422–31.
(1979), The causes and consequences of rising industrial concentration, *J.L.E.*, **22**, 191–208.
(1980), *Industrial market structure and economic performance*, Chicago, Rand McNally.
, Beckenstein, A., Kaufer, E. and Murphy, R.D. (1975), *The economics of multiplant operation*, London: Harvard U.P.
Schmalensee, R. (1972), *The economics of advertising*, Amsterdam: North Holland.
(1973), A note on the theory of vertical integration, *J.P.E.*, **81**, 442–9.
(1974), Brand loyalty and barriers to entry, *Southern E.J.*, **40**, 579–88.
(1976), Advertising and profitability: further implications of the null hypothesis, *J.I.E.*, **25**, 45–54.

(1977), Using the *H* index of concentration with published data, *R.E. Stats.*, **59**, 186–93.
(1978), Entry deterrence in the ready to eat breakfast cereal industry, *Bell J.*, **9**, 305–27.
(1979), Market structure, durability and quality: a selective survey, *Economic Inquiry*, **17**, 177–96.
(1980), The new industrial organisation and the economic analysis of modern markets, M.I.T. working paper 1133-80.
(1981*a*), Economies of scale and barriers to entry, *J.P.E.*, **89**, 1228–38.
(1981*b*), Output and welfare implications of monopolistic third-degree price discrimination, *A.E.R.*, **71**, 242–7.
(1982), Product differentiation advantages of pioneering brands, *A.E.R.*, **72**, 349–65.
Schumpeter, J.A. (1943), *Capitalism, socialism and democracy*, London: Unwin.
Schupack, M.B. (1972), Dynamic limit pricing with advertising, Mimeo, Brown University.
Seade, J. (1980), The stability of Cournot revisited, *J.E.T.*, **23**, 749–52.
Shapiro, C. (1980), Advertising and welfare: comment, *Bell J.*, **11**, 749–52.
Shapley, L. (1953), A value for *n* person games, *in* H.W. Kuhn and A.W. Tucker, *Contributions to the theory of games*, Princeton: Princeton U.P.
Sharkey, W.W. (1982), *The theory of natural monopoly*, Cambridge: Cambridge U.P.
Shepherd, W.G. (1967), What does the survivor technique show about economies of scale, *Southern E.J.*, **34**, 113–22.
(1972), The elements of market structure, *R.E. Stats.*, **54**, 25–35.
Sherman, R. (1971), Experimental oligopoly, *Kyklos*, **24**, 30–49.
and Willett, T.D. (1967), Potential entrants discourage entry, *J.P.E.*, **75**, 400–3.
Shrieves, R.E. (1978), Market structure and innovation: a new perspective, *J.I.E.*, **26**, 329–47.
Shubik, M. (1959), *Strategy and market structure*, New York: John Wiley.
(1980) (with R. Levitan), *Market structure and behaviour*, London: Harvard U.P.
Simon, H.A. (1955), On a class of skew distribution functions, *Biometrika*, **42**, 425–40.
and Bonini, C.P. (1958), The size distribution of business firms, *A.E.R.*, **48**, 607–17.
Simon, J.L. (1970), *Issues in the economics of advertising*, Urbana, Ill.: Illinois U.P.
Smithies, A. (1940), Optimum location in spatial competition, *J.P.E.*, **49**, 423–9.
Spence, A.M. (1975), The economics of internal organisation: an introduction, *Bell J.*, **6**, 163–72.
(1976*a*), Product differentiation and welfare, *A.E.R.*, **66**, 407–14.
(1976*b*), Product selection, fixed costs and monopolistic competition, *R.E. Studs.*, **43**, 217–35.
(1977), Entry, capacity, investment and oligopolistic pricing, *Bell J.*, **8**, 534–44.
(1980), Notes on advertising, economies of scale and entry barriers, *Q.J.E.*, **95**, 493–504.
Spindler, Z.A. (1974), A simple deterministic solution for bilateral monopoly,

Journal of Economic Studies, 1, 55–64.
von Stackleberg, H. (1952), *The theory of the market economy*, Oxford: Oxford U.P.
Stewart, M.B. (1979), Monopoly and the choice of product characteristics, *Economics Letters*, 2, 79–84.
Stigler, G.J. (1954), The economist plays with blocs, *A.E.R.*, 44, 7–14.
  (1964), A theory of oligopoly, *J.P.E.*, 72, 44–61.
  (1968), *The organisation of industry*, Homewood, Ill.: R.D. Irwin.
Stoneman, P. and Ireland, N. (1983), The role of supply factors in the diffusion of new process technology, *E.J.* (supplement), 93, 66–78.
Strickland, A.D. and Weiss, L.W. (1976), Advertising, concentration and price-cost margins, *J.P.E.*, 84, 1109–21.
Sutton, C.J. (1974), Advertising, concentration and competition, *E.J.*, 84, 56–69.
Swan, P.L. (1970), Market structure and technological progress: the influence of monopoly on product innovation, *Q.J.E.*, 84, 627–38.
  (1972), Optimum durability, second-hand markets and planned obsolescence, *J.P.E.*, 80, 575–85.
Sweezy, P.M. (1939), Demand under conditions of oligopoly, *J.P.E.*, 47, 568–73.
Sylos-Labini, P. (1962), *Oligopoly and technical progress*, Cambridge, Mass.: Harvard U.P.
Telser, L.G. (1964), Advertising and competition, *J.P.E.*, 72, 537–62.
  (1969), Another look at advertising and concentration, *J.I.E.*, 18, 85–94.
  (1972), *Competition, collusion and game theory*, London: Macmillan.
Theil, H. (1967), *Economics and information theory*, Amsterdam: North Holland.
Theocharis, R.D. (1960), On the stability of the Cournot solution on the oligopoly problem, *R.E. Studs.*, 27, 133–4.
Triffin, R. (1949), *Monopolistic competition and general equilibrium theory*, Cambridge, Mass.: Harvard U.P.
Usher, D. (1964), The welfare economics of invention, *Eca.*, 31, 279–87.
Vernon, J.M. and Graham, D.A. (1971), Profitability of monopolisation by vertical integration, *J.P.E.*, 79, 924–5.
Vickrey, W.S. (1964), *Microstatics*, New York: Harcourt, Brace and World.
Von Neumann, J. and Morgernstern, O. (1953), *Theory of games and economic behaviour*, (3rd. ed.), Princeton, N.J.: Princeton U.P.
von Weizsäcker, C.C. (1980a), A welfare analysis of barriers to entry, *Bell J.*, 11, 399–420.
  (1980b), *Barriers to entry: a theoretical treatment*, Berlin, Springer Verlag.
Warren-Boulton, F.R. (1974), Vertical control with variable proportions, *J.P.E.*, 82, 783–802.
  (1978), *Vertical control of markets: business and labour practices*, Cambridge, Mass.: Ballinger.
Waterson, M. (1980), Price cost margins and successive market power, *Q.J.E.*, 94, 135–50.
  (1981), On the definition and meaning of barriers to entry, *Antitrust Bulletin*, 26, 521–39.
  (1982a), The incentive to invent when a new input is involved, *Eca.*, 49, 435–45.
  (1982b), Vertical integration, variable proportions and oligopoly, *E.J.*, 92, 129–44.
Weiss, L.W. (1963), Factors in changing concentration, *R.E. Stats.*, 45, 70–7.

(1966*a*), Business pricing policies and inflation reconsidered, *J.P.E.*, **74**, 177–8.

(1966*b*), Concentration and labour earnings, *A.E.R.*, **56**, 96–117.

(1969), Advertising, profits and corporate taxes, *R.E. Stats.*, **51**, 421–30.

(1971), Quantitative studies of industrial organisation, *in* M.D. Intriligator (ed.) *Frontiers of quantitative economics*, Amsterdam: North Holland.

(1974), The concentration-profits relationship and antitrust, *in* Goldschmid *et al.* (1974).

Wenders, J.T. (1967), Entry and monopoly pricing, *J.P.E.*, **75**, 755–60.

(1971*a*), Collusion and entry, *J.P.E.*, **79**, 1258–77.

(1971*b*), Excess capacity as a barrier to entry, *J.I.E.*, **20**, 14–19.

Westfield, F.M. (1981), Vertical integration: does product price rise or fall?, *A.E.R.*, **71**, 334–46.

White, L.J. (1972), A note on the influence of monopoly on product innovation, *Q.J.E.*, **86**, 342–5.

(1976), Searching for the critical concentration ratio . . . , *in* S.M. Goldfeld and R.E. Quandt (eds.) *Studies in nonlinear estimation*, Cambridge, Mass.: Ballinger.

(1977), Market structure and product varieties, *A.E.R.*, **67**, 179–82.

Williamson, J. (1966), Profit, growth and sales maximisation, *Eca.*, **31**, 1–16.

Williamson, O.E. (1963), Selling expense as a barrier to entry, *Q.J.E.*, **77**, 112–28.

(1964), *The economics of discretionary behaviour: managerial objectives in a theory of the firm*, Englewood Cliffs, N.J.: Prentice-Hall.

(1968), Economies as an antitrust defense, *A.E.R.*, **58**, 18–31.

(1971), The vertical integration of production: market failure considerations, *A.E.R.*, **61**, 112–23.

(1975), *Markets and hierarchies: analysis and antitrust implications*, New York: Free Press.

(1979), Assessing vertical market restrictions: . . . the transactions approach, *University of Pennsylvania Law Review*, **127**, 953–93.

Willig, R.D. (1976), Consumers' surplus without apology, *A.E.R.*, **66**, 589–97.

(1979), Multiproduct technology and market structure, *A.E.R.*, **69**, 346–51.

Wolf, G. and Shubik, M. (1975), Teams compared to individuals in duopoly games with an artificial player, *Southern E.J.*, **41**, 635–48.

Worcester, D.A. (1957), Why 'dominant firms' decline, *J.P.E.*, **65**, 338–46.

Yamey, B.S. (1972), Notes on secret price cutting in oligopoly, *in* M. Kooy (ed.) *Studies in economics and economic history in honour of Professor H.M. Robertson*, London: Macmillan.

(1974), Monopolistic price discrimination and economic welfare, *J.L.E.*, **17**, 377–80.

Yarrow, G.K. (1976), On the predictions of the managerial theories of the firm, *J.I.E.*, **24**, 267–79.

Zeuthen, F. (1930), *Problems of monopoly and economic welfare*, London: Routledge.

Index

Adelman, M.A. 169, 223
administered pricing hypothesis 14
advertisability 134
advertising
  barriers to entry 134–6, 202–3
  basic framework 128–30
  consumer attitudes 130
  Dorfman–Steiner condition 128–9
  economies of scale 134–5, 201, 204
  elasticity of demand 129–33
  empirical effects 201–3
  information 136–8, 139–41
  literature 141
  market structure, effects upon 130–4, 203–4
  welfare 138–41
Akerlof, G.A. 127, 223
Allen, R.D.G. 94, 223
Andrews, P.W.S. 69, 223
Archibald, G.C. 30, 223
  and Rosenbluth, G. 114, 119, 127, 223
Arrow, K.J. 97, 147, 148, 149, 164, 224
average cost pricing 14
average variable and marginal cost 14, 19, 221

Bacharach, M. 55, 106, 224
Bain, J.S. 57, 62, 69, 79, 81, 191, 193, 224
Baran, P.A. and Sweezy, P.M. 12, 15, 224
bargaining within coalitions 47–52, 103–5
Baron, D.P. 75, 77, 78, 197, 224
barriers to entry
  advertising 135–6
  Bain's basic concepts 57
  Bain–Sylos–Modigliani analysis 57–66
  blockaded entry 57, 62, 63
  brand proliferation 120
  cost, fixed and sunk 72–4
  definitions 57, 79
  effects on pricing 56, 57, 62, 73, 74–9
  growth 197, 215
  impeded entry 57, 63, 64, 72
  innovation 160–1
  legal restrictions 73
  limit price 57–61, 69, 74–9; Sylos

Postulate 58–65
  literature 81
  measures of: Bain, 193–4; Comanor and Wilson 193–9
  post-entry outcome 69–73
  potential entrants: beliefs 67–70, 80; threat of 69–70
  product proliferation 120–1
  scale economies 72
  Stackleberg equilibrium 61, 62, 63
  vertical integration 98, 99
  welfare 79, 80
barriers to exit 73
barriers to mobility 74, 81, 210, 211
Bator, F. 15, 224
Baumol, W.J. 15, 80, 81, 224
  Panzar, J.C. and Willig, R.D. 73, 188, 224
behavioural theory 12, 14
Benham, L. 201, 224
Benishay, H. 191, 224
Berkowitz, M.K. and Kotowitz, Y. 164, 224
Bernhardt, I. 98, 224
Bertrand, J. 25, 224
Bertrand model 25, 26, 53, 73, 80
Bertrand–Nash equilibrium 159
Bhagwati, J.N. 69, 224
bilateral power 198–200
Bishop, R.L. 36, 55, 103, 104, 106, 224
Blackorby, C., Donaldson, D. and Weymark, J.A. 164, 187, 224
Böbel, I. 200, 225
Bradburd, R.M. 204, 225
  and Over, A.M. 198, 225
brand loyalty 135
Bresnahan, T.F. 26, 225
Brooks, D.G. 199, 225
Brozen, Y. 73, 138, 200, 225
Brunner, E. 72, 225
Butters, G.R. 141, 202, 225
buyer concentration ratio 199

Cable, J. 133, 204, 225
capacity as entry barrier 71–2
capital 73–4, 81, 98–9, 194–6
  advertising 202–3

238